Hong Kong

Hong Kong is a small city with a big reputation. As mainland China has become an 'economic powerhouse' Hong Kong has taken a route of development of its own, flourishing as an entrepot and a centre of commerce and finance for Chinese business, then as an industrial city and subsequently a regional and international financial centre.

This volume examines the developmental history of Hong Kong, focusing on its rise to the status of a Chinese global city in the world economy. Chiu and Lui's analysis is distinct in its perspective of the development as an integrated process involving economic, political and social dimensions, and as such this insightful and original book will be a core text on Hong Kong society for students.

Stephen Chiu is Professor of Sociology at the Chinese University of Hong Kong, Hong Kong.

Tai-Lok Lui is Professor of Sociology at the Chinese University of Hong Kong, Hong Kong.

Asia's Transformations
Edited by Mark Selden
Cornell University, USA

The books in this series explore the political, social, economic and cultural consequences of Asia's transformations in the twentieth and twenty-first centuries. The series emphasizes the tumultuous interplay of local, national, regional and global forces as Asia bids to become the hub of the world economy. While focusing on the contemporary, it also looks back to analyse the antecedents of Asia's contested rise.

This series comprises several strands:

Asia's Transformations
Asia's Transformations aims to address the needs of students and teachers. Titles include:

Debating Human Rights
Critical essays from the United States and Asia
Peter Van Ness

Hong Kong's History
State and society under colonial rule
Tak-Wing Ngo

Japan's Comfort Women
Sexual slavery and prostitution during World War II and the US occupation
Yuki Tanaka

Opium, Empire and the Global Political Economy
Carl A. Trocki

Chinese Society
Change, conflict and resistance
Elizabeth J. Perry and Mark Selden

Mao's Children in the New China
Voices from the Red Guard generation
Yarong Jiang and David Ashley

Remaking the Chinese State
Strategies, society and security
Chien-min Chao and Bruce J. Dickson

Pan-Asianism in Modern Japanese History
Colonialism, regionalism and borders
Sven Saaler and J. Victor Koschmann

The Making of Modern Korea, second edition
Adrian Buzo

Re-writing Culture in Taiwan
Fang-long Shih, Stuart Thompson and Paul-François Tremlett

Asia's Great Cities
Each volume aims to capture the heartbeat of the contemporary city from multiple perspectives emblematic of the authors' own deep familiarity with the distinctive faces of the city, its history, society, culture, politics and economics, and its evolving position in national, regional and global frameworks. While most volumes emphasize urban developments since the Second World War, some pay close attention to the legacy of the longue durée in shaping the contemporary. Thematic and comparative volumes address such themes as urbanization, economic and financial linkages, architecture and space, wealth and power, gendered relationships, planning and anarchy, and ethnographies in national and regional perspective. Titles include:

Bangkok
Place, practice and representation
Marc Askew

Hong Kong
Global city
Stephen Chiu and Tai-Lok Lui

Representing Calcutta
Modernity, nationalism and the colonial uncanny
Swati Chattopadhyay

Singapore
Wealth, power and the culture of control
Carl A. Trocki

The City in South Asia
James Heitzman

Global Shanghai, 1850–2010
A History in Fragments
Jeffrey N. Wasserstrom

Hong Kong
Becoming a Chinese global city
Stephen Chiu and Tai-Lok Lui

Asia.com is a series that focuses on the ways in which new information and communication technologies are influencing politics, society and culture in Asia. Titles include:

Japanese Cybercultures
Mark McLelland and Nanette Gottlieb

Asia.com
Asia encounters the internet
K.C. Ho, Randolph Kluver and Kenneth C.C. Yang

The Internet in Indonesia's New Democracy
David T. Hill and Krishna Sen

Chinese Cyberspaces
Technological changes and political effects
Jens Damm and Simona Thomas

Mobile Media in the Asia-Pacific
Gender and the art of being mobile
Larissa Hjorth

Literature and Society
Literature and Society is a series that seeks to demonstrate the ways in which Asian Literature is influenced by the politics, society and culture in which it is produced. Titles include:

The Body in Postwar Japanese Fiction
Douglas N. Slaymaker

Chinese Women Writers and the Feminist Imagination, 1905–1948
Haiping Yan

Routledge Studies in Asia's Transformations
Routledge Studies in Asia's Transformations is a forum for innovative new research intended for a high-level specialist readership, and the titles will be available in hardback only. Titles include:

The American Occupation of Japan and Okinawa*
Literature and memory
Michael Molasky

Koreans in Japan*
Critical voices from the margin
Sonia Ryang

Internationalizing the Pacific
The United States, Japan and the Institute of Pacific Relations
in war and peace, 1919–1945
Tomoko Akami

Imperialism in South East Asia
'A fleeting, passing phase'
Nicholas Tarling

Globalization, Culture and Society in Laos
Boike Rehbein

Transcultural Japan
At the borderlands of race, gender, and identity
David Blake Willis and Stephen Murphy-Shigematsu

Post-Conflict Heritage, Post-Colonial Tourism
Culture, politics and development at Angkor
Tim Winter

Education and Reform in China
Emily Hannum and Albert Park

Writing Okinawa: Narrative Acts of Identity and Resistance
Davinder L. Bhowmik

Maid in China
Media, mobility, and a new semiotic of power
Wanning Sun

Northern Territories, Asia-Pacific Regional Conflicts and the Åland Experience
Untying the Kurillian Knot
Kimie Hara and Geoffrey Jukes

* Now available in paperback

Critical Asian Scholarship
Critical Asian Scholarship is a series intended to showcase the most important individual contributions to scholarship in Asian studies. Each of the volumes presents a leading Asian scholar addressing themes that are central to his or her most significant and lasting contribution to Asian studies. The series is committed to the rich variety of research and writing on Asia, and is not restricted to any particular discipline, theoretical approach or geographical expertise.

Southeast Asia
A testament
George McT. Kahin

Women and the Family in Chinese History
Patricia Buckley Ebrey

China Unbound
Evolving perspectives on the Chinese past
Paul A. Cohen

China's Past, China's Future
Energy, food, environment
Vaclav Smil

The Chinese State in Ming Society
Timothy Brook

China, East Asia and the Global Economy
Regional and historical perspectives
Takeshi Hamashita
Mark Selden and Linda Grove

The Global and Regional in China's Nation-Formation
Prasenjit Duara

Hong Kong

Becoming a Chinese global city

Stephen Chiu and Tai-Lok Lui

Routledge
Taylor & Francis Group

LONDON AND NEW YORK

First published 2009
by Routledge
2 Park Square, Milton Park, Abingdon, Oxon OX14 4RN

Simultaneously published in the USA and Canada
by Routledge
270 Madison Avenue, New York, NY 10016

*Routledge is an imprint of the Taylor & Francis Group,
an informa business*

© 2009 Stephen W.K. Chiu and Tai-Lok Lui

Typeset in Times New Roman by Swales and Willis Ltd, Exeter, Devon
Printed and bound in Great Britain by
CPI Antony Rowe, Chippenham, Wiltshire

British Library Cataloguing in Publication Data
A catalogue record for this book is available from the British Library

Library of Congress Cataloging in Publication Data
Chiu, Stephen Wing-kai.
Hong Kong: becoming a Chinese global city/Stephen Chiu and Tai-Lok Lui.
p. cm.—(Asia's great cities) (Asia's transformations)
1. Hong Kong (China)—Economic policy.
2. Hong Kong (China)—Economic conditions. 3. Hong Kong (China)—
Social conditions. I. Lü, Dale II. Title. III. Series. HC470.3.C446 2009
330.95125'05—dc22
2008050123

ISBN 10: 0–415–22010–6 (hbk)
ISBN 10: 0–415–22011–4 (pbk)
ISBN 13: 978–0–415–22010–1 (hbk)
ISBN 13: 978–0–415–22011–8 (pbk)

Contents

Figures

Tables

Acknowledgements

The research for this book is an outcome of several smaller projects and has received financial support from the HKSAR Research Grants Council (HKUST6054/02H) and the Department of Sociology, The Chinese University of Hong Kong. We would also like to thank Mark Selden and David Levin for their comments and suggestions for improving the text. Winnie Chan's assistance in data analysis and editorial matters is gratefully acknowledged. The maps were prepared by Kelvin Cheung. Alex Po Lun Chung kindly allowed us to adopt his work entitled 'Tourists' Hong Kong' for our book cover. We are grateful to the Census and Statistics Department for giving us access to the public use data file and generating statistical tables for our analysis in Chapter 4. The continual support and understanding of the editorial staff at Routledge is also critical in allowing this book to see the light of the day during this ten years' gestation.

Parts of Chapter 4 and Chapter 5 have been published as journal articles in *Urban Studies* and *The China Review* respectively. Chapter 4 is a revised version of 'Testing the global city – social polarization thesis: Hong Kong since the 1990s' (*Urban Studies* Vol. 41, No. 10, 2004: 1863–1888). Chapter 5 is based upon 'Governance crisis in post-1997 Hong Kong: a political economy perspective' (*The China Review* Vol. 7, No. 2: 1–34). We thank the editors and publishers of these journals for their permission for reproducing parts of these articles in this book.

Introduction

Since its inception, Hong Kong has been a key intersection of different worlds, forever a strategic exchange node for firms from China to the rest of the world and from the rest of the world to China, as well as among all the overseas Chinese communities.

(Sassen 2001: 174)

At the top we find the cities that are [the] subject of Saskia Sassen's researches: the command and control centres of the global economy, New York, London, and Tokyo. After that, the going becomes more contentious because we lack unambiguous criteria for assigning particular cities to a specific place in the global system. There are cities that articulate large national economies into the system, such as Paris, Madrid, and Sao Paulo; others have a commanding multinational role, such as Singapore and Miami; and still others, such as Chicago and Hong Kong, articulate important subnational (regional) economies.

(Friedmann 1995: 23)

The centralization of intelligence and control resulting from the annihilation of space by modern means of communication has given to individual cities or chains of cities specialized roles as collectors and distributors of different kinds of information. The great produce and financial exchanges centralize in strategic cities or groups of cities and thereby create primary and secondary centers of dominance with respect to the differentiated functions.

(McKenzie 1968 [1927]: 211)

Hong Kong: a small city with a big reputation. Its total area is only 1,104 square kilometres but, according to the Hong Kong Special Administrative Region Government, in 2007 it was the world's 11th largest trading economy, the 15th largest banking centre according to external banking transactions, the sixth foreign exchange market on the basis of turnover, and the seventh worldwide and third largest stock market in Asia in terms of market capitalization (Hong Kong Special Administrative Region Government 2008: 66). Almost 4,000 international corporations have established regional headquarters or offices in Hong Kong.

Hong Kong is resilient. Many projected a grim outlook for this city before 1997. In 1995, *Fortune* magazine predicted that the return of Hong Kong to China would bring about the demise of the city as an international hub. The title of the magazine article was simply 'The death of Hong Kong' (*Fortune* 1995). *Fortune* published another leading article on Hong Kong in 2002. This time the question was 'Who needs Hong Kong?' (*Fortune* 2002). Fears of Hong Kong's political regression from an open and liberal polity as a result of integration with a socialist regime might have proved unfounded, its economic vitality, however, was called into question by recession. Yet, on the eve of the tenth anniversary of Hong Kong's return to China, *Time* magazine (2007), *Fortune*'s sister publication, ran a cover story on Hong Kong, with its special report entitled 'Sunshine with clouds, 1997–2007'. Hong Kong was congratulated for staying in 'great shape'. Of course, whether Hong Kong has really bounced back is still open to discussion. But clearly it has weathered the storm of a major economic recession and a period of political adjustment. Furthermore, it reappeared, again, on the cover of *Time* magazine in 2008. This time the heading was 'Ny-lon-kong', referring to New York City, London and Hong Kong – three connected cities, exemplars of globalization, which have 'created a financial network that has been able to lubricate the global economy' (*Time* 2008: 32).

Hong Kong as a global city

Hong Kong always appears in writings on the world city or the global city that contain a list of what are considered to be leading cities in the world economy (see Friedmann's quotation on p. 1). Few observers neglect Hong Kong's place in this stratified system of global cities even though they differ in what they understand to be its role and significance in the global urban hierarchy. Some view it as a secondary city in the semi-periphery (Friedmann 1986). Others characterize Hong Kong as a high-connectivity gateway city (Taylor 2004: 92). Differences in placement and characterization notwithstanding, Hong Kong was classified as a world city or global city in 13 out of 16 world city research monographs or journal articles reviewed by Taylor (2004: 40).

When Hong Kong is cited as an example of a global city in the commonly adopted 'roster of world cities' (Beaverstock, Taylor and Smith 1999), little else is usually said about it (a notable exception is Meyer 2000). Hong Kong is mentioned more for the purpose of showing where it fits in the bigger map constructed of the global urban hierarchy than for studying the case in its own right (but see Chiu and Lui 2004; Breitung and Gunter 2006; Chu 2008). Hong Kong quite often appears to be treated merely as a case of honourable mention.

This book makes the case for Hong Kong as a global city. It is not simply just another piece to fit into a worldwide mapping of the global city hierarchy. It is more than just another case of a city with global connectivity and important economic functions. Nor is its significance limited to its phenomenal economic growth and rapid pace of urban development. As Sassen well puts it in the above quotation, 'Hong Kong has been a key intersection of different worlds'. Going beyond Sassen and other writers, we have a longer and larger story to tell about the making of Hong Kong as a global city. It is longer because we seek to develop a grounded understanding of how Hong Kong has become a global city by examining this process

from an historical perspective. 'Traders and financiers in Hong Kong always operated in multitiered national, world-regional, and global economies. Recognition of
that business scope provides one key for unlocking the enigma of Hong Kong as the
global metropolis for Asia' (Meyer 2000: 2). This was the case in the nineteenth
century, and very much the same applies to the twentieth century (and perhaps the
twenty-first century as well). Chapter 1 opens our discussion of Hong Kong's pathway to the status of a global city with a macro historical analysis that emphasizes
the historical origins of its global connections. We focus in particular on the nature
of Hong Kong's central position in Chinese capitalism or, in Hamilton's phrase,
Chinese-led capitalism (Hamilton 1999: 15), a regional and global network of economic ties via organizational and personal linkages facilitated by Chinese migrants
in different parts of the world. Our longer historical perspective highlights two
issues. The first concerns the historical origin of the rise of Hong Kong as an entrepot, a commercial city and a financial centre. We emphasize in this respect the
interactions between its colonial status and connections with the world economy
and its regional linkages through Chinese networks. The second concerns the
deeper roots, as well as the breadth and depth of economic ties, that have led to the
structuring of Hong Kong into a global city.

We continue our historical account and analysis of global city formation in
Chapter 2, with a discussion of the structuring and restructuring of the Hong Kong
economy in the post-Second World War decades. We highlight how Hong Kong
quickly became an 'industrial colony' by specializing in labour-intensive manufacturing for export as the world economy underwent major restructuring after the
war. On the basis of its strong commercial linkages with the regional and world
economies, Hong Kong was able to capitalize on new opportunities created by this
restructuring to develop a manufacturing sector that was highly responsive to
changing market needs abroad. During the 1980s, Hong Kong consolidated its status as a major financial centre and seized the opportunities created by the reopening
of socialist China's economy to move its manufacturing offshore, mainly to the
newly established special economic zones and the nearby region of the Pearl River
Delta just across the border. The relocation of manufacturing triggered a highly
compressed process of economic restructuring that caused a drastic decline in the
manufacturing sector's contributions to Hong Kong's employment (from 47.0 per
cent in 1971 to 4.7 per cent in 2006) and gross domestic product (from 28.2 per cent
in 1971 to 3.1 per cent in 2006). These drastic socio-economic changes reflect a
major transformation in the economic geography of Hong Kong and its neighbouring region. Hong Kong is the major driving force for a new local and regional division of labour. It also needs to adjust to such changes.

The socio-economic impacts of economic restructuring will be examined in
Chapter 4. There we shall look at Hong Kong critically with reference to the debate
in the global city literature about whether rising inequalities and growing social
polarization are inevitable outcomes of becoming a global city. We draw for this
purpose upon our empirical analysis of the changing employment structure and patterns of income inequality in contemporary Hong Kong. And, in Chapter 6, we
extend our discussion of economic restructuring with an examination of Hong

Kong's reintegration, economic as well as political, with China before and after 1997, the year when China resumed sovereignty over Hong Kong. Not only has Hong Kong become a part of China politically, its economic future has also become increasingly dependent on China's integration with the global economy. Contrary to the expectation that globalization loosens a city's connection with its national and regional economies, Hong Kong is becoming increasingly re-embedded in the broader regional and national, economic environment of China as well as its neighbouring economies. Cross-border economic activity and flows of people have increased exponentially in both directions. Furthermore, Hong Kong is eager to find new opportunities on the mainland as China deepens its economic reform and emerges as an economic powerhouse in the Asian regional and global economy.

Not only is our story longer, it is also broader than what is available in existing accounts. Chapter 3 traces Hong Kong's pathway to its status as a commercial and financial centre. We underline the effects of geo-politics and institutions on the well-rehearsed story of Hong Kong as a financial centre. Our historical analysis of the emergence of Hong Kong as a regional and then global financial centre in the post-war decades echoes our emphasis on the formation of global city. It is also an attempt to unravel the economic and political dynamics in the shaping of opportunities for development and the institutional responses to such openings.

In Chapter 5, we examine urban governance in detail, with the intention of demonstrating the importance of bringing politics back in to the study of the global city. It is often simply assumed that the rise and fall of a global city hinges upon adaptation to the changing environment. A core-centric approach, which views the dynamics of the global economy from the angle of the core economies, assumes that global cities in the semi-periphery are dependent and reactive. They respond to whatever opportunities are presented by the changing market environment. But how these opportunities are seized at the right time and utilized fully is left unexamined. We argue that the institutional configuration of a global city helps to explain why and whether opportunities are effectively captured or missed.

Our larger story of Hong Kong as a global city, therefore, addresses broader theoretical issues. In particular, we use the experience of Hong Kong to reflect upon the theoretical adequacies of existing global city studies. It is our contention that the case of Hong Kong can help to illuminate the nature of global city formation – that is, the processes whereby cities have come to develop their linkages with the world economy and to assume global city status. Global city formation is not simply an outcome of the changing world economy. Some cities do, and others do not, become global cities. Those that become global cities do so because they have developed the institutional structures that facilitate and strengthen global linkages and better prepare their urban economies to meet new challenges.

Global city studies

Our study of Hong Kong as a Chinese global city is informed by the literature on the world city (Friedmann and Wolff 1982; Friedmann 1986, 1995) and the global city (Sassen 1991, 2000, 2001, 2002). Readers whose interests lie in the historical pathways that Hong Kong has gone through in making itself into a global city may want to go directly to our analysis in Chapter 1 and the following chapters. For those who are interested in finding out more about the theoretical framework upon which this book is based, our discussion here summarizes our critique and an elaboration of a sociological framework for studying global cities. Global city studies, which have proliferated since the 1980s and cover a wide range of cities in different parts of the world (for a summary, see Taylor 2004), promise to cast new light on our understanding of both the city (and inter-city networks) and the changing world economy. The growth of this literature itself reflects the impacts of economic restructuring on the world economy in the past decades, namely the intensification of global flows of economic activity, the deepening of economic penetration through global finance and multinational corporations into different parts of the world, and the consolidation of major cities as nodal points of global business. Cities, and not nation-states, are becoming the key nodes of all these globally connected activities (Abrahamson 2004: 2).

The notion of the world city is not new. Gottmann (1989: 62) notes that Goethe, with Rome and Paris in mind, used the term when describing the leading cultural centres. Geddes (see Taylor 2004: 21) introduced the idea of a world league of cities, hinting at a world hierarchy of cities within which some cities assumed major positions and roles. Writing from the perspective of human ecology, McKenzie hinted at the formation of a spider-web-like hierarchy of world cities (see quotation above). Hall (1966), whose interests lie more in urban planning than in analysing inter-city networks, developed Geddes's idea and identified six leading urban centres in the world. But the systematic study of the world city or the global city really took off in the 1980s following Friedmann's (Friedmann and Wolff 1982; Friedmann 1986) observation that a 'new international division of labour' (Frobel *et al*. 1980) had facilitated a more global penetration by multinational corporations with the result that major cities had emerged as centres of economic control and coordination. Though cities have always played a significant economic role historically, now they had become even more important in the context of intensified global flows of people and economic activity.

Against this background, a network of global cities arises from the spatial manifestation of capital accumulation in the new global economy. What drives this emergence of global cities is posited to be the dual processes of dispersal of production and centralization of control. As the global mobility of capital and commodities accelerated, production dispersed geographically, especially manufacturing. Firms have aggressively globalized their operations since the 1980s in search of cheaper labour and lucrative markets. It is not only corporations originating from the core countries that have pursued this strategy; some firms from the developing semi-periphery of the world economy have followed a similar strategy.

As spatial dispersion grows, so does the need for more effective mechanisms of coordination and control of a firm's economic activities. This leads in turn to greater centralization in coordination and control functions. The concentration of ownership in a smaller number of mega-corporations reinforces this trend. But it is the sheer scale and complexity of global transactions that brings about the expansion of top-level multinational operating headquarters and the concomitant growth of services firms that cater to them: insurance, banking, financial services, real estate, legal services, accounting, consultancy and professional associations. Sassen classifies these firms as producer services that include 'not only services to production firms narrowly defined but also those to all other types of organizations' (1991: 91). The distinctive feature of producer services is thus the fact that they are intermediate outputs produced not for final consumers but for other organizations. While the firms providing producer services do not typically depend on proximity to final consumers, they do need to keep abreast of new developments in their field and of what firms are doing. Producer services therefore often exhibit a tendency towards locational concentration. New York and London are global cities essentially for their extraordinary concentration of a variety of service firms. In sum,

> Global cities are, however, not only nodal points for the coordination of processes; they are also particular sites of production. They are sites for (1) the production of specialized services needed by complex organizations for running a spatially dispersed network of factories, offices, and service outlets; and (2) the production of financial innovations and the making of markets, both central to the internationalization and expansion of the financial industry. To understand the structure of a global city, we have to understand it as a place where certain kinds of work can get done, which is to say that we have to get beyond the dichotomy between manufacturing and services. The 'things' a global city makes are highly specialized services and financial goods.
>
> (Sassen 2001: 5)

The three theses of global cities research

The essence of the theses about the world city and the global city put forward by Friedmann (1986, 1995; also Friedmann and Wolff 1982) and Sassen (1991, 2000, 2001) lies in their attempt to capture the impacts of the structural transformation of the world economy towards accelerated globalization and increasing interconnectedness on urban development. Though their arguments and their implications differ in some respects (see Sassen 2001: xix), they can be summarized in three basic theses. The first thesis, *the global urban network and hierarchy thesis*, suggests that a network of global cities arises as the spatial manifestation of capital accumulation in the world economy. The second thesis, *the global city function thesis*, posits that the location of each individual global city in the global urban network is determined by the 'functions assigned to the city' (Friedmann 1986: 70). Alternatively, as Sassen (2000: 4) puts it, by its contribution to the operation of the global economy as command points in the organization of the world economy, that is, as key locations and marketplaces for the leading industries of the current period – finance and specialized services for firms, and major sites of production and innovation for these industries.

These two theses highlight the existence of a dual process of dispersal of production and centralization of control in the structuring of the emergent global cities.

The linkages among the global cities that result from the changing division of labour in the global economy constitute a 'complex spatial hierarchy' (Friedmann 1986: 71). Implicit in the global city function thesis is the idea that cities' contribution to the coordination and control of global economic activity and the production of specialized services would be reflected in their positioning in the different tiers constituting the hierarchy of global cities. Those belonging to the first tier are expected to be key global players, while those in the second tier assume a more important role at the sub-national or regional level.

The third thesis, *the dual city thesis*, is that the functions performed by each global city would shape in turn the nature of its socio-economic structure. More specifically, the socio-economic structure of the global city will come to be characterized by rising social inequalities and social polarization. There are two aspects of growing inequalities in global cities. First, the gap between global and globalizing cities on the one side and those in the peripheries on the other is growing. Second, social inequalities within a global city are also found glaring. The idea of the dual city is primarily an attempt to address the latter question, examining the changing social structure and its social consequences within a global city.

The growing literature on world cities and global cities (useful surveys include Friedmann 1995; Beaverstock, Taylor and Smith 1999; Short and Kim 1999; Brenner and Keil 2006) can be grouped into three main areas that roughly correspond to the proposition expressed by these three theses: the mapping of the global city network and hierarchy (Taylor 2004); case studies illustrating the changing urban functions and cityscape (Abu-Lughod 1999; Sassen 2001); and issues concerning the socio-economic consequences (rising income inequalities and social polarization) of becoming a global city (Mollenkopf and Castells 1991; Sassen 2001). A number of questions have been raised as a result of this research, about the theoretical and empirical validity of the original theses put forward by Friedmann and Sassen. Rather than going into specific details of criticism by individual commentators targeted at either theoretical problems or the empirical basis of the claims made in the literature, we concentrate instead only on those criticisms that question the basics of the global city theses.

Methodological issues

The global city thesis has been criticized first for its methodological inadequacy on the grounds that 'Ideas are asserted more than demonstrated' (Short and Kim 1999: 8). Taylor (2004) goes further in confronting directly the key texts on global city analysis by arguing that the claims about inter-city networks and the existence of an urban hierarchy, which together form the major contentions of this line of research, are not supported by the evidence. Drawing upon Jacobs' (1986) analysis of the city economy, Taylor argues for a city-centred approach, and therefore rejects the notion of a national urban hierarchy, implicit in global city analysis, for the study of the development of inter-city connections.

Taylor's attempt to provide a rigorous empirical mapping and a theoretical foundation for studying inter-city relations and connectivity is a valuable contribution to global city research. His work provides us with both a city-centred perspective (thus giving us a framework that is closer to the original idea of the world city or the global city) for analysing the development of inter-city networks and a data-driven structural mapping for understanding the position of the individual city in the macro context. He has made an important contribution in going beyond the mapping of the hierarchy of world cities originally formulated by Friedmann (1986), by giving it the necessary analytical and empirical substance. Yet, because of his focus on structural mapping and related analytical issues, Taylor has paid little attention to questions concerning global city formation, particularly the processes by which it occurs and the role of governance (Olds and Yeung 2004).

Second, the literature on global cities has been criticized for being ahistorical in viewing contemporary developments as a sharp break from the past, for neglecting the diverse ways that cities respond to global forces, and for rarely taking space seriously (King 1991; Ward 1995; Abu-Lughod 1999: 2; Smith 2001). Again, Taylor's global urban analysis is relatively sensitive to these problems. Not only has he emphasized the need to restore historical understanding of global city development in different phases of the development of the world economy (see Taylor 2004: Chapter 1), he also includes in his analysis a disaggregation and a geography of different types of services. Yet his treatment of history and the networking process at the structural level has its limitations. Structural analysis is good at mapping linkages and spelling out the broader framework of inter-city competition, but has little to offer on the question of how global cities come into being (Robinson 2002; Olds and Yeung 2004; Wang 2004). How mobility in the global urban hierarchy is materialized cannot be explained solely by an analysis of opportunities and possibilities at the macro level. Although the structural mapping can explain the broader context and the availability of opportunities for development, it tells us very little about how individual cities are able to capitalize on the opportunities opened to them by the process of macro restructuring in the world economy. In addition to a structural analysis of networking, we also need to look into the processes of global city formation. For a more complete understanding of the making of global cities, meso-level institutional analysis and an examination of the role of agency are required.

The above criticisms point to an inherent problem in global city analysis. In the first instance, the foci on structural mapping of global urban hierarchy and inter-city relations and linkages at the global level have led to a de-emphasis or downright neglect of agents and/or actors in the making of global city. Furthermore, the emphasis on the global economic context and the focus on mobile global capital have prematurely written off the active role of the state (Wang 2004) and other critical players (e.g. the formation of a pro-growth coalition within a city for the promotion of policy conducive to becoming a global city) in global city formation. The discussion has often taken the form of crude economism: the broader global economic structure, or more directly the functions to be performed by global cities, determines the structure of the global urban hierarchy and the fate of individual cities in this stratified urban system. This economism also takes the form of core-centric functionalism – that is, economic functions required by the core of global capitalism largely determine the role to be played by different layers of global cities. Yet, as Brenner and Keil (2006: 12) emphasize, 'local agents act and react to pressures of global restructuring, but they are also active producers of globalization processes. They are the builders of the global city'.

Furthermore, underlying this emphasis on the global economy and its power to shape the fortune of global cities, lies a Euro-American-centric perspective (Ward 1995; Robinson 2002; Gugler 2003). This is most evident in the difference in research focus between the studies of global cities in the USA and Europe on the one side, and Asia (perhaps with the exception of Tokyo) on the other. In the study of existing global cities, especially those well-documented global cities like New York, London and Tokyo, 'All too often structures of city governance are either taken as a "given", or are ignored altogether' (Ward 1995: 298). This Euro-American-centric perspective is, as noted above, closely connected with core-centric functionalism and structural hierarchy and ranking built into the literature on global city research. The fact that these cities almost command unchallenged status in the literature leads to an under-emphasis on local politics and the institutional basis of governance (Ward 1995). By contrast, studies of potential and aspiring global cities in developing countries, whether in East Asia (Wang 2004) or South America (Ward 1995), are keen to 'put politics and government back into the world cities agenda' (Ward 1995: 298). Research on global cities outside the core, largely driven by the concern about how to push major cities in developing countries further up the global urban hierarchy, is far more attentive to the importance of institutional and political analysis and the role of actors/agencies. In other words, it pursues a research agenda concerning the processes that facilitate some cities to become (or fail to become) global cities. This leads in turn to a focus on the question of urban governance, which has been unduly neglected, as an important component of the research on global city formation.

The significance of place

Critiques of global cities research for its weak empirical basis and over-reliance on structural analysis also point out that global cities research tends to see such leading cities too broadly in terms of their functions in the global economy. Equally pertinent is the temptation, dangerous indeed, of viewing the city as a globalizing and autonomous economic unit, and thus the global economy as no more than networks and flows linking up cities through nodes in the global urban hierarchy. While the value of these criticisms is noted, it should be pointed out that world cities researchers have long recognized the significance of place in understanding the development of global cities (see Sassen's reinstatement of her arguments, 2001: 349–50):

> The place-ness of the global city is a crucial theoretical and methodological issue in my work. Theoretically it captures Harvey's notion of capital fixity as necessary for hypermobility. A key issue for me has been to introduce into our notions of globalization the fact that capital even if dematerialized is not

simply hypermobile or that trade and investment and information flows are not only about flows. Further, place-ness also signals an embeddedness in what has been constructed as the 'national,' as in national economy and national territory. This brings with it a consideration of political issues and theorizations about the role of the state in the global economy which are excluded in more conventional accounts about the global economy.

Short *et al.* (2000: 318) also put forward the thesis of the gateway city with the intention of shifting the attention 'away from which cities dominate to how cities are affected by globalization'. By focusing on 'the transmission of economic, political and cultural globalization', the gateway city thesis highlights the interconnectedness of the global city and its surrounding region. Indeed, it points to the interactions between the local and the regional.

This emphasis on the significance of place makes it easier to connect global cities research with the new concept of the global city-region (Scott 2001). This regional dimension of global city underlines the fact that the development of global city, despite its articulation with the global economy and thus a strong connection with distant economic locations and activity, is always embedded in a wider and yet proximate social, political and spatial context. The key implication of this emphasis on embeddedness of global cities is that instead of seeing global cities as globalizing economic units that are disembedded from their immediate environment, we need to tease out how they are contextualized in different layers of the broader socio-economic and political structures.

One of the key features of our analysis of Hong Kong becoming a global city underlines the embeddedness of the global city and the significance of national and regional factors in shaping global city development. Instead of seeing global cities as globalizing economic units that are disembedded from their immediate environment, we try to analyse how different layers of the broader socio-economic and political structures impact on the making of a global city. A focus on the significance of place in understanding the global city requires taking seriously the interplay of the global and the local, the interactions of national, regional and local levels, and the issue of urban governance.

Governance: without and within

There are different layers of political embeddedness. What is especially relevant to our present discussion is that the national is more than just the backdrop for the rise and fall of global cities (Massey 2007: 17–21). Despite the fact that globalization brings with it new challenges to the capacity of the nation-state to deal with new issues relating to the management of the national economy, the power and effects of the national remain real enough in shaping the parameters that structure the development of global cities (on the myth of the powerlessness of the state under globalization, see Weiss 1998). State policy at the national level defines and redefines how global cities are connected with their neighbouring regions, and thus draws and redraws the boundary with their hinterland. The state can also develop new rules and regulations that either expand or restrict global cities' interconnectedness with the regional and the world economy. This is not to deny or to underestimate the significance of the sub-national and the impacts of new regionalism (i.e. local regions taking the initiative in carrying out economic, political and social mobilization to deal with economic restructuring in the face of globalization) in the shaping of economic development. Our point rather is to highlight the fact that whether and how the national is relevant or otherwise is an empirical question. Globalization per se does not make the role of the nation-state irrelevant. The state continues to exert its influence, albeit in different ways, on regional social formation (and thus the configuration of the global cities' hinterland).[1] The re-scaling of a global city is always closely connected to the state's re-scaling project. As Brenner (1998) puts it, 'Global city formation cannot be adequately understood without an examination of the matrices of state territorial organization within and through which it occurs.' In other words, the question of development for global cities is always a project embedded in a broader regional and national context. Indeed, the question of governance for a global city is, by default, a city-region or city-nation issue. The global city's management of its growth and development always requires coordination and collaboration that go beyond its city boundary. How inter-city as well as city-region 'development coalitions' (Keating 2001) are created to foster the growth and development of global cities is a crucial issue in urban governance that lies beyond the boundary and scope of the global city itself.

Equally important is the question of governance within the global city (also see Brenner and Keil 2006: 130–1). Ward (1995: 299–300) criticizes existing research for giving insufficient attention to 'the political-administrative structures through which such cities are governed and managed'. The political and institutional basis for the success of leading global cities in attaining their current positions has been largely taken for granted. As noted above, this neglect of the political question is partly an outcome of the use of structuralist (the focus on positioning within the world economy and the global urban hierarchy) and functionalist (the focus on contributions to global financial and producer services) explanations in global city research. It is partly a consequence also of an under-emphasis on the processes of global city formation (i.e. of ignoring how a place is governed and managed in order to capitalize on the opportunities opened by economic restructuring in the world economy). In brief, global city research can benefit from incorporating a political economy of place.

Research on the urban growth machine (Molotch 1976; Logan and Molotch 1987; Jonas and Wilson 1999) and urban regime (Lauria 1997) does not address the question of governance of the global city directly but is still relevant to our discussion here. Despite their differences (Harding 1995; Stoker 1995), research on the urban growth machine and urban regime has pointed to some crucial aspects of urban politics, namely the need to go beyond a focus on the local state, the interplay of public and private agencies in shaping urban development, the internal politics of coalition building, the building of capacity for action, and a choice of policy or path of development. For a deeper understanding of the growth and development of global cities in developing countries, how a global city project (often expressed in the forms of heavy investments in infrastructure construction, the building of spectacular architectural landmarks, hosting of mega-events, etc.) is made viable in terms of capacity building, mobilization of resources and the construction of a hegemonic alliance to support such a venture is always an open question. Through examining the nature of urban governance, we probe the institutional configuration and the role of actors/agencies in the making of global cities. As noted above, opportunities come and go. It is important to know how a city is capable of capturing the new openings or otherwise in changing its position and fortune in the global urban hierarchy. Governance is one of the key variables in determining a city's capacity for action in becoming a global city.

Dual social structure

So far we have discussed the processes of global city formation. As noted earlier, equally important in studies of global cities is the issue of the outcomes of becoming a global city (i.e. the dual city thesis). One view is that global city formation has a similar impact everywhere on urban social structure. By contrast, our emphasis on the significance of place and the institutional as well as political configuration of global city formation points to the possibility that globalization can have diverse outcomes for urban social structure. While the hypothesis put forward by Friedmann and Sassen on dualism in the social structure of the global city should be taken seriously, how and why social polarization and rising inequalities come about is an analytical and empirical question deserving our attention.

The relationship between global city development and social polarization has generated a rich body of literature debating and testing the validity of the thesis. Most of the relevant studies have focused on global cities in the USA and Europe. Baum's contributions (1997, 1999) are among the few exceptions that go beyond such geographical limits. In this book we intend to contribute to this ongoing discussion by examining the case of Hong Kong, another global city outside of the primary axes of London, New York and Tokyo. Hong Kong is an ideal site for testing the dual city thesis because it has undergone the critical transformation postulated in the global city literature in the most striking manner in that the decline of secondary production and expansion of services, and especially producer services, has been rapid and extensive. Hong Kong can thus serve as a critical case for assessing whether social polarization is in fact an inevitable outcome associated with the development of global cities. Moreover, by using the Hong Kong population census micro-data rather than published aggregate data, we can conduct a more direct test of the polarization thesis by examining the relationship between structural and occupational changes.

One of the most interesting and controversial aspects of the global city thesis concerns the impact of the emergence of global cities as post-industrial production sites, and the ascendance of finance and producer services on the broader social and economic structure of major cities – the so-called polarization thesis. Friedmann and Wolff (1982: 320) noted that, 'The dynamism of the world city economy results chiefly from the growth of a primary cluster of high level business services which employs a large number of professionals – the transnational elite – and ancillary staffs of clerical personnel.' Allied to this primary cluster are other poles of employment growth. One is the personal services and other amenities catering for the new elite: restaurants, hotels, luxury boutiques, entertainment, real estate, domestic services and security. The other growing sectors are international tourism and government services. All these sectoral and occupational trends are argued to have negative consequences for social equity in the form of rising social inequality and a more skewed income distribution. Sassen (1998: 137) drew our attention to growing differences in the earning capacities of different kinds of employees working in different economic sectors, the casualization of the employment relation and the rise of urban marginality. In global cities, 'class polarization has three principal facets: huge income gaps between transnational elites and low-skilled workers, large-scale immigration from rural areas or from abroad, and structural trends in evolution of jobs' (Friedmann 1995: 324). Employment expansion tends to cluster at the top and bottom ends of the occupational/income distribution at the expense of the middle. The processes of deindustrialization and expanding service industries have both contributed to this phenomenon. Manufacturing jobs that once provided middle-level income have been replaced by a duality of jobs in services that tend to be either relatively well paid or poorly paid. Sassen (1998) underlines the casualization of the employment relation in the form of rising job insecurity and part-time jobs at the lower end of the labour market and in the labour-intensive service industries. As a result of the dualization in the organization of service industries, jobs at the bottom are often filled by marginal workers, primarily documented or undocumented migrants from countries with a lower level of development. The image of an 'hourglass' has also been invoked to describe the social structure of the global city (Marcuse 1989: 699).

The polarization thesis has been subjected to considerable critical review (see especially Hamnett 1994, 1996). First, the concept as presented by Sassen is found to be ambiguous and ill-defined. To test whether there is polarization, we need to distinguish between relative and absolute polarization – that is, whether it means a widening of the gap between the top and the bottom in the occupational hierarchy, or whether it means that globalization will create a larger number of low-skilled and/or low-paid jobs in addition to the increase in professional and managerial jobs. Furthermore, it is also necessary to assess whether polarization occurs in the occupational structure or is largely manifested in income distribution.

Second, the polarization thesis is also said to contradict findings from the wider literature on the changing occupational structure in advanced capitalist societies, especially the evidence for the growth of professionalization and the new middle class. Third, it is also questionable whether the hypothesis can be generalized to other advanced countries because it could be contingent on the experiences of New York and Los Angeles, where high levels of immigration accentuated the processes of dualization and casualization in the service sector. A more general issue therefore is to what extent polarization, if it occurs, is a result of the economic restructuring forced by globalization and how much it is shaped by local institutional contexts such as policies on immigration. Finally, there is the issue of gender: to what extent are the growing inequalities in the global city gender-specific? These are the key questions that need to be addressed in discussing the social consequences of becoming a global city.

Summary

In the following chapters we shall take up the questions raised above in our analysis of Hong Kong as a Chinese global city. We contextualize Hong Kong's emergence as a global city in the structuring and restructuring of the world economy as well as in its national and regional economic and political environment. In emphasizing the broader regional and national context of global city, our discussion aims to be sensitive to geo-politics, and the changing parameters and effects of both the national and the regional levels. Global city formation, in other words, is not simply an outcome of exogenous factors in the world economy. How specific cities are able to capitalize on opportunities in the changing world economy is crucial to our understanding of the processes through which some cities are able to reach global city status and others are not. The formation process itself needs to be addressed. Our case study of Hong Kong is intended to unpack this formation process.

We shall also examine the socio-economic consequences of becoming a global city, particularly in terms of rising social inequalities and social polarization. We not only look at the socio-economic outcomes empirically, we also underline through our analysis the pertinence of the institutional configuration of the global city in shaping the social fabric and contours of the city itself. By analysing both the institutional settings and the social consequences of global city development, we gain a better understanding of the complexities of global cities. There are different types of global city. Local institutional settings have their impacts on shaping the social fabric of the global city. An awareness of how local specificities matter is important to future comparative global city research.

1 Global connections

Centre of Chinese capitalism

> Hong Kong, as a place, was and continues to be at the organizing center of Chinese-led capitalism. Hong Kong assumed this role shortly after its founding in the nineteenth century and continued it until World War II. Then after the war and the Chinese revolution, Hong Kong was the first location where Chinese capitalism reemerged, although in a somewhat changed form.
>
> (Hamilton 1999: 15)

Introduction

Exposure to globalization is hardly new to Hong Kong. Right from its beginnings as a British colony in the nineteenth century, Hong Kong was declared a free port (by Elliot in June 1841) with no restrictions on foreign trade and investment. It subsequently became an important trading port as well as a commercial city not only for advancing the economic and political interests of the British Empire but also for facilitating regional trade and finance between China and other Asian economies. Indeed, Hong Kong's strength as a commercial city and trading port lies in her interconnectedness with not one but a variety of economic networks. This chapter provides a historical backdrop to our discussion of the emergence of Hong Kong as a centre of Chinese capitalism for the past 160 years.

The beginning

Archaeological findings suggest that human settlements in Hong Kong date back to 6000 BC. The discovery of an Eastern Han (AD 25–220) tomb in Kowloon is another piece of archaeological evidence of a long historical connection with the southern region of the mainland. But regular Chinese settlement in the New Territories began only during the Song dynasty (Hayes 1977: 25). During the Tang dynasty, garrisons were established in Tuen Mun, where the Portuguese landed in 1514. According to the official gazetteer records that first appeared in the late sixteenth century, what was later to become Hong Kong, Kowloon and the New Territories were included in San On County. In brief, the history of Hong Kong does not begin with the arrival of the British. But, once it became a colony, Hong Kong was channelled towards a different path of development.

Hong Kong was first occupied by British troops in 1841 and then formally ceded to Britain under the Nanjing Treaty in 1842. Hong Kong island was, by British accounts, sparsely populated at that time. A statement on the conditions of the Island of Hong Kong prepared in 1844 reported that:

> On taking possession of Hong Kong, it was found to contain about 7,500 inhabitants, scattered over 20 fishing hamlets and villages. The requirements of the fleet and troops, the demands for labourers to make roads and houses, and the servants of Europeans, increased the number of inhabitants, and in March 1842, they were numbered at 12,361. In April, 1844, the number of Chinese on the island is computed at 19,000, of whom not more than 1,000 are women and children. In the census are included 97 women slaves, and the females attendant on 31 brothels, eight gambling-houses, and 20 opium shops, &c. ... There is no trade of any noticeable extent in Hong Kong.
>
> (Jarman 1996: 9, 11)

R. Montgomery Martin, the Colonial Treasurer who prepared this statement on Hong Kong, objected to the choice of the island for British occupation, arguing that, 'On a review of the whole case, there are no assignable grounds for the political or military occupancy of Hong Kong, even if there were no expense attending that occupancy' (Jarman 1996: 16). This echoed the comment by Lord Palmerston, the British Foreign Secretary, to Elliot concerning his occupation of Hong Kong that it was, in his eyes, 'a barren island with hardly a house upon it' (quoted from Welsh 1997: 108). Palmerston further remarked that 'it seems obvious that Hong Kong will not be a Mart of Trade' (Welsh 1997: 108). The acquisition of Hong Kong was not without controversy among the British (Carroll 2005: 38–46) and this controversy continued for years afterwards (Zhang 2001: 21–2). Chusan, which was strategically located for future interests in Guangzhou, was repeatedly cited as a better choice for the advancement of British interests. In fact, as shown in Martin's exchanges with the British government, even after the exchange of the ratifications of the Treaty of Nanjing, arguments about the desirability of the acquisition of Hong Kong continued. Our point here is that while British descriptions about the barrenness of Hong Kong might have been overstated, they did point to an important fact about the motivation for the colonization of Hong Kong: the British had their eyes on expanding business opportunities with China, and Hong Kong was not an obvious choice of acquisition for that purpose.

The British had in fact seriously entertained the idea of surrendering Hong Kong in exchange for other, more economically promising concessions from China. But Pottinger, who was initially hugely disappointed by the Chuenpi agreement, was later convinced of 'the necessity and desirability of our possessing such a settlement as an emporium for our trade and a place from which Her Majesty's subjects in China may be alike protected and controlled' (quoted in Endacott 1973: 22). To conduct business with China, the British needed a sheltered harbour and a land base for related logistics. These, and not Hong Kong's natural resources nor a population constituting an attractive market, were the primary advantages of Hong Kong

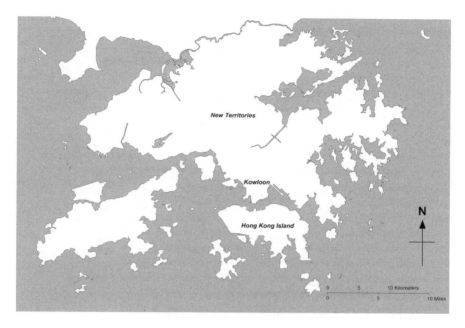

Figure 1.1 Map of Hong Kong

for the British. Because of these considerations, the British did not develop their base in existing major settlements in the Eastern and southern parts of the island but set up their military and administrative operations on the northern shore instead (Ho 2004: 17). This area was developed into the City of Victoria. Later, with the cessation of Kowloon in 1860 and the lease of the New Territories in 1898, the territorial boundaries of colonial Hong Kong were finalized (see Figure 1.1). Despite her long historical linkages with China, Hong Kong's subsequent development into a trading port and commercial city, boosted by an influx of Chinese, was largely an outcome of the rise of the City of Victoria.

The rise of a city of trade, commerce and finance

As one might have guessed from the above discussion about the controversy among the British over the acquisition of Hong Kong, there were few signs during the early years of colonization foretelling Hong Kong's subsequent economic success. Contrary to Pottinger's prediction in 1842 that 'Within six months of Hong Kong being declared to have become a permanent Colony, it will be a vast emporium of commerce and wealth' (quoted in Endacott 1973: 72), the City of Victoria soon found itself in a difficult situation. The opening of five treaty ports to the British, as stipulated in the Treaty of Nanjing, actually undermined Hong Kong's role as a centre of transhipment. Indeed, in the 1840s, 'Hong Kong survived ..., not primarily through the development of a free trade between Britain and China (which took place slowly at the mainland ports), but as a depot for two semi-monopolistic and still technically illegal enterprises: the importation of opium into China and the traffic in labourers out of China' (Munn 2001: 23). Hong Kong thus did not develop into an important port for entrepot trade immediately after the arrival of the British.

It did not take long, however, before the City of Victoria was turned from a British frontier colony into a vibrant trading and commercial city. Following closely behind the military troops, major British traders almost immediately moved their head offices for their business operations in the region to Hong Kong (Endacott 1973: 76; Tsang 2004: 56–7). In this connection, Hong Kong was also gradually developed into a centre for services, more precisely shipping and repair services, for the businesses concerned.

It was during the 1850s, however, that Hong Kong's prospects 'were becoming brighter' (Fairbank 1969: 239) as the island experienced a rapid growth of economic activity. The Chinese population in Hong Kong increased sharply during this period, rising from 28,297 in 1849 to 85,280 in 1859 (Tsai 1993: 22, 299). Two external factors facilitated this turnaround in Hong Kong's business fortunes. First, the discovery of gold and the resultant gold rush in California in 1848 and then a couple of years later in New South Wales, Australia, created a strong demand for labourers. Hong Kong became, as a result of increasing activity related to the dispatch of Chinese coolie emigrants abroad, 'the key staging post for Chinese emigration' (Tsang 2004: 58). Second, political and social disorder on the mainland drove people from the southern part of China, both merchants and labourers, to seek refuge in Hong Kong (Fan 1974: 1). This experience was to be repeated a number of times in the course of Hong Kong's history: 'trouble in China was a "god-send" for Hong Kong' (Munn 2001: 49; also see Eitel 1983: 259). As Carroll (2005: 50) notes, 'The combination of the Taiping Rebellion and the growth of Chinese communities overseas did more than save Hong Kong from an economic depression; it changed the island's basic reason for being. Hong Kong was transformed from a colonial outpost into the center of a transnational trade network stretching from the China coast to Southeast Asia and then to Australia and North America.' And Hong Kong was quick to capitalize on these new opportunities, changing itself in the process into a seaport with growing business activity.

The business of exporting Chinese labourers began in Xiamen in 1845 (Peng 1981: 181). The huge demand for Chinese labourers sprang from the gold rush in the United States of America and Australia, and the intensification of colonization and capitalist penetration into Asia and Latin America. Chinese labourers, who were cheap and productive, were much in demand and were exported not only to the USA and British colonies, but also to more remote places such as Cuba and Peru (Peng 1981: 191). The emigration business enabled the shipping companies, brokers and labour recruiters to make huge profits from the coolie trade. But the impacts of the emigration business extended far beyond benefiting those directly involved in the organization of coolie labour. Closely related to the emigration business were rope manufacturing, shipbuilding, repairing and refitting, and provisioning for ships. As a result of the growth of coastal and international shipping services, the demand for professional services increased so that medical facilities, legal advice, money exchange and insurance services became available. The growth of overseas Chinese communities (and their demands for supplies from their native places) stimulated an increase in international commercial and trading activities. Indeed, 'both European and Chinese mercantile communities in Hong Kong prospered by providing commercial, financial and professional services' (Tsai 1993: 26). More critically, the demand for financial services, particularly services driven by the emigrant labourers' remittances to their hometowns (Hamashita 1997a), created the conditions for the growth of banking and financial activities in Hong Kong from the 1860s.

As noted above, the emigration business involved more than simply human trafficking. The rise of Chinese communities abroad created demands for commercial and financial activities. The establishment of the so-called 'jinshan zhuang' and 'nanyang zhuang' in Hong Kong, firms specialized in shipping supplies to North America and Australia, and Southeast Asia respectively, served as intermediaries between the growing overseas Chinese communities and the emigrants' hometowns (Zhang 2001: 182–7). In addition to the shipment of supplies to overseas Chinese communities, these 'jinshan zhuang' and 'nanyang zhuang' also assumed the role of recruitment agents for emigrant labourers and financial intermediaries. They handled in particular the remittances of emigrant labourers. And that business gradually evolved into commercial lending and credit as well.

In brief, Hong Kong's participation in the transhipment of emigrant labourers and goods had a much bigger impact on its economy and society than merely promoting shipping and related activities. A whole cluster of economic activities, from shipping and related manufacturing activities to commerce and finance, grew concomitantly with the rise of Hong Kong as a seaport. Internal trade within China also reinforced the momentum of economic growth and development in Hong Kong. As Kose (1994) argues, major centres of commerce and finance like Hong Kong and Shanghai benefited enormously from Chinese internal trade. First, they were centres of regional economies. Second, internal trade was controlled primarily by Chinese merchants. Because of a shortage of currency, most of the trading activities and the related financing (e.g. the issuing of certificates of credit) were carried out by a settlement system under the Chinese merchants' control. This settlement system worked as a clearing house for business transactions among the local merchants. As a result, Hong Kong and Shanghai functioned both as a centre of trade and of settlement. And because of their international connections, Hong Kong and Shanghai had an additional advantage:

> The settlement system was profitable for the Chinese import–export merchants and promoted bartering. It made trade expansion possible even when little silver cash was available. ... Foreign merchants did not have locally produced Chinese goods which could be exchanged together with their goods. ... This placed foreign merchants at a disadvantage, and in the late nineteenth century foreign merchants withdrew from local ports to trading centres at Shanghai or Hong Kong.
>
> (Kose 1994: 140–1)

There are two points to note here. First, once Hong Kong's pace of development picked up from the 1850s, the different kinds of economic activity worked to reinforce each other in strengthening Hong Kong's role as a commercial and financial intermediary in the changing global economy (Endacott 1964a: xiii, xv). Hong Kong became a base of operations for British traders' head offices, a centre for the transhipment of emigrant labourers, a seaport with growing supporting industries for interregional and international trades, and a financial hub for remittances and the settlement of payment for commercial activities. Not only did each of these activities develop its forward and backward linkages, thus reinforcing the momentum of growth and development, more importantly together they brought Hong Kong into world and regional trading, financial and migration networks. They literally put Hong Kong on the map of the world economy.

Second, Hong Kong's rise as a centre of trade and finance was not simply an outcome of Western colonialism (also see Carroll 2005). Nor can we explain Hong Kong's changing path of development in the nineteenth century simply from the perspective of the metropolitan centre of imperialism (cf. Stoler and Cooper 1997: 29). The socio-economic development of Hong Kong was not determined by the metropolitan centre. Pre-existing interregional and transnational networks of economic activity were equally, if not more, important in shaping Hong Kong's path of development:

> The growth of Hong Kong after 1842 into an entrepot owed a great deal to the interregional and international trades already developed in the region centuries before the Opium War. In fact, British Hong Kong inherited these trades, which had long been carried on, with Canton and Whampoa as a transhipment port for commodities from various parts of China, Northeast Asia, Southeast Asia, and the Western world.
>
> (Tsai 1993: 17)

And Hong Kong was not alone in finding that the immediate impacts of colonialism were more limited than expected. Singapore, another British colony and an important trading port in Southeast Asia, was also a case that experienced little direct benefit from British imperial connections. In fact, Britain was 'not a very important trading partner' (Latham 1994: 158–9) for both Singapore and Hong Kong. Singapore's rise to the status of important trading port had a lot to do with its intra-Asian trading networks:

> [T]he dynamic element in Singapore's trade was Western purchases of tin and rubber, which drew imports to Singapore which were then re-exported West. The purchasing power which was thus transmitted to Singapore and Asia was not then channelled back to Britain, America and other Western countries, but retained in Asia where it was spent to a considerable extent on rice and other foodstuffs, and the manufacturers of Asia's emergent industries.
>
> (Latham 1994: 151)

In sum, the significance of Singapore and Hong Kong, both being British colonies, lay not in distributing British exports within the region, but in assuming the role of reallocation and distribution of Asian goods within Asia. 'They were the twin hubs of intra-Asian trading activity, not merely British trading outposts' (Latham 1994: 145).

The pre-existing intra-Asian trading networks played a crucial role in facilitating Hong Kong's economic development after 1841. The formation of these trading networks can be traced back to the tributary system in Asia, which 'consisted of a network of bilateral relationships between China and each tribute-paying country, with tribute and imperial "gift" as the mediums of exchange and the Chinese Capital as the center' (Hamashita 1997b: 120; also see Hamashita 2003). More importantly, the tributary system grew in parallel with or 'was in symbiosis with a network of commercial trade relations' within the region (Hamashita 1997b: 120). Hong Kong's success in locking in to these pre-existing commercial networks, and not its trade and finance with the metropolitan centre of the imperial power, marked the first major turning point in its economic development. Hong Kong captured such opportunities through inheriting the historical trading centre of Canton, and developing into a centre of trade and finance for the intra-Asian economic networks and the international market. It transformed itself in the process from a colonial outpost that served other economic purposes into a city of trade, commerce and finance.

Consolidation of a regional and international business centre

In an article entitled 'A glance at Hongkong in 1850', Dr J. Berncastle, a physician passing through the colony on his way to England from Canton, described Hong Kong as 'a dull place for a stranger to remain in more than a few days' (quoted in Bard 1993: 42–3). In Berncastle's description, the main street, Queen's Road, 'extends the whole length of the town. In it are the principal offices of the merchants, banks, and shops ... filled with all sorts of European goods' (Bard 1993: 41). And piracy was a problem. 'There is seldom a week without some attack taking place upon fishing boats or passage-boats, in these waters' (Bard 1993: 41). The description by the famous Russian playwright Anton Chekhov, who visited the colony in October 1890, was very different: '[Hong Kong] has a glorious bay, the movement of ships on the ocean is beyond anything I have seen even in pictures, excellent roads, trolleys, a railway to the mountains, museums, botanical gardens; wherever you turn you will note evidences of the most tender solicitude on the part of the English for men in their service; there is even a sailors' club' (Bard 1993: 50).

Between 1850 and 1890, Hong Kong consolidated its position as an entrepot within the region. Indeed, once Hong Kong entered into the regional and international networks of trade, commerce and finance, it was able to capitalize quickly on the opening of new opportunities. Despite growing competition from other treaty ports in the region, Hong Kong remained the location for the head offices of the leading British companies (see, for example, Bard 1993: 51–79; Meyer 2000: 103–5): 'The main British firms were centred at Hong Kong, and other ports were regarded as out-ports, and this remained broadly true, even when Shanghai out-stripped Hong Kong in commercial importance' (Endacott 1964a: xv). The avail-ability of commercial, financial and professional services constituted an essential component of Hong Kong's competitive advantage.

Equally significant for the socio-economic development of Hong Kong society in the second half of the nineteenth century was the rise of a Chinese business elite. As early as 1854, Governor Bowring noted that economic development in Hong Kong had 'created a class of Chinamen daily becoming more influential and more opulent to whom we may look for future cooperation' (quoted in Carroll 2005: 52). In his cor-respondence in 1863 to the Colonial Office, Governor Robinson recognized that the Chinese merchants had played an important role in Hong Kong's economic growth when he noted that 'it is the Chinese who have made Hong Kong what it is and not its connection with the foreign trade' (Carroll 2005: 53). The rise of the Chinese mer-chants was reflected in their contribution to the government's revenue. In 1876, only eight names on the official list of the 20 highest rate payers in Hong Kong were Chinese individuals or firms. In 1881, there were 17 Chinese names; only three European companies were listed (Chan 1991: 107). Robinson's observation about the emergence of the Chinese merchants was confirmed by Governor Hennessy's report on the census findings (seemingly in an attempt to explain whether the huge amount of money expended by the Chinese merchants on the acquisition of land property was speculation or otherwise) in his speech to the Legislative Council in 1881:

> Total value of [land] properties bought by Chinese from foreigners, $1,710,0366 [sic] ... Now, this large item of $1,710,000 on the transfer of prop-erty, almost entirely for commercial purposes, to the Chinese community since January last year, is undoubtedly an event of great importance. ... The Chinese Trading hongs, – that is, the Nam-pak hongs and other wealthy merchants who now send the manufacturers of England into China, – have increased from 215 to 395 [between 1876 and 1881]. Chinese traders have increased from 287 to 2,377; Chinese brokers, from 142 to 455. Taking the Chinese engaged in deal-ing in money; – the Shroffs have increased from 40 to 208; the Teachers of shroffing have increased from 9 to 14; the Bullion dealers, who do not appear in any former census, are now returned at 34; the Money Changers, 111 in 1876, still remain at 111, but in 1876 there were no Chinese Bankers returned, and now we have in this census 55 Chinese Bankers. ... Looking to the increase I have pointed out in the ordinary machinery for commercial movement in the harbour, to this remarkable increase of the mercantile community, and to the well-known magnitude of the mercantile transactions of our Chinese mer-chants, it seems clear that this large expenditure, since January 1880, of $1,710,000 by Chinese for commercial property was a necessary expenditure.
>
> (Endacott 1964a: 146–7)

And the scope of Chinese business was by no means confined to trade, commerce and finance. As noted by Governor Hennessy in the same speech, 'I find many local Chinese manufacturers in this Colony' (Endacott 1964a: 148).

It is true that many of these rising Chinese merchants were compradors of foreign hongs. But it would be misleading to assume that the Chinese compradors were completely subordinated to foreign interests. The employment of compradors was a reflection of changes in the business environment and operations (particularly the decline of the traditional commission agency business) (Hao 1970: 21). Diversification of economic activities and the increasingly direct involvement in Asian business meant that the Western merchants had to find support from Chinese compradors for developing a bridge between themselves and the local market. And these Chinese compradors were not simply local agents of the Western merchants. They developed their own lines of business, ranging from trade and shipping to banking and insurance. In short, a Chinese capitalist class was forming and these Chinese capitalists played an important role in the facilitation of Hong Kong's growth and development into a centre of regional as well as international trade, commerce and finance.

Hong Kong's status as a regional and international centre of trade, commerce and finance is best reflected in the rapid growth of activity of the Hongkong and Shanghai Banking Corporation (HSBC), established in 1864 as 'a local bank ... for Hong Kong and the Treaty Ports of China and Japan' (King 1988: 4), which con-

Table 1.1 The Hongkong and Shanghai Banking Corporation branches and agencies, 1918

Location	Year of opening	Location	Year of opening
Hong Kong	1865	Calcutta	1867
Foochow	1867	Rangoon	1891
Saigon	1870	Bombay	1869
Amoy	1873	Colombo	1892
Bangkok	1888		
Canton	1909	Mania	1875
		Iloilo	1883
Shanghai	1865		
Hankow	1868	Batavia	1884
Tientsin	1881	Sourabaya	1896
Peking	1885		
Hongkew	1909	Singapore	1877
Tsingtau	1914	Penang	1884
Harbin	1915	Malacca	1909
Vladivostok	1918	Kuala Lumpur	1910
		Ipoh	1910
London	1865	Johore	1910
San Francisco	1875		
New York	1880		
Lyons	1881		
Hamburg	1889		
Yokohama	1866		
Kobe/Hiogo	1869		
Nagasaki	1891		
Taipei	1909		

Source: Based on King (1988: 92)

firmed its head office status in regional and international networks. More interestingly, the spread of branches and agencies of the Hongkong and Shanghai Banking Corporation, shown in Table 1.1, covering many major ports connected with Chinese emigration and serving commerce and trade via Chinese migrants, also confirms our earlier discussion about the impacts of the long established Chinese networks, particularly in terms of remittances and the flow of the Chinese population (Hamashita 1997a: 111–14), on Hong Kong's economic development as a business centre for trade and finance.

In brief, by the late nineteenth century, Hong Kong was clearly a key participant in international and regional networks and flows of economic activity. In commenting on the commercial revolution in China in the nineteenth century, Hao (1986: 341–2) noted:

> New commercial centers, such as Shanghai and Hong Kong, rose to national and international prominence. They were great population centers, which, unlike earlier Chinese cities as centers of political administration, were primarily great emporiums of trade. It was in these economic centers that those who traded could usually count on a quick sale, prompt payment, and a broad choice of opportunities to invest the proceeds. It was here, too, that one found expert knowledge of market conditions the world over, skill in appraisal and classification of merchandise, informed brokerage services, and sophisticated facilities handling credit, exchange, insurance, and distribution.

Hong Kong's subsequent rise to the status of a global city did not happen overnight, but had long historical roots.

2 An industrial colony

Hong Kong manufacturing from boom to bust

Until we examined the position we were as a body inclined, with others of the community, to consider the industry of Hong Kong as being of very minor importance. As the result of research and evidence, however, we have come to the conclusion that it has assumed a proportion which can by no means be disregarded and that while it has arisen in somewhat haphazard style it does contribute substantially to the welfare of the economic unit of South China and Hong Kong. We are of the opinion, however, and all the evidence which we have heard bears this out, that the industry of Hong Kong cannot develop much beyond its present stage except inasmuch as it can form an economic part of the whole industrial development of South China and even to some extent of North China. While some of the factories at present existing in Hong Kong are solely Hong Kong units, some of the more important are but sections of industrial concerns, the other parts of which operate in Canton or in Shanghai.

(quoted in Faure and Lee 2004: 84)

Introduction

The above excerpt from the 'Report of the Commission Appointed by His Excellence the Governor of Hong Kong to Enquire into the Causes and Effects of the Present Trade Depression in Hong Kong and Make Recommendations for the Amelioration of the Existing Position and for the Improvement of the Trade of the Colony' (circa 1935) reminds us that Hong Kong's manufacturing industries, commonly believed to be a product of the industrial take-off in the 1950s, have a much longer history (see Leeming 1975). This reminder serves to connect our discussion in Chapter 1 of the macro-historical and nineteenth-century backgrounds to Hong Kong's pathway to a global city to our review in this chapter of Hong Kong's rise to the status of an important newly industrialized economy in the world economy during the post-war decades. More interestingly, it also reminds us of the close connections between Hong Kong's industrial and economic development and that of the mainland. Hong Kong's early industrialization was embedded in the broader economic milieu of the mainland. The relocation of manufacturing to the Pearl River Delta since the 1980s can be seen as a rediscovery of a hinterland from which it had been disconnected (see Chapter 6).

What follows is a review of the post-war development of Hong Kong's manufacturing industry. We trace its spectacular rise to global prominence in the early post-war decades, as well as its equally swift 'hollowing out' in the last decades of the twentieth century. Hong Kong's manufacturing peaked in the 1980s in terms of both the number of industrial establishments and the scale of employment. By the 1990s local production had already shrivelled so much that it was but a pale shadow of what it had been during the peak years. Rarely has such an industrial cycle been compressed within such a short period of time. Yet alongside this 'hollowing out' of the manufacturing sector there has also occurred a process of expansion of Hong Kong's industrial production in terms of both the spatial redistribution and scale of production of manufacturing establishments. The relocation of manufacturing production across the border has been one of the major forces reshaping the economic landscape of South China since the 1980s (Sit and Yang 1997). Yet, as noted in the report concerning the condition of Hong Kong's economic development after the world depression in 1929, this relocation of manufacturing plants from Hong Kong to the Pearl River Delta marks more of a rediscovery of its hinterland in mainland China than a radical break in Hong Kong's path of industrial development. The regional dimension of Hong Kong's economic and urban development has always been pertinent (So 1999), only shaped and reshaped by changing geo-politics and the configuration of the regional economy.

We will come back in Chapter 6 to this issue of how Hong Kong as a global city has extended its activities beyond its administrative boundary and has as a result transformed itself and the neighbouring areas into a global city-region (Scott 2001) in recent years. In this chapter we will provide a brief account of how Hong Kong built up its manufacturing industries, through reliance on its commercial linkages in the post-Second World War decades, in the context of restructuring in the world economy. As we will show in our subsequent discussion, the strengths of these commercial linkages, a legacy of the historical roots in trade, commerce and finance, are an important factor in structuring the course of industrial development. Local manufacturers made the best use of these strengths to plug in to the world market when Hong Kong's manufacturing took off. These strengths continued to impact on industrial development by facilitating Hong Kong's restructuring into a control centre for product development, marketing and coordination of production as the production processes began moving offshore in the 1980s. Such industrial restructuring processes constitute an integral part of the history of Hong Kong's rise to the status of global city.

The golden age of Hong Kong industries

We will not provide here a detailed historical account of Hong Kong's industrialization since such accounts are available elsewhere (see Chen 1984; So 1986; Chiu, Ho and Lui 1997). Without repeating what has, by now, become a well-known story of the rapid transformation of Hong Kong from an entrepot into an industrial colony after the embargo on China during the Korean War, it is perhaps worth quoting Reidel's (1973: 3) comments, which sum up succinctly the key features of the 'Hong Kong model of industrialization' in the early post-war decades:

Hong Kong (1) specializes in the manufacture of standardized consumer goods (2) for export (3) to high income countries in the West, and at the same time, the Colony (4) relies on Asian countries for the provision of raw materials and (5) on Western countries for capital goods. Another essential feature is the method of marketing exports. Hong Kong relies on manufacturers, wholesalers and large retail chain-stores in Europe and America to market her products. This feature, combined with the fact that the goods manufactured are highly standardized, requiring little 'research and development', means that Hong Kong entrepreneurs are left to do what they can do best: produce. These features, taken together, constitute what shall be called the 'Hong Kong model of industrialization'.

From modest beginnings in the 1950s, Hong Kong's manufacturing sector grew rapidly. By 1961 it accounted for 23.6 per cent of GDP and 43.0 per cent of total employment (see Table 2.1). Hong Kong's rapid industrial growth has been attributed to a number of factors, including entrepreneurship, particularly management and skills from emigrant entrepreneurs from mainland China (Wong 1988; Wu 1988), the economic culture of the population (Wong, S. 1986), the Hong Kong government's pursuit of a 'positive non-interventionist' policy towards the economy and its contribution to the building of the infrastructure for economic development (Friedman and Friedman 1980: 54–5; Haddon-Cave 1984; but, for a critical review of the colonial government's intervention in economic activities, see Deyo 1987: 243–5; Schiffer 1991; Chiu 1994; Choi 1997; Ngo 1999a; Goodstadt 2007), and the supply of a hard-working and flexible labour force (see, for example, Lethbridge and Ng 1984: 96). Without denying the importance of all the above factors to the success of Hong Kong's industrial development, it is also clear that the changing world economy played a significant part in stimulating export-led industrialization in East Asia in general and Hong Kong in particular. The spectacular growth of the Hong Kong economy through export-led industrialization was essentially conditioned by the restructuring of the world economy in the early post-war years (Landsberg 1979; Frobel *et al.* 1980; Dicken 1986; So 1986; Gereffi and Korzeniewicz 1994).

The restructuring of the global economy changed the previous international division of labour that was based upon a small core of industrialized and developed capitalist countries trading with developing Third World countries that supplied raw materials. In effect, the restructuring entailed a spatial relocation of manufacturing production in the world economy. During this process of relocation, partially driven by the maturity of the product cycle of consumer goods, like garment making, toys and electrical appliances (Dicken 1986), some developing economies emerged as the manufacturing sites for exports. This reorganization of the international division of labour was the precondition for Hong Kong's export-led industrialization. The emergence of international subcontracting networks has facilitated the incorporation of Hong Kong into the global manufacturing system through a network of transnational corporations (Germidis 1980; Dicken 1986; Chu 1988). Hong Kong was also well suited to take advantage of the opportunities

Table 2.1 GDP and employment by industry (percentage), 1961–1981

Industry/year	GDP			Employment		
	1961	1971	1981	1961	1971	1981
Agriculture and fishing	3.4	1.8	0.7	7.3	3.9	2.1
Mining and quarrying	0.3	0.2	0.2	0.7	0.3	0.1
Manufacturing	23.6	28.2	22.8	43.0	47.0	41.2
Electricity, gas and water	2.4	1.8	1.4	1.1	0.6	0.6
Construction	6.2	4.9	7.5	4.9	5.4	7.7
Wholesale and retail trades, restaurants and hotels	19.5	19.5	19.5	14.4	16.2	19.2
Transport, storage and communication	9.6	6.8	7.5	7.3	7.4	7.5
Financing, insurance, real estate and business services	10.8	17.5	23.8	1.6	2.7	4.8
Community, social and personal services	17.7	18.9	13.3	18.3	15.0	15.6
Ownership of premises	6.5	—	9.8	NA	NA	NA
Nominal sector	—	—	–6.5	NA	NA	NA
Unclassified	—	0.6	—	1.4	1.5	1.3

Sources: Zheng (1987: 187); *Estimates of Gross Domestic Product* (Census and Statistics Department various years); Census and Statistics Department (1982: 138); Census and Statistics Department (1987: 38); *Hong Kong Annual Digest of Statistics 1991* (Census and Statistics Department various years)

Notes:
NA = not applicable
— = not available or negligible

in the world market due to its abundant supply of low-cost labour in the 1950s and 1960s, which allowed for the development of labour-intensive consumer goods production. Furthermore, the pre-existing network of commercial transactions that had evolved during the entrepot years helped to ease Hong Kong's manufacturers' integration into the emerging global subcontracting system.

It could be argued that, given the absence of natural resources and the limited size of Hong Kong's domestic market, it had no alternative to developing export-orientated industries when entrepot trades were adversely affected by the United Nations' trade embargo on China during the Korean War. However, the lack of an alternative to industrialization obviously does not explain the success of Hong Kong's manufacturing industries. Chu's study (1988) of the development of the garment industry in Hong Kong helps to shed light in this regard on the effects of the changing international economy on the industrialization of the colony. The gist of her argument is as follows. First, contrary to the thesis of a 'transferred industrialization' (that Hong Kong's industrial development was a result of the relocation of enterprises from Shanghai because of political changes on the mainland) (Sit and Wong 1989), she contends that while it is true to say that the influx of Shanghainese industrialists, who brought with them capital and skills, facilitated the growth of manufacturing in general and the textile industry in particular, their influence on the industrialization process should not be overstated. There is no evidence that the textile industrialists played an active role in the development of garment production (Chu 1988: 121). The influence of these industrialists on other production activities is thus more limited than is sometimes supposed. Second, though the British merchants and their Commonwealth connections were pertinent to developing markets for local exports in the early 1950s, their role became less significant as the USA emerged as the major importer of Hong Kong garment products. Third, foreign direct investment in manufacturing has been rather insignificant, at least during the initial stage of the colony's industrial development (also see Hung 1984: 186). Chu's close scrutiny of the validity of the above explanations leads to her argument that the major factor that accounts for Hong Kong's industrialization lies elsewhere. She claims that 'it is the multinational trading groups or the "commercial form" of international subcontracting system that has been at work' (Chu 1988: 74). The international subcontracting system has provided Hong Kong with the opportunities to develop low-cost, labour-intensive, export-orientated industries.

The outcome of Hong Kong's incorporation into the global manufacturing and marketing networks was phenomenal industrial growth that transformed Hong Kong from an entrepot into an industrial colony. During the 1960s the manufacturing sector continued to grow in terms of its contributions to GDP and employment. In 1971, manufacturing accounted for 28.2 per cent of GDP and 47.0 per cent of total employment (see Table 2.1). The driving force behind this phenomenal industrial growth was small local manufacturers (Sit *et al.* 1979; Sit 1982; Sit and Wong 1989). In 1971, among the 17,865 establishments in the manufacturing sector, only 242 entailed foreign direct investment (1.4 per cent). The majority of industrial establishments in Hong Kong were owned by local capital. Around 70 per cent of all manufacturing establishments employed fewer than 20 persons, with an average establishment size of 33 persons. These small establishments were original equipment manufacturing (OEM) manufacturers, relying heavily on local trading companies and overseas buyers as intermediaries to connect them to the global economy. Hong Kong's connections with the world economy are an example of what Gereffi (1994) has called the 'buyer-driven' type in his classification of governance structures in global commodity chains. The commercial intermediaries, from large retailers to brand-named merchandisers to trading firms, link up manufacturers in developing countries with the global economy. The key feature of this type of governance structure is that production is decentralized. Local manufacturers are OEM producers – that is, their main task lies in handling assembly processes according to the specifications provided by trading companies, overseas retail chains or sourcing agents, who also take care of distribution and marketing of finished products made by the OEM manufacturers. This form of trade-led arrangement is common in labour-intensive, consumer goods industries. Hong Kong's success in plugging into these commercial, 'buyer-driven' global manufacturing networks is based, at least partially, upon its commercial history and long established trading linkages (see our discussion in Chapter 1). A vibrant commercial sector, with dynamic import–export houses and institutional support from finance and banking, has been crucial in making Hong Kong's export-led industrialization a success.

The decade of the 1970s was an important moment in changing the path of development of Hong Kong's economy. It was not only a period when the tertiary sector began to overtake the leading economic role of manufacturing, it was also the period when local manufacturers increasingly felt the pressure of competition from other newly industrializing economies and of growing protectionism in export markets. The responses to these pressures generated different strategies of industrial diversification. In the first place, the electronics industry emerged and, by 1980, had surpassed the textile industry in terms of its contributions to employment and share of domestic exports. Second, major industries like garment making began to 'trade up' and broaden their product ranges.

Recognizing the challenges arising from international competition and growing protectionism, the then Governor noted the 'urgency to the long term desirability of broadening our industrial base' (Advisory Committee on Diversification 1979: 1) and appointed an advisory committee in 1977 to study this matter. The *Report of the Advisory Committee on Diversification* was finally published in late 1979. But, as noted by Chen and Li (1988: 137), it 'was out of date as soon as it was published because of the new role for Hong Kong as a result of China's opening up in 1977'. While China's open-door policy was to bring about the revival of entrepot trade and open new opportunities for local manufacturing, a change in the political atmosphere and a relaxation in border controls triggered the influx of legal and illegal migrants from mainland China from the mid-1970s. Like previous waves of migration from across the border, this one brought Hong Kong a new pool of low-wage labour for the manufacturing sector (see Skeldon 1986; Greenwood 1990). Census statistics suggest that 58.0 per cent of the population growth in the period 1976–1981 was composed of net immigration. Moreover, the composition of this incoming population was predominantly male (60.7 per cent) and a large proportion were in the age group 15 to 34 (59.9 per cent) (Census and Statistics Department 1982: 76). It is also noted that 'The unemployment rate of 3.4 per cent for immigrants is significantly lower than the 4.0 per cent recorded for the local population possibly because immigrants were more willing than local workers to take up jobs requiring lower levels of skill' (Census and Statistics Department 1982: 77). A large proportion of the economically active immigrants (73.9 per cent) were found in production occupations, which provided the entry point for their participation in the labour market. Hong Kong's development as a global city has therefore been intricately tied to the inflow of migrant workers, who overwhelming came from mainland China.

The above discussion should be adequate to highlight the pertinence of this incoming population for the supply of labour to local manufacturing. But what interests us here is not only the point that the arrival of immigrants increased the supply of labour available to work in Hong Kong's industries – more importantly, it had the unintended effect of perpetuating the strategy of developing labour-intensive industries. The consequence was, as cogently put by Greenwood (1990: 21), that 'the growth of Hong Kong's GDP in the 1960s and 1970s was made up, in significant degree, by the "horizontal" expansion of the labour force, i.e. the arrival of large numbers of relatively unskilled workers, rather than by the "vertical" upgrading of skills of resident employers and employees'.

The fact that successive waves of immigrants from mainland China replenished the labour supply and thereby enabled manufacturers to better cope with labour shortages (Sit *et al*. 1979: 360, 390; England and Rear 1981: 77–80; Chen 1984: 13) should not lead us to assume that the continuation of a low-wage, labour-intensive production strategy was simply the outcome of 'historical accidents'. On the contrary, the effects of the 'timely' arrival of immigrants on the structuring of local manufacturing have to be explained in the context of an industrial structure dominated by small manufacturing establishments.

As noted earlier, small industrial establishments have played a critical role in Hong Kong's export-led industrialization (Sit *et al*. 1979). Small establishments (those employing fewer than 50 persons) have made up the bulk of local industrial establishments. This was the case in 1961 (78.7 per cent), and continued to be so in 1981 (92.1 per cent). Indeed, the figures show that, during this period, there was no increase in the average size of industrial establishments or decline in the proportion of small establishments in Hong Kong's industrial structure. There were two sides to this dynamism of small industrial establishments. On the one hand, the fact that Hong Kong's industries were mainly labour-intensive and producing for overseas markets provided the conditions for the growth of small manufacturing establishments in the major industries. Because these small factories relied on import–export houses and local larger factories for orders, designs and marketing, they could concentrate on production. Moreover, the labour-intensive character of local factories made entry into the industrial system relatively easy since small factories were able to deliver products of the required quality without heavy investment in technology and other infrastructural items of production. These small industrial establishments were responsive and adaptable to a changing business environment. This is particularly important given the heavy dependence of Hong Kong's industries on overseas markets (Sit 1982: 406). On the other hand, because these small factories faced a constant struggle to survive in competitive and fluctuating markets, given their limited access to working capital, they were poorly equipped to take the initiative to switch to less labour-intensive forms of production. They were more survivors, occupying narrow economic niches, than venturers taking the lead in innovation and structural transformation. Small factory employers were thus happy to capitalize on the arrival of immigrants as an additional source of supply of secondary labour because this enabled them to continue with their labour-intensive production processes.

To recap, Hong Kong's manufacturing in the 1970s, despite facing fierce international competition, growing protectionism, and the call for more industrial diversification, did little collectively to prepare for the process of economic restructuring. Technology and product upgrading, as well as diversification, sometimes occurred, but these were more in the nature of individual responses than collective efforts to enhance the long-term competitiveness of industry through implementing major organizational changes.

Industrial restructuring in the 1980s

By the 1980s, industries in Hong Kong found it increasingly difficult to maintain their competitiveness by continual reliance on labour-intensive manufacturing, for three reasons. First, and most important, labour costs had been increasing in both real and nominal terms during the 1980s. The average daily money wage in manufacturing more than doubled from HK$73 in 1982 to HK$184 in 1990, while the average real wage in 1982 prices increased from HK$73 in 1982 to HK$101 in 1990 (Census and Statistics Department 1991: 22). This posed serious problems for Hong Kong's manufacturers because such increases made it difficult for them to compete with producers in other newly industrialized economies (NIEs) with lower labour costs. Second, equally pertinent was the labour shortage situation (Joint Associations Working Group 1989; Ng, Chan and Wong 1989). The problems in this case were two-fold. First of all, there were long-term causes behind the shortage of labour. The most important was the trend of decline in population growth. Also contributing to the labour shortage was a vicious cycle arising from the failure to restructure the manufacturing sector. Manufacturers were eager to keep wages low in order to maintain their competitiveness, and so, whenever possible, they moved their production to places with abundant supplies of low-wage labour. These practices tended to discourage young Hong Kong workers from joining the manufacturing sector and, in turn, exacerbated problems of labour recruitment. (On problems related to the recruitment of women manufacturing workers, see Ng, Lui and Chan (1987: 70–72).) Third, another critical factor in rising production costs was the soaring property market. Between 1981 and 1990, rentals for private flatted factories had more than doubled, while their prices had increased by 66.6 per cent (Rating and Valuation Department 1991: Table 44). The high cost of factory premises was obviously unfavourable for industrial development, especially for those industries where cost-sensitive, cut-throat competition prevailed.

In a government survey conducted in the early 1990s on the manufacturing environment, 1,589 manufacturers were asked to indicate whether they perceived any of a given list of 18 factors as constraints on the growth of their industries. Almost 90 per cent of the respondents perceived high labour costs as a constraint, and 37.4 per cent perceived it as a serious constraint. Other labour problems, such as labour shortage and labour turnover, were also high on the list of constraints, with 24.5 per cent and 24.4 per cent of the respondents regarding them respectively as serious constraints on growth. The high cost of factory premises was also perceived as a serious constraint by 37.4 per cent of the responding firms, making it the second most widely perceived constraint on industrial growth (Industry Department 1992: 287).

We have argued elsewhere that in spite of the government's lame efforts to 'diversify' local industries, Hong Kong's manufacturing industries in general, and electronics and garment making in particular, continued in the 1980s to rely on labour-intensive methods of production to survive and compete in the world market (Lui and Chiu 1993; Chiu, Ho and Lui 1997). Garment manufacturers continued to produce high-quality fashion clothing as subcontractors for international brand-name fashion houses. This was done, however, without significant modernization and automation of the production process. The strength of the industry lay in its experience and skills, as well as its reputation in the world market for manufacturing good-quality clothing items. 'The large number of small and medium-sized factories contributes to the strength of the clothing industry as providers of a variety of fashion products, and respond quickly to constant shifts in market demands under an efficient subcontracting network' (Industry Department, 1992: 40). The electronics industry, on the other hand, similarly thrived by locating and producing for niche markets (e.g. fax machines, video games, application of specific integrated circuits, and talking toys). It had largely avoided competing in mass markets such as that for standardized microchips, which require a large initial outlay and a high technological content. Also, it did not significantly upgrade the technology- and capital-intensity of its production process. Instead, relocation of the labour-intensive assembly lines to China began to gather momentum from the mid-1980s onwards. If it was mostly a case of 'business as usual' amid marginal adjustments in the 1980s, what was the picture for the 1990s and beyond? Below we shall take a closer look at the trajectory of development of Hong Kong's electronics industry, in order to illustrate the rise and demise of a key industry in the manufacturing sector.

The electronics industry: an illustration

The electronics industry was one of the first to move production to East Asia, with multinational corporations starting production in Hong Kong in the late 1950s. Labour-intensive manufacturing for consumer electronics was a common entry point. Hong Kong was one of the world's leaders in transistor radio assembly in the early 1960s when the electronics industries around the region were not much different from one another. The territory, if not a leader, managed to keep up with the other three 'Asian Dragons' by the 1970s, only to lag behind in the regional race since the restructuring era of the 1980s. A number of studies have identified a strong resemblance between Hong Kong's electronics industry and its counterparts in East Asia until the mid-1980s (Ernst and O'Connor 1992; McDermott 1992; Hobday 1995).

The divergence between Hong Kong and the other three 'Asian Dragons' became increasingly apparent only from the 1980s, a decade of economic restructuring when the emergence of new protectionism in the West, together with the rise of new low-cost competitors in Asia, forced the four NIEs to reorientate their development strategies (Chiu 1994). South Korea and Taiwan were subsequently found to be most successful in building a globally competitive electronics industry, but Hong Kong was still not too far behind them in the mid-1980s in terms of production value and technology level (Ernst and O'Connor 1992: 95–180). However, the industry had stagnated in Hong Kong by the 1990s as a contract manufacturer mainly for consumer gadgets. Meanwhile, Taiwan transformed itself into one of the market leaders in various high-tech segments, including notebook and desktop computers, optical scanners, multimedia cards and high-speed modems, to name but a few notable examples (*Business Week* 1996). Likewise, South Korea is not only a powerhouse in consumer electronics, but also a key supplier for some critical components, including LCD (liquid crystal display) and CRT (cathode ray tube).[1] In addition to product upgrading, both South Korea and Taiwan took bold steps to catch up technologically by, for example, developing locally a dynamic semiconductor industry (Hong 1992).

The difference in restructuring strategies helps explain the contrasting performances in industrial upgrading, as the four NIEs all responded to the challenge of economic restructuring by a combination of three strategies. The strategy set includes: first, expanding outward investment and relocating production processes in other developing countries; second, raising the level of regional integration in trade; and, third, increasing the value-added content of their exports and upgrading the industrial structure (Chiu 1994). Indeed, South Korea shifted its emphasis from an 'imitation strategy' towards an 'innovation strategy' by intensifying in-house R&D (Kim 1997). Taiwan likewise has been so keen to acquire cutting-edge capability in various technology areas that a globally orientated strategy became a real possibility for a handful of firms (Lee and Pecht 1997). Even Singapore developed locally a world-class engineering capability despite the predominance of multinational corporations (MNCs) since; strong precision engineering industries have, for example, been built up around the HDD (hard disk drive) sector (Wong 2001). Given Hong Kong's overwhelming reliance on the relocation strategy (Chiu, Ho and Lui 1997), its failure to pursue upgrade possibilities is not surprising.

Growth without catching up

By the early 1980s, Hong Kong's electronics industry was found to be mainly orientated towards consumer electronics, in contrast with that in Japan, South Korea, Taiwan and Singapore, among others, where high value-added sectors such as computer, office automation and industrial electronics had by then become major growth areas (Hong Kong Productivity Centre 1983). Indeed, the share of consumer products in Hong Kong electronics exports increased sharply, from 52 per cent in 1974 to 71 per cent in 1980, and that of parts and components decreased from 48 per cent to 29 per cent over the period (Hong Kong Productivity Centre 1983: 13–14).

This trend persisted, making consumer electronics a consistent leader among all electronics sectors in Hong Kong throughout the 1980s in terms of output, number of firms and employment. As shown in Figure 2.1, consumer electronics constituted over 50 per cent of the industry's gross output throughout the 1980s, followed by parts and components, with computer products comparatively insignificant.[2] Not until consumer electronics declined sharply after 1988 did the other two sectors start to catch up slowly. But, in terms of number of firms, the leading position of consumer electronics has not been challenged since the late 1970s. As Table 2.2 shows, the number of firms often exceeded, and sometimes was even double or triple, the sum of firms for all other electronics sectors during the period from 1979 to 1995.

The predominance of consumer electronics did not however mean a better competitive performance. Quite the opposite: this sector has consistently under-performed compared to the computer and component sectors in terms of value-added ability (measured by value-added as a percentage of gross output). This explains why the Hong Kong Productivity Centre (1983) discovered that value-added per unit sales in the electronics industry plunged during its fast growth in the 1970s, with the figure falling to around 25 per cent of the output value in 1980 from an average of 30 per cent between 1973 to 1977 (Hong Kong Productivity Centre 1983: 11–12). A contraction in consumer electronics in the late 1980s in both gross output (Figure 2.1) and number of firms (Table 2.2) further demonstrates its relative weakness. By contrast, the component and computer sectors that include comparatively higher value-added activities provided steadier employment during the 1980s, with the computer sector even showing an increase in the number of firms.

But neither the components nor the computer sectors were able to achieve a satisfactory competitive performance by international standards. That Hong Kong electronics had long relied heavily upon imported parts and components illustrated the weakness of the local component sector. Critical components often had to be imported from Japan, Taiwan, South Korea, the USA and Europe, with less than half of the total purchased materials composed of locally available parts (Dataquest Inc. 1991: IV-9). The computer sector likewise remained a junior partner in international trade (Boston Consulting Group 1995: 80–1).

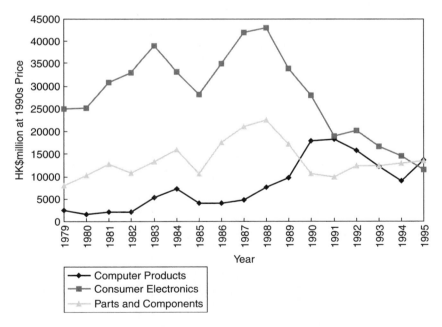

Figure 2.1 Gross output of major sectors in Hong Kong's electronics industry at 1990s constant price, 1979-1995

Source: *Annual Survey of Industrial Production* (Census and Statistics Department, various years)

Table 2.2 Relative scale of major sectors of the electronics industry in Hong Kong, 1979–1995

Year	Consumer electronics		Parts and components		Computer products		Office automation equipment		Industrial apparatus		Others	
	No. of firms	No. of persons engaged	No. of firms	No. of persons engaged	No. of firms engaged	No. of persons	No. of firms	No. of persons engaged	No. of firms	No. of persons engaged	No. of firms	No. of persons
1979	757	N/A	153	N/A	42	N/A	3	N/A	2	N/A	90	N/A
1985	1295	60177	326	30218	133	11936	12	175	4	519	189	8538
1990	733	33200	372	24363	213	21495	20	2050	52	324	112	3613
1995	405	9277	173	18421	123	9437	63	3448	18	137	25	653

Source: *Annual Survey of Industrial Production* (Census and Statistics Department, various years)

All in all, the electronics industry failed as a whole to upgrade production in order to catch up with its competitors during the 1980s. In 1989, the average value-added and output per worker of electronics manufacturing in Hong Kong were US$16.10 and US$79.10 respectively, lagging far behind Singapore's level of US$30.60 and US$108.50. Squeezed by intensifying regional competition on the one hand and surging local costs on the other, the industry's gross output began to decline after peaking in 1988 (Figure 2.2). A look back at Figure 2.1 confirms that consumer electronics led the downturn, but the statistics from Table 2.2 show that both the computer and component sectors did little more than postpone the decline of local production. The early 1990s thus saw a continuous decline in virtually all sectors in terms of gross output, number of firms and employment.

Entering the 'made by Hong Kong' era

The sharp decline of the electronics industry by the early 1990s reflects in a way the failure of Hong Kong to catch up with South Korea, Taiwan and Singapore on the one hand, and the intensifying competition from Thailand and Malaysia on the other (Dataquest Inc. 1991; Boston Consulting Group 1995). But the decline of local production resulted mostly from a collective strategy of the industry – relocation of production to mainland China – in the face of a surge in local production costs since the mid-1980s. With most firms choosing the relocation route instead of the upgrading alternative, offshore production multiplied at the expense of local production in

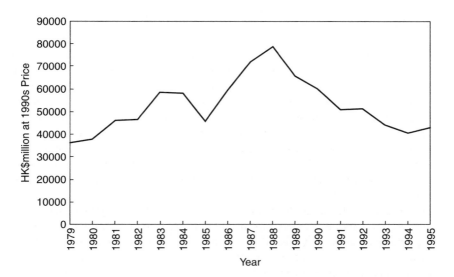

Figure 2.2 Gross output of electronics manufacturing in Hong Kong at 1990s constant price, 1978–1995

Source: *Annual Survey of Industrial Production* (Census and Statistics Department, various years)

the 1990s, marking the end of 'made in Hong Kong' and the start of the era of 'made by Hong Kong' (Berger and Lester 1997).

A study conducted by the Federation of Hong Kong Industries (FHKI) on industrial investments in the Pearl River Delta confirms the trend for electronics firms to relocate (Federation of Hong Kong Industries 1992). Almost 70 per cent (69.4 per cent) of the electronics establishments covered by the study had investment in the region (Federation of Hong Kong Industries 1992: 63), with the average employment size of 905 persons for these relocated establishments (Federation of Hong Kong Industries 1992: 69). The strategy of going offshore was by no means confined to larger firms. Many small and medium-sized firms were also eager to take advantage of the abundant supply of cheap labour in Guangdong (Federation of Hong Kong Industries 1992: 67).

As a result, the Guangdong Province of China recorded spectacular growth in the electronics industry. The vast majority of the foreign investment enterprises (FIEs) in Guangdong were Hong Kong based. The Boston Consulting Group (1995: 10) estimated that Hong Kong-backed electronics enterprises accounted for 77 per cent of all electronics enterprises, or 83 per cent of all electronics FIEs in Guangdong around the mid-1990s. By the 1990s, therefore, the scale of Hong Kong-backed electronics enterprises in Guangdong far exceeded those remaining in Hong Kong. That is why the MIT research group refers to this situation as 'made by Hong Kong' (i.e. Hong Kong coordinated manufacturing with production carried out offshore) (Berger and Lester 1997).

By moving their labour-intensive processes to mainland China, local manufacturers turned their operations in Hong Kong into controlling headquarters (Chiu, Ho and Lui 1997). R&D activities are mainly conducted in their Hong Kong establishments. The more sophisticated processes are also retained in their Hong Kong premises, while assembly is done in their offshore plants. Therefore, even though the industry showed a sharp increase in value-added per person from the late 1980s onwards, we cannot infer from this that Hong Kong had introduced a systemic transformation in its industrial activities. Quite the opposite: the majority still remained largely OEM suppliers for overseas buyers (Hobday 1995; Berger and Lester 1997; Chiu, Ho and Lui 1997; Enright *et al.* 1997). Some Hong Kong manufacturers even transformed themselves into traders by making use of their business contacts with local subcontractors and manufacturers based in mainland China. In other cases, they assumed the role of just a sourcing agent for transnational corporations (Berger and Lester 1997). Even in the case of those better-performing firms that upgraded to original design manufacturing (ODM), their in-house design activities ranged only from hardware design to software programming, mechanical drawing, building prototype samples and tool-making. Only occasionally did they become involved in industrial or conceptual design. Successful upgrading to 'own brand manufacturing' (OBM) was rare (Hong Kong Trade Development Council 1997). Not surprisingly, Hong Kong's status as a cost-based competitor in the international marketplace remained unchanged, as the Boston Consulting Group International Inc. (1995: 199) noted:

The Hong Kong domestic electronics industry is among the smallest in the region, and is the only one which has been contracting in real value over the past five years. In terms of capabilities, the Hong Kong industry is grouped with the new low-cost manufacturing bases in Thailand, Malaysia and China as a cost-based competitor with relatively few capabilities in product innovation and development. The other four industries in the region have, or are developing, capabilities at a much higher rate and face the future as value based competitors.

Inertia in upgrading as a strategic choice

But if Hong Kong has stagnated over the past three decades as a cost-based competitor in the international marketplace, it may well be the case that the territory kept doing what it did best: international subcontracting. Indeed, 'local manufacturers have traditionally profited from moving quickly in and out of products and markets' (Dataquest Inc. 1991: IV-64). On the one hand, its strength lies in quick responses to market changes. Most producers can complete product designs in less than 12 months and produce from order to shipment in less than six months (Dataquest Inc. 1991: Appendix IV-15). On other hand, they are more reliant on market intelligence than advances in core technological development for survival, preferring to catch up with new developments of parts and components by acquiring them in the market instead of internalizing such processes of technological innovation (Chiu, Ho and Lui 1997). With the constantly changing global division of labour offering ample business opportunities in various market segments, Hong Kong firms just expanded into those product lines that producers in other advanced countries abandoned when upgrading their product portfolios.

Underlying Hong Kong's excellence in international subcontracting is a strategic preference for following behind over catching up with other rivals in the global competitive race. A good illustration of Hong Kong's preoccupation with the low-end market is the audio-visual (AV) sector, a consistent leader in the industry. Hong Kong started to assemble transistor radios in the late 1950s, making it the first Asian economy outside Japan to develop consumer electronics (Gregory 1985: 12). Closely following the invention of the radio cassette recorder in the mid-1970s and the introduction of stereo systems in 1979, Hong Kong's radio industry was in full swing from the late 1970s through to 1981, when there were some 400 firms in the field (Hong Kong Trade Development Council 1984). By the late 1970s, in fact, Hong Kong even shared world leadership in radio production with Japan by almost dominating the lower end of the market (Gregory 1985: 9–13).

But while Hong Kong was the first to benefit from Japan's upgrading from simple to multifunctional audio products, its propensity to catch up in the international race kept slowing as Japan shifted its focus to such items as personal stereos, high-fidelity audio equipment, colour TVs and video tape/cassette recorders (VTRs/VCRs). The production of simple radios – portable radios, clock radios and portable radio recorders – thus dominated Hong Kong's exports of audio-visual products throughout the 1980s. Higher value-added items including car audio, colour TVs and VTRs/VCRs never came close to accounting for even half the export value of simple radios before the late 1980s.

While massive relocation resulted in the decline in output of simple radios after the late 1980s, other product segments fared no better. By the late 1980s, there was virtually no VTR/VCR manufacturers in Hong Kong, and only a few TV manufacturers, producing mostly 14-, 20- and/or 21-inch colour models (Hong Kong Trade Development Council 1990). The audio segment was a bit better off than its video counterpart, with a few manufacturers already developing CD players in 1989 (Hong Kong Trade Development Council 1990). However, even by the mid-1990s when many manufacturers were capable of producing laser-based audio equipment, radio receivers were still the only AV product for which Hong Kong claimed to be the world's leading exporter (Hong Kong Trade Development Council 1997).

A similar pattern can also be found in the case of the local computer industry. It basically stagnated along the value-added chain despite its early start and the fact that, by the late 1980s, Hong Kong could still claim a healthy computer industry that was producing both desktop and laptop PC systems, and all kinds of peripherals including keyboards, monitors, disk drives, modems, memory cards, various add-on cards and even printers (Hong Kong Trade Development Council 1988). As technological advances stimulated the multimedia boom in the 1990s, the territory could barely claim a steady business only in parts and accessories and, to a much lesser extent, in peripherals. This assessment remains more or less valid even after we take the massive relocation into consideration, as local manufacturers were mostly engaged in the production of computer parts and accessories likes motherboards, add-on cards, disk controllers, keyboards, multimedia cards, CD-ROM drives and game controllers by the mid-1990s (Hong Kong Trade Development Council 1997).

The semiconductor industry in Hong Kong also moved along the same trajectory. As in the case of consumer electronics, Hong Kong was the first Asian economy outside Japan to get into the semiconductor industry (Gregory 1985). In an attempt to defend themselves against Japanese rivals, Fairchild led US semiconductor manufacturers in seeking cost-competitive production sites in Asia by the early 1960s. Its first choice was Hong Kong, 'the only location that then offered the essential conditions for a successful assembly operation' (Mackintosh Consultants Ltd 1982: 71). By the late 1960s the territory had become the principal Asian assembler of semiconductors for the US market (Henderson 1989: 98). By the early 1980s three or four local firms had even acquired the capability to fabricate up to four-inch wafers for LSI (large-scale integration) devices (Mackintosh Consultants Ltd 1982: 72). Indeed, the strength of its semiconductor industry in this earlier phase is shown by the fact that even though a very large proportion of the output of these semiconductor devices was consumed locally, the annual export value amounted to HK$1,000 million or more throughout the 1980s.

By 1986, 21 companies in Hong Kong (six of which were locally owned) were engaged in the manufacture of semiconductors, making the territory an emerging core of the regional division of labour in the industry (Henderson 1989: 112). The 1990s saw Hong Kong steadily expanding into testing and packaging activities as reflected in the export value of integrated circuits (ICs) (Figure 2.3). Another interesting fact in this connection is that Vitelic from Taiwan and Motorola from the USA formed a joint venture in Hong Kong in 1996 only to make memory ICs that were generations behind the technological frontier. It produced watch and clock ICs, voice and melody ICs and electronic toy ICs that had been fabricated locally for almost 20 years (Hong Kong Trade Development Council 1997). This shows that the Hong Kong semiconductor sector remained only a technological follower, especially bearing in mind the successful technological catch-up of both Taiwan and South Korea.

These episodes all point to a strategic preference for the international subcontracting that Hong Kong electronics manufacturers have practised so consistently

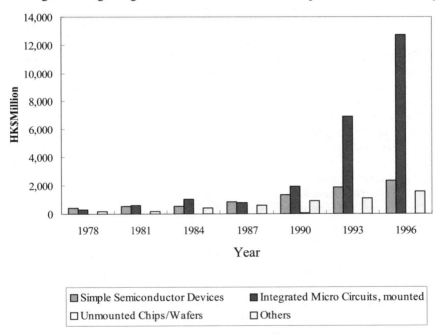

Figure 2.3 Hong Kong domestic exports of semiconductor devices at 1990s constant price, 1978–1996

Source: *Hong Kong Trade Statistics* (Census and Statistics Department, various years)

Notes:

1. Each category in this figure is composed of one or more six-digit items listed in *Hong Kong Trade Statistics*. 'Simple semiconductor devices' includes 'diodes', 'transistors', 'photocells' and 'other simple semiconductor devices'; 'Integrated micro circuits, mounted' includes 'integrated micro circuits, unmounted'; 'Unmounted chips/wafers' includes 'integrated micro circuits, unmounted chips wafer'; and 'Others' includes 'electronics components and parts within group 776'.
2. The constant price is calculated by deflating the nominal price by the volume index as listed in *Estimates of Gross Domestic Product* (Census and Statistics Department 1998).

since the early stage of development of the industry (see also Chiu and Wong (1998) for a similar case in the LCD industry). The industry's quick take-off in the 1970s demonstrates how effective the model was in the earlier phase of an industry's development, while the subsequent decline of local production points to the inherent systemic limits to a cost-based competitive strategy. It is worth emphasizing that Hong Kong survived the challenge not by industrial upgrading but, instead, by revitalizing the business model through massive relocation. And, as a result of relocation, Hong Kong's manufacturers expanded the scale of production. Manufacturing under the so-called 'made by Hong Kong' strategy is in a sense more of a continuation of the 'made in Hong Kong' practice but on a larger scale because few manufacturers have taken the opportunity to relocate in order to upgrade their technology and production sophistication.

A glance at the leading export items over the period 1978–1996 confirms the clustering of Hong Kong electronics around mature and/or fad products whose profit margins usually stagnate, or sometimes even decline, over time (Table 2.3). Notable examples include LCD/LED watches and TV games from the late 1970s to early 1980s, telephone sets during the mid-1980s, video tapes in the late 1980s, radio telephonic receivers (including such telecommunications equipment as CB radios and transceivers) from the late 1980s to the early 1990s, among others from the three product segments – AV, computer and semiconductor – just discussed. Even the parts and component sector follows a similar trajectory, as the early 1990s saw the rise of discrete components (static converters, rectifiers and transistors) and printed circuits, together with parts and components for RF apparatus (i.e. TV and radio), audio equipment and telecommunications equipment.

Product upgrading is modest in scale at best, and process innovation and technology catch-up are hardly evident. Going back to the 1970s, when international subcontracting prevailed in the field, the industry's expenditure on technology development (including product design and process improvement) was relatively minimal compared to the large value of output and turnover. This is especially true in consumer electronics, where it was found that the whole sector spent only HK$13 million on product design and process improvement in 1978 (Hong Kong Productivity Centre 1983: 32). Thus the Hong Kong Productivity Centre (1983: 32) was right to suggest that 'the industry has not been accumulating experience and know-how in technology development'. For small and medium-sized enterprises (SMEs) in Hong Kong, even in the 1980s, there was a low level of awareness among the entrepreneurs of the importance of technology development and upgrading (Sit and Wong 1989: 168–70): 'it is evident that much attention has been paid to new machinery as a cure for production and technological problems ... their perspective on improving technology is very narrow ... When asked about their opinion on low cost automation, 2/3 of the sample firms claimed that they had not heard of it'.

But while Hong Kong manufacturers are supposed to prefer capital investment to other forms of process innovation, the performance of the electronics industry from the early 1980s to the mid-1990s, with respect to gross addition to fix assets, seems to suggest a different story. This is again most evident in consumer electronics,

Table 2.3 Leading domestic export items in Hong Kong electronics industry, 1978–1996

Rank	1978	1981	1984	1987	1990	1993	1996
1	LCD watch (1.88)	LED/LCD watch (4.27)	Computer parts (6.13)	Quartz analogue electronic watch (7.07)	Quartz analogue electronic watch (11.71)	Computer parts (12.12)	Mounted IC (12.06)
2	Portable radio (1.85)	Computer parts (3.09)	Quartz analogue electronic watch (3.12)	Computer parts (5.38)	Computer parts (9.63)	Parts for RF apparatus (7.51)	Computer parts (7.22)
3	Clock radio (1.47)	Portable RCR (1.99)	LED/LCD watch (2.98)	Portable RCR (2.35)	Radio parts (3.22)	Electronic watch (6.97)	Electronic watch (5.80)
4	Computer parts (1.33)	Portable radio (1.98)	Portable RCR (1.87)	Radio parts (2.30)	TV parts (2.56)	Mounted IC (6.70)	Parts for RF apparatus (3.85)
5	Portable RCR (0.99)	Clock radio (1.49)	Portable radio (1.82)	LED/LCD watch (2.29)	Computer system (2.37)	Printed circuit (2.58)	Printed circuit (3.23)
6	Transistor (0.72)	TV game (1.46)	Telephone set (1.80)	Telephone set (1.78)	Mounted IC (1.95)	Cassette tape sound recorder for office use (1.67)	Cassette tape sound recorder for office use (2.02)
7	Mounted IC (0.61)	Quartz analogue electronic watch (1.28)	Radio parts (1.63)	Video-tapes (1.47)	Printed circuit (1.92)	Parts for audio equipment (1.67)	Parts for audio equipment (1.95)
8	Pocket calculator (0.60)	Mounted IC (0.86)	Clock radio (1.34)	Color TV (1.45)	Radio telephonic receiver (1.85)	Transistor (1.46)	Transistor (1.87)
9	TV game (0.49)	Cassette recorder (0.64)	Mounted IC (1.15)	Portable radio (1.33)	Static converters/rectifiers (1.65)	Static converters/rectifiers (1.38)	Other semiconductor device (1.44)
10	Cassette recorder (0.47)	Electronic clock (0.59)	Computer peripheral (0.86)	Computer system (1.20)	Photocopying apparatus (1.55)	Parts for telecoms equipment (1.23)	Parts for telecoms equipment (1.26)

Source: *Hong Kong Trade Statistics* (Census and Statistics Department, various years)

Note: Figures in brackets denote the value in HK$ billion at 1990s price.

which seldom invested more than 3 per cent of its gross output in fixed assets. The computer sector was not much better in this respect, averaging an annual rate of gross addition to fixed assets of just 3.39 per cent over the period. Not surprisingly, a study report on industrial automation carried out in the early 1990s found Hong Kong electronics to be lagging two to three years behind Taiwan and Singapore in upgrading to SMT (surface-mount technology) by using automatic pick-and-place machines (Hong Kong Productivity Council 1992).

Size limitation counts much less than management attitude in various types of process upgrading, since a major barrier to automation in Hong Kong is 'the lack of appreciation of the contribution of manufacturing operations to the value-added of a business in industry' (Hong Kong Productivity Council 1992: 59). Fong's (1992) study on JIT (just-in-time) systems highlighted the weakness of Hong Kong companies in inventory control and also found that management misconceptions more than any other factor hindered Hong Kong's upgrade to a JIT system.

As in the case of process innovation, investment in technology innovation – usually carried out in a company's R&D section – is small in Hong Kong (Reif and Sodini 1997). In fact, electronics firms in Hong Kong have had a relatively weak R&D section. Chiu, Ho and Lui's (1997: 64) survey in the mid-1990s found that more than two-thirds (73.9 per cent) of electronics firms employed no more than three R&D professional staff. One may again be tempted to attribute this limitation to the plethora of SMEs in the industry but even larger firms were not much better in this regard. Yu (1997: 125) highlights this point when he notes that 'large electronics companies in Hong Kong spent money on R&D mostly for the transfer of technology or for imitation, not for technological breakthrough or designing brand new products'. Therefore, even though Hong Kong was quick to switch to CAD (computer-aided design) software in product design, the weakness in corporate R&D was so widespread that the electronics industry was still at its early stage in the application of ASICs (application-specific integrated circuits) (Industry Department 1991). Not surprisingly, Hong Kong has the lowest R&D spending, estimated at 0.08 per cent of GDP in 1992, among the four 'Asian Dragons' (Barker and Goto 1998: 256). Given the preoccupation with OEM, this situation is understandable (Dataquest Inc. 1991: IV-20):

> Most of the respondents were involved in electronic system designs and the design of mechanical parts. In most cases, the designs were worked out according to the product specifications and product cosmetics provided by the parent companies or the customers. Only half of the respondents performed product cosmetic designs for some of their products, and design of tooling and molds were not widely provided by the respondents.

The electronics industry in Hong Kong thrived from the 1960s to the 1980s. Yet its pace of growth had slowed considerably by the late 1980s, especially when compared to what was achieved by South Korea, Taiwan and even Singapore over the same period (Dataquest Inc. 1991). While Hong Kong's electronics industry has been renowned for its flexible adaptation to changes in market demand, the territory did little to transform its role in the global division of labour as an OEM supplier in low value-added sectors even when opportunities for industrial upgrading became more abundant from the 1980s onwards. A review of the development of the Hong Kong electronics industry since its inception confirms the predominance of the production of mature or fad products whose profit margins usually stagnate, or even decline, over time. Indeed, Hong Kong's electronics industry became so attached to international subcontracting that it failed to pursue upgrading systematically through process innovation or technological catch-up, thereby restricting itself to the status of being a follower. This is exactly why some highlight flexible adaptation to frequent market change as a 'Hong Kong advantage' (see, for example, Enright *et al*. 1997; Yu 1997) while others question whether a strategy of this kind is sustainable in the long run (see, for example, Berger and Lester 1997; Eng 1997; Chiu and Wong 1998).

The institutional context of restructuring

It is our contention that the restructuring strategies sketched above are best comprehended within the broader institutional context in Hong Kong. Firm and sectoral characteristics interact with Hong Kong's particular institutional configuration of state policy, industrial relations and the financial system, to produce various corporate responses to the changing environment. Elsewhere (Lui and Chiu 1993, 1994; Chiu, Ho and Lui 1997) we have argued for a perspective on restructuring that emphasizes the institutional 'embeddedness' of firm behaviours. Pure market signals do not dictate firm responses. The East Asian NIEs that were mentioned in our earlier discussion have by and large faced the same set of pressures from the mid-1980s onwards. Yet the responses of the manufacturers in different localities are by no means identical. We suggest that each of the East Asian NIEs has followed a distinctive trajectory of economic development that conditioned its pattern of industrial restructuring in the 1990s. In the case of Hong Kong, it is a case of massive relocation without technological upgrading.

In the above discussion of the industrial restructuring process, we have concentrated on the performances of local small factories in garment making and electronics production. It appears from the picture we have described as if local small manufacturers have been left almost entirely on their own to cope with problems arising from increasing protectionism, rising production costs and changes in global capitalism. It is in fact exactly our contention that this represents the effects of the institutional setting of Hong Kong's industrial economy – Hong Kong is a case of unorganized late industrialization (Chiu and Lui 1995). More specifically, we contend that local small manufacturers have been neither assisted nor pushed to follow a different course of industrial restructuring.

In discussions of late industrialization, the state is often portrayed as the major agent of socio-economic transformation (Gerschenkron 1966; Amsden 1989). For instance, Amsden (1989) argues that late industrialization is based upon borrowed technology, which presumably requires large doses of investment, a high level of technological sophistication and a long period of learning. That is why the state must come into the picture, since state intervention is required to help individual firms to finance their investments in technology, promote technological upgrading, and bear the initial costs or losses in adopting foreign technologies. The case of Hong Kong casts doubt upon the functionalist logic of the statist interpretation of late industrialization. From our earlier discussion of local manufacturers' responses to the changing economic environment, it is clear that state intervention remains tangential to the structuring of corporate strategies.

Turning to the role of the colonial state in economic development, few observers of the Hong Kong economy have failed to recognize the relatively limited role assumed by the colonial state in economic development under the rubric of 'positive non-interventionism'. Nor have they failed to notice the positive aspects of entrepreneurship and competition in fostering rapid growth. However, contrary to the picture portrayed by Friedman and Friedman (1980: 54–5), the colonial state is far from passive in facilitating economic growth (Schiffer 1991). A notable example is the massive public housing programme since the 1950s. State provision of public housing has now been widely recognized as one of the most important factors contributing to the success of local industries (Castells, Goh and Kwok 1990: Chapter 2). In functional terms, the public housing programme (the current population living in public and aided housing, including those in home ownership estates, is 48.8 per cent of the total population) helps tackle the problem concerning the reproduction of labour power.[3] This matter is particularly pertinent as Hong Kong's industries are mainly labour-intensive and their competitiveness depends heavily on the supply of cheap labour. The public housing programme has in this connection the effect of subsidizing the pay of the low-wage population – the working-class families are able to survive on the low wages they receive from their employers and the latter are assisted indirectly to continue their pursuit of low-wage, labour-intensive manufacturing. So, the assumption that the colonial state stays aloof from all aspects of social and economic affairs is basically inaccurate. In short, what we mean by 'positive non-interventionism' is not the picture of *laissez-faire* conjured up in neo-classical economics texts. As Youngson (1982: 132) puts it, 'Hong Kong and *laisser-faire* have only an occasional acquaintance.' Also, it is important to note that it is one thing to say that the Hong Kong government has not attempted any direct intervention in the structuring of local manufacturing, but it is quite another to infer from this that it practises the *laissez-faire* philosophy in each domain of economic activities. In fact, the government assumes an important role in the regulation of matters concerning finance and banking, and at moments of crisis, comes to the rescue (Jao 1988: 53–4; Goodstadt 2007). Put differently, it is more accurate to describe the policy of the colonial state as 'selective intervention' rather than wholesale 'non-interventionism'.[4]

We should not go to the opposite extreme, however, by including the Hong Kong colonial state within the family of capitalist developmental states (cf. Johnson 1987). We have analysed elsewhere the role of the colonial state in Hong Kong's industrialization (Chiu and Lui 1995; Lui and Chiu 1996). The gist of our argument is that local industrialists have not been able to secure strategic linkages with the colonial state, and the latter, therefore, has a tendency to stay aloof from managing industrial development (Lui and Chiu 1993; also cf. Henderson 1991: 174). The government–industry relationship is actually well captured by the notion of 'positive non-interventionism' (Haddon-Cave 1984). Whereas various state policies regarding the provision of medical care and housing have the effect of lowering the cost of reproducing labour power (cf. Schiffer 1991), the colonial state steers clear of playing any interventionist or directive role in the development of industries. Compared with other NIEs in the region (for a brief summary of major research, see Weiss and Hobson 1995), the role of the Hong Kong government falls far short of being a capitalist developmental state. Not only has it not formulated any strategic industrial policy, it has also refused to provide any long-term national strategy of industrial development or direction for the operation of the market economy. The aforementioned public housing programme, as an example of the type of intervention of the colonial state in the economy, illustrates the strength as well as weakness of the approach of 'positive non-interventionism'. While the provision of public housing helped to make low-wage, labour-intensive manufacturing a viable strategy for industrialization in the 1960s and 1970s, this form of indirect intervention does not provide any incentives for local industries to follow the track of industrial upgrading. The emphasis of government policy towards industrial development continues to be indirect involvement under the 'non-interventionist' banner. This indirect involvement takes the form mainly of infrastructural and institutional supports (see Wong, T.Y.C. 1991 on the Hong Kong government's industrial policy).

As regards infrastructural support, the colonial state had long been active in financing education, and building communication and transportation networks. However, in terms of human resources development, there was no industry-specific manpower training. Generally speaking, there was practically no coordination between manpower training and industrial development. Concerning institutional supports in the 1980s and 1990s, government expenditures focused mainly on financing the work of the Industry Department and subventing the activities of various industry-related bodies like the Hong Kong Productivity Council and the Hong Kong Design Innovation Company. On the whole, however, the government maintained its detachment by not subsidizing any one industry and by not directly assisting any particular industrial activity in terms of support for R&D and other matters related to technological development. The colonial state essentially stayed aloof from the operations of industrial production. Returning to our discussion of the electronics industry, local manufacturers found themselves very much on their own in meeting the challenges of industrial restructuring (particularly in the area of technological innovation and upgrading), with minimal support from the government. Short-term economic calculations therefore had come to predominate among local manufacturers given the nature of the government's non-interventionist policy. And this short-term orientation was further reinforced by political uncertainties affecting the business environment during the 1980s and 1990s (i.e. the 1997 question concerning the future political conditions of Hong Kong after its decolonization).

In our 1992 Survey of Industrial Restructuring in Hong Kong, we sought to verify our generalizations about the state–industry relationship in Hong Kong by asking a sample of respondents from establishments in the garment and electronics industries for their assessment of this relationship.[5] The scant support given by the colonial state to industrial development, and the arm's length relationship between the state and industry are illustrated by our respondents' answers to questions concerning their opinions about the public support system. When asked whether they thought support from a number of public bodies was adequate for their business, manufacturers on the whole gave low ratings to the public support systems for industrial development. Apart from the Trade Development Council, which over half of the respondents said provided adequate support, more than half of all responding firms regarded support from the Productivity Council, Industry Department, Labour Department and Vocational Training Council as inadequate. Evaluations of infrastructural facilities were mixed, with slightly less than half of all respondents claiming they were adequate. As can be seen in Table 2.4, electronics firms were less critical of public support than garment-making firms. For every aspect of the public support system, negative ratings were more common among garment-making respondents.

The relatively more positive ratings given to the Trade Development Council and infrastructural facilities also reflect the colonial state's mode of involvement in industrial development. As argued above, the colonial state refrained from pursuing a sectoral industrial policy that gave priority to manufacturing in the allocation of resources. It offered ample support and incentives to private capital accumulation *in general*, while refraining from interfering with the flow and distribution of resources and capital across different sectors. Infrastructural provision certainly served this purpose well. Furthermore, the state was also constrained in exercising intervention in the marketplace by its limited resource base. On the one hand, the home government expected the colony to be self-sufficient so that it would not have to rely on subsidies from the sovereign state. Following the Sino-British

Table 2.4 Industrialists' evaluation of public support of industries (%)

	Supportive	*Neutral*	*Unsupportive*	*Supportive*	*Neutral*	*Unsupportive*
	Trade Development Council			*Vocational Training Council*		
Electronics	63	10.9	26.1	25.5	19.1	55.3
Garment	44.1	13.2	42.6	25.5	19.1	55.3
making All	51.8	12.3	36	18.3	17.4	64.3
	Productivity Council			*Labour Department*		
Electronics	34.8	21.7	43.5	27.1	29.2	43.8
Garment	11.9	23.9	64.2	10.4	25.4	64.2
making All	21.2	23	55.8	17.4	27	55.7
	Industry Department			*Infrastructural Provisions*		
Electronics	15.6	28.9	55.6	53.3	17.8	28.9
Garment	16.7	12.1	71.2	44.6	12.3	43.1
making All	16.2	18.9	64.9	48.2	14.5	37.3

Source: 1992 sample survey (see Chiu and Lui 1995)

Agreement on the future of Hong Kong, the Chinese government began to pay closer attention to Hong Kong's fiscal policy. The obligation of the Hong Kong administration to follow a balanced-budget policy is actually included in the Basic Laws, the mini-constitution approved by the National People's Congress in April 1990 for the administrative region of Hong Kong after the 1997 handover. Since the Asian Financial Crisis and the period of globalization, it is also apparent that the international financial community's perception of the fiscal viability of the SAR government is increasingly a significant factor in its policy calculations, as evident in the following quotation from the Chief Executive's Policy Address in 2003 (http://www.policyaddress.gov.hk/pa03/eng/policy.htm):

> ... we must ensure our economy returns to growth by adopting proactive steps to attract foreign investment and retain domestic investment. These investors pay close attention to our credit ratings, which take into account the Government's fiscal position. In making their assessments, international rating agencies mainly focus on the outlook for revenue and expenditure, especially in the recurrent account. Recently, Standard & Poor's announced that it would downgrade its outlook for Hong Kong's long-term local currency credit rating from stable to negative. This, in effect, is a warning that this rating will be downgraded if the fiscal deficit does not improve in the future. A downgraded rating will inevitably have an adverse effect on both the public and private sectors, resulting in higher financing costs. This would lead to a worsening investment environment and a general erosion of the attractiveness of Hong Kong to foreign investors. We cannot overlook the importance of maintaining a favourable investment environment which is crucial to our economic recovery and restructuring.

It is also interesting to note that the principle of fiscal restraint is very much internalized in the policy-making process of the Hong Kong government, both in the colonial and SAR period, and is not a direct result of the actual size of the surplus or deficit. Hong Kong has been running a sizeable accumulated surplus since much of the post-war period, but this has not prevented the government talking up the need for fiscal prudence and a balanced budget.

Given these external constraints, the colonial state had to be very prudent in public spending. At the same time, apart from land sales and taxation, the state did not possess any other means (e.g. financial system, foreign aid and loans, public enterprises) of acquiring resources to implement interventionist strategies. Consequently, the state's support of industrial development is necessarily limited in scale and cannot involve a major increase in public spending or subsidies. Hence, the various public bodies geared towards assisting industrial development (the Productivity Council, Industry Department and Vocational Training Council) were either limited in their scale of operation, or operated on a self-financing basis. Most of them served as a medium for disseminating information to the private sector, with the Trade Development Council being most successful in such undertakings.

In short, state assistance to manufacturing appeared to local industrialists as too little in scale and too limited in scope to be of much help. Local manufacturers' reliance on restructuring strategies like relocation, flexible production and concentrating on narrow market niches amid the continuation of a labour-intensive mode of production was understandable given the nature of this state–industry relationship.

An even more illuminating finding from the survey is that, when asked what kind of measures they would like the state to undertake for them, about 40 per cent and 46 per cent of the respondents in electronics and garment-making respectively replied 'none'. Some added by way of further explanation that they did not believe that the government could do much. Four garment-making and two electronics firms responded that they hoped the government would establish an industrial loan scheme to help them weather the process of restructuring. A minority of seven electronics firms (none in garment making) hoped the government would concentrate more effort on technological development. Apart from these isolated cases, our findings clearly suggest that industrialists did not have high expectations that the state would be able or willing to assist their restructuring.

A second component of the institutional context of industrial restructuring is Hong Kong's financial system. It has been argued that the banking system has been the pillar of the development of manufacturing industries in East Asia (Wade 1990). Under the influence of the state's selective credit policy, banks in Japan, Korea and Taiwan channelled substantial funds to the industrial sector. Singapore has an industrial bank responsible for the provision of long-term capital. This type of active partnership between finance and industry found in other East Asian countries hardly exists in Hong Kong. Hong Kong's situation appears instead to be closer to that of Britain, where an 'institutional separation of finance and industry' predominated historically (Ingham 1984). There is no industrial bank in Hong Kong. As shown in Lui and Chiu (1996: 235), the share of local bank loans and advances to the manufacturing industries accounted for less than 20 per cent of the total in the 1960s, and declined further in the 1970s and 1980s. Hong Kong manufacturing industries' share in bank loans is obviously not commensurate with their contributions to the national product and is far below corresponding figures for the other East Asian NIEs.

The inadequate support from the banking sector is most noticeable when we consider medium-sized and small manufacturing firms. Larger firms, with substantial collateral, manage to solicit assistance from the banks, but smaller firms are often denied financial assistance. As a study conducted in the early 1960s observed, 'The degree of self-financing in Hong Kong industry is indeed abnormally high; a number of substantial firms rely exclusively on their own resources' (Economist Intelligence Unit 1962: 16). The same study also pointed out that, even for the larger firms, long-term capital investment tended to be self-financed and most bank loans were directed to the financing of short-term working capital. Later studies also revealed the same pattern of 'institutional separation' of the small-scale manufacturing sector from the financial sector. For example, surveys of small and medium-sized enterprises carried out in the 1990s again identified insufficient bank finance as a problem (see Schenk 2004a: 584). This institutional feature discourages restructuring strategies, which require heavy capital investment, and encourages capital-saving strategies, especially among the smaller firms.

We are not saying, however, that the banking system is entirely irrelevant to industrial enterprises.[6] In terms of general banking services, Hong Kong's banking sector is one of the most advanced in Asia. Both the range and quality of banking services in Hong Kong are impressive. Industrialists in general hold positive views of the banking sector. It is in the area of lending, especially long-term lending for capital investment, that local manufacturers find the banking sector most wanting. Again our survey findings testify to the same weak linkages between manufacturing firms and the banking sector. More than 80 per cent of the electronics firms in the sample of our 1992 survey were founded with the entrepreneurs' own savings, as were about three-quarters of garment-making firms. Only three electronic firms and five of the garment makers started with 50 per cent or more of their capital coming from banks and finance companies. After their founding, more than 50 per cent of the electronics manufacturers successfully borrowed money from banks. Garment-making firms had less luck, with only about one-third of them managing to borrow from the banks. More revealing is the finding that less than half of all responding garment firms had ever attempted to solicit financial support from the banks. 44 per cent of the electronics firms in the sample responded that they had never borrowed from banks.

We also asked our respondents to evaluate the adequacy of banks' assistance with respect to three aspects of their operation: working capital, trade credit and fixed capital. Since most of them had no previous experience of soliciting banking assistance in some of these three areas, the number of 'no answer' responses was rather high in the survey. As shown in Table 2.5, among those who had an opinion about these banking services (i.e. excluding the 'No comments' column), most were satisfied with banks' assistance in providing trade credits. This is not surprising given the origin of Hong Kong's banking sector in financing entrepot trade. The self-liquidating and short-term nature of trade credits also minimizes the risk borne by the banks. The evaluation of banks' assistance to the lending of working capital was mixed, split between positive and negative assessments. The majority of the firms, however, regarded the banking sector's assistance in the lending of fixed capital as inadequate. Electronics firms had more positive ratings of the banking sector on the whole than did the garment-making firms. In all three areas, the proportion of electronics firms indicating that banking assistance was adequate outweighed the proportion giving a negative evaluation. The majority of garment-making firms in our sample, on the other hand, regarded banks' assistance to be inadequate with respect to the lending of both working capital and fixed capital. The influence of the size factor is evident here. As shown earlier, the electronics firms are larger on average than garment-making firms in our sample, as well as in the population as a whole. The smaller firms in the sample were more likely to feel left out in terms of receiving the banking sector's services to the manufacturing industries. Hence while larger firms enjoyed international standard banking services, small-scale firms found few channels to obtain funding forrestructuring and

Table 2.5 Industrialists' evaluation of support from the banking sector

		No comments	Adequate	Neutral	Inadequate
Working capital	Electronics	8.3	43.8	22.9	25
	Garment making	22.2	20.6	20.6	36.5
	All	16.2	30.6	21.6	31.5
Trade credits	Electronics	14.6	50	18.8	16.7
	Garment making	28.6	27	15.9	28.6
	All	22.5	36.9	17.1	23.4
Fixed capital	Electronics	18.8	35.4	25	20.8
	Garment making	34.9	12.7	11.1	41.3
	All	27.9	22.5	17.1	32.4

Source: 1992 sample survey (see Chiu and Lui 1995)

upgrading. The lack of long-term funding perhaps explains to a large extent why industrial automation has been progressing so slowly in Hong Kong.

Although firms have not received much direct assistance from the state and the banking sector, they are given a free hand by their employees and the trades unions to restructure their production (on the recent development of unionism, see Chiu and Levin (2003)). Private firms are not required by the state to bear any 'social responsibility' that limits their options, nor are they constrained by a strong labour movement in making decisions on restructuring production. Hong Kong's union movement is numerically weak, with less than 20 per cent of all employees belonging to unions. Union density in the manufacturing sector is even lower – less than 10 per cent. Unions are also organizationally fragmented into three 'federations' of different political persuasions (England 1989). Union organization at the shop-floor level is particularly weak, so that unions have very limited power to mobilize collective actions such as strikes to resist restructuring. At the community level, the political clout of the union movement is equally limited. Consequently, in devising various strategies for restructuring, industrial firms are almost completely free from problems of union-led resistance or interference. Hence, they have considerable flexibility in changing their production strategies. In particular, unions are unable to resist the relocation of production to China. Employers have no need to negotiate with workers over the schedule of relocation, nor do they have to honour or feel bounded by union contracts. Not surprisingly, then, most respondents (74 per cent in garment making and 71.4 per cent in electronics) reported having 'cooperative' labour relations within their firms. The overwhelming majority (over 95 per cent) of the respondents also regarded unions as having negligible influence on the management of their enterprises.

Hollowed-out manufacturing in the late 1990s

By the late 1990s, the restructuring of Hong Kong's manufacturing industries was almost complete. This restructuring, however, was largely in the form of massive relocation rather than local upgrading of production processes. The official *Hong Kong Yearbook: 2000* has this to say about the manufacturing sector at the end of the twentieth century:

Automation, technology upgrading and relocation of lower value-added operations to the Mainland have accelerated the development of more knowledge-
based and higher value-added manufacturing, as well as manufacturing-
related services or producer services. Expansion of manufacturing activities
offshore since the 1980s has also turned Hong Kong into a strategic control
centre of an increasingly globalized production network. In spite of the
structural change, the manufacturing sector remained an important sector of
the economy providing employment to 229 445 persons (9.8 per cent of the
total private sector employees) in 2000.

(http://www.yearbook.gov.hk/2000/eng/06/c06-04.htm)

Despite the official reassurance that manufacturing had emerged leaner but fitter
from the restructuring, and was still an important source of economic growth and
employment, there could be no doubt about its much diminished significance in the
local economy.

As the above discussion plainly points out, relocation of low value-added operations to the mainland has not been accompanied by the growth of knowledge-based
and higher value-added manufacturing in Hong Kong. The latter has occurred to a
certain extent, but the much diminished weight of the manufacturing sector at the
turn of the century is a clear testament to the massive and rapid contraction of manufacturing industries in Hong Kong. Accounting for close to 40 per cent of local
employment at its peak in 1981, manufacturing's share by the turn of this century
had dropped to less than 10 per cent (Table 2.6). Consistent with its labour-intensive nature, the sector also contributed to only about 5 per cent of GDP, much lower
than its share of employment (Table 2.7). By now it is at roughly the same level in
this respect as minor industries such as construction and the public utilities (electricity, gas and water).

Hong Kong manufacturing has thus passed through the equivalent of a life cycle
in less than 50 years, from the post-war take-off to its current mutation into a main-
land-based industry with few local linkages. It had brought much wealth to a whole
generation of industrialists, and provided a means of livelihood and avenues of
upward mobility for workers. While it brought wealth and opportunities to Hong
Kong people, its phenomenal decline has also brought disruption and misery to the
lives of plenty of them. We will delve into the human side of the restructuring
process in Chapter 4. Here we close this chapter by summarizing the key points of
our earlier discussions: the historical legacy of trade, commerce and finance
assisted Hong Kong manufacturing in building its connection with the world market; the phenomenal growth of the manufacturing sector has, in turn, confirmed
Hong Kong's position in the global economy; finally, with their strengths in commerce and responsiveness to the changing market, Hong Kong's manufacturers
have been quick to tap in to new resources, and have opted for the strategy of relocation that subsequently rescaled their production and paved the way for the formation of a global city-region with Hong Kong becoming the centre of control,
marketing and business services.[7] This industrial restructuring process is also a part
of the history of Hong Kong's formation into a global city.

Table 2.6 Distribution of employment by sectors (%), 1981–2001

Year	Manufacturing	Construction	Commerce	Transport and communication	Finance and business	Services	Others	Total (000s)
1981	39.2	8.8	20.8	7.0	5.0	17.3	1.9	2407.0
1990	27.7	8.3	25.9	9.9	7.7	18.9	1.6	2741.0
1991	26.1	8.2	26.7	10.0	8.3	19.3	1.5	2793.8
1992	23.9	8.5	27.4	10.7	8.4	19.6	1.4	2787.2
1993	21.5	8.0	28.5	11.2	9.5	20.0	1.3	2865.0
1994	18.8	7.9	28.6	11.4	11.5	20.2	1.5	2968.5
1995	17.5	8.1	28.9	11.4	11.6	21.5	1.1	3012.7
1996	15	9.4	29.8	10.9	12.1	21.6	1.1	3063.2
1997	13.4	9.8	30.3	10.9	13.1	21.5	1.0	3253.4
1998	11.8	9.5	30.5	11.2	13.7	22.3	0.9	3232.5
1999	11.5	9.2	30.2	10.9	13.9	23.5	0.9	3148.5
2000	10.2	9.5	30.7	11.2	14.1	23.6	0.8	3254.9
2001	9.6	8.9	30.1	10.7	15.0	25.0	0.7	3230.1

Source: *Quarterly Report on General Household Survey* (Census and Statistics Department, various years)

Note: Year-end figures

Table 2.7 Gross domestic product (GDP) by economic activity, 1980–2000 (percentage contribution to GDP at factor cost)

Economic activity	1980	1985	1990	1995	2000
Agriculture and fishing	0.8	0.5	0.2	0.1	0.1
Mining and quarrying	0.2	0.1	0.0	0.0	0.0
Manufacturing	**22.8**	**21.3**	**16.7**	**7.7**	**5.4**
Electricity, gas and water	1.5	2.8	2.4	2.4	2.9
Construction	6.5	4.8	5.2	5.1	4.9
Services	**68.3**	**70.5**	**75.4**	**84.7**	**86.6**
Wholesale, retail and import and export trades, restaurants and hotels	19.4	21.5	23.7	24.8	24.6
Transport, storage and communications	6.9	7.7	9.0	9.4	9.5
Financing, insurance, real estate and business services	21.7	15.1	18.9	22.6	21.4
Community, social and personal services	11.9	16.3	14.1	16.5	19.9
Ownership of premises	8.4	9.9	9.7	11.4	11.3
GDP at factor cost	**100.0**	**100.0**	**100.0**	**100.0**	**100.0**

Source: Hong Kong Census and Statistics Department (http://www.censtatd.gov.hk/hong_kong_statistics/statistical_tables/index.jsp?charsetID=1&tableID=036, retrieved 17 April 2006)

Notes: 0.0 = less than 0.05%

3   The building of an international financial centre

From the functional point of view, Hong Kong, unlike the traditional centres such as London and New York, did not begin its career as a net exporter of capital. At the same time, unlike many other newly emergent centres, it does not confine its activities to entrepot financial services or offshore banking, since the domestic market is also highly dynamic. The most appropriate appellation is therefore 'regional financial centre'. As the designation implies, it is a focal point for the flow of funds across national boundaries in the Asian-Pacific area.

(Jao 1980: 161)

In judging Hong Kong's entitlement to the label IFC [international financial centre], we must consider Hong Kong in its historical context. This includes the strong commercial heritage of banking and financial services, which continued to dominate the activity in the colony throughout the 1950s and 1960s, and positioned Hong Kong as the regional centre for the exchange of information and expertise on Asian and Western market opportunities. ... The diversification of financial activity in the 1950s and 1960s set Hong Kong on its path to becoming a major IFC in the 1980s.

(Schenk 2001: 120–1)

Introduction

The driving force behind Hong Kong's rise to the status of global city is its connectivity with the global economy through plugging in to the global system of industrial production and the global flows of commercial and financial activities. Of course, as we have shown in the previous chapter, the division between industry on the one side and commerce and finance on the other is always more for analytical convenience than substantive. Industry, commerce and finance, at least in Hong Kong's case, have always been closely intertwined, each reinforcing the other, and creating the synergy for further growth and development. Following our review of the development of manufacturing in Hong Kong, we examine in this chapter Hong Kong's path of development as a centre of finance and commerce, from an entrepot to a regional financial centre in the early post-war decades and then to an international financial centre in the 1980s.

How Hong Kong has come to assume the status of one of the global cities, and in the process has developed and expanded producer services and taken up a major role in the coordination of global flows of commercial and financial activities, requires explanation. The debate between Schenk and Jao (see the quotations on p. 56) involves more than simply a disagreement about the chronology of Hong Kong's emergence as a leading player in the world of commerce and finance. Underlying the discussion about the timing of Hong Kong's rise to the position of a key financial centre is a deeper historical process shaping its emergence and changing roles in the regional and global contexts. In the following discussion, we shall examine the course of Hong Kong's development into an international financial centre and how this development is shaped by local, regional and global dynamics. While regional and global dynamics facilitated Hong Kong's emergence as a financial centre, local institutional responses have also been crucial in enhancing the city's capacity to deliver much-demanded services.

Trade-driven financial development

It is widely accepted that Hong Kong has a long history of involvement in global trade and finance (see our discussion in Chapter 1), but vibrant participation in commercial and financial activities does not by itself confirm the status of the locale concerned as a centre, be it regional or global, of such activities. In this regard, Jao's argument (1979, 1980, 1997; also see Li 2004) that Hong Kong became a regional financial centre in the late 1960s (around 1969) serves as a convenient starting point for our discussion of the city's changing fortunes in the global flows of commercial and financial activities. According to Jao (1979: 675), one of the indicators of Hong Kong's emergence to the position of regional financial centre is 'the presence of a large and still increasing number of international banking institutions and other non-bank financial intermediaries'. Between December 1969 and October 1978, the number of representative offices of foreign banks increased from 21 to 104. Yet, Jao is also quick to point out the mere presence of foreign banks, which given Hong Kong's colonial background is hardly a new phenomenon, is not in itself sufficient to make a city a regional financial centre. He argues that:

> The essence of such a center is that non-domestic financial intermediaries congregate not only to transact business in the host city's or host country's domestic financial markets, but also to engage actively in the channelling of funds to and from third countries. Even before 1970, Hong Kong could boast of a cosmopolitan banking structure where all the major trading nations, with the exception of the Soviet bloc and the poorer Third World countries, were represented. But most foreign banks then were content to confine their activities to financing Hong Kong's external trade and domestic economic activities. There was little thought of using Hong Kong as a regional base for conducting offshore banking business. Notwithstanding its earlier roots, the growing internationalization of banking operations and financial activities has become evident only in the past eight or nine years.
>
> (Jao 1979: 677)

Important changes reflecting structural shifts in Hong Kong's financial sector were, first, 'the emergence of depository institutions other than the licensed commercial banks' and, second, 'the trend toward greater banking concentration' as shown by foreign banks' acquisition of local Chinese counterparts (Jao 1979: 679–80).

Jao's observations (1979) point to the fact that, during the first 100 years of British colonial rule, Hong Kong's financial activities were closely connected to its trade and commerce. In the very early days of the colony, large agency houses, such as Jardine Matheson, Dent and Company, also performed most of the banking functions (Ghose 1987: 2). The growth of trade and commerce attracted British banks based in India to expand their operations to the colony. This was soon followed by other European banks. 'Between the founding of the Colony and 1866, no fewer than 11 banks opened their offices in Hong Kong and gradually a banking sector with a distinct local flavour evolved' (Ghose 1987: 3). The Hongkong and Shanghai Banking Corporation (HSBC) was founded in 1865 by representatives of major hongs in Hong Kong as a local bank to meet the financial requirements of the expanding commercial activities in the region, with an emphasis on servicing Hong Kong and the treaty ports of China and Japan. Its business soon surpassed that of the Oriental Banking Corporation, the first British bank to open in Hong Kong. And, as noted in Chapter 1, the HSBC quickly extended the scale and scope of its business and established its own organizational networks in the region. Because of its local and regional emphasis, it became active in financing intra-regional business and

> developed a truly broad local base and financed many important projects both in Hong Kong and in China, although it can be argued that many of these ventures, such as insurance, shipping, docks, wharfs and godowns etc were directly related to foreign trade.
>
> (Ghose 1987: 6)

The native Chinese banks (*qian zhuang*, *yin hao*, or *piao hao* in Chinese) provided financial services to Chinese businesses, and handled transactions related to remittances to and from overseas Chinese communities. With the rise of the Chinese bourgeoisie and the emergence of Chinese businesses with overseas connections, like the Wing On and Sincere department stores, the services carried out by these native banks proliferated (Ghose 1987: 8). And the growing complexity of local Chinese financial services is best shown by some Chinese bankers' attempts to develop Western-style banks. The National Bank of China was established in 1891 (but closed down in 1911), followed by the Bank of Canton in 1912 and the Bank of East Asia in 1918. The growth of Chinese banking services further facilitated the formation of the Chinese Bankers' Association in 1919.

Other financial and business services were also quite well developed in the first 100 years of Hong Kong's colonization. Immediately after the occupation of Hong Kong by the British, Jardine Matheson, Dent and Company relocated Canton Insurance Office Limited from Guangzhou and set up its office in the colony. Insurance services proliferated hand in hand with the growth of trade and commerce. Stock trading activities began in the late nineteenth century with the establishment of the Hong Kong Stock Exchange in 1891 and later the Hong Kong Sharebrokers' Association in 1921. The Gold and Silver Exchange Company was founded in 1910, and registered in 1920 as the Chinese Gold and Silver Exchange Society, to facilitate trade and exchange in gold and silver. The Exchange Fund was set up in 1935 to act as a mechanism to ensure the backing of Hong Kong bank notes issued by the note-issuing banks. Reed's (1981) ranking of world financial centres, which is based upon the number of private banks, the number of international banks with their headquarters stationed in the centre, and the presence of foreign banks, classifies Hong Kong in the second-rank international financial centres (IFCs) in 1900–30. It is suggested by Reed (1981) that Hong Kong was then in an important position to finance China's international trade.

Geo-politics in the early post-Second World War decades

Further development in Hong Kong's trade, finance and business services in the post-Second World War decades was more than simply a repetition of its earlier path of growth. The picture is well captured by Schenk (2001: 121):

> Hong Kong clearly fits into the model of an IFC emerging from an international commercial entrepot. … The collection of banking, merchant/marketing and insurance expertise that had serviced the entrepot of Hong Kong in the nineteenth and early twentieth centuries combined with the regulatory environment to make Hong Kong a major target for new entrants in the decades that followed. … In the first two decades after the Second World War, the colony began this transition from an exclusively commercial to an increasingly financial focus. With the stagnation of the re-export trade in the 1950s, many banks shifted toward new activities such as financing domestic industry, collecting capital from abroad, and channelling the increasing wealth in Hong Kong overseas. The dramatic rise in deposits and the influx of foreign banks into Hong Kong in the early 1960s shows that the colony was developing into a collection centre in these years. The flurry of activity in the first stock market and property booms in the early 1960s also attracted investors and speculators, establishing Hong Kong as a centre where fortunes unrelated to international trade could be won (and lost). The increasing sophistication of foreign security transactions and the growth of the exchange markets in these years further contributed to the emergence of Hong Kong as an IFC. The diversification of financial activity in the 1950s and 1960s set Hong Kong on its path to becoming a major IFC in the 1980s.

Two observations are particularly pertinent here. First, in addressing Jao's argument about Hong Kong's becoming a regional financial centre in 1969–70, Schenk does not deny that it experienced a major transformation in the structure of its financial and commercial services in the late 1960s but she does contend that development in the early post-Second World War decades was crucial for inserting Hong

Kong into the global financial economy. Second, while it is quite true to say that Hong Kong had been an international commercial entrepot prior to the Japanese invasion, with financial development closely linked with the colony's participation in world trade and particularly commercial activities related to China, its subsequent development into an international financial centre began from the 1950s and early 1960s and not, as argued by Jao, since 1969–70.

Schenk (2001) points to the significance of changes in the international monetary and financial system in the first two decades after the Second World War and the colony's geo-politics in shaping Hong Kong's connection with the flows of money in various segments of the international financial market. First, the sound institutional framework for finance, a stable currency (backed by the Exchange Fund) and free exchange together constituted one of the key factors for Hong Kong's success in attracting the inflow of money and capital from neighbouring countries. It provided a safe haven for the savings of the region's overseas Chinese. More importantly, in 1945–9 Hong Kong quickly overtook Shanghai as a centre for China's trade and finance. Because of the nationalist government's trade control and exchange rate policy, mainland merchants flocked to the colony with the aim of capitalizing on Hong Kong's free foreign exchange market. Because of political and economic instability on the mainland and the free convertibility of the Hong Kong dollar, Hong Kong currencies circulated widely in China (Schenk 2000).

Hong Kong's economic connections with mainland China continued despite the latter's shift to a socialist economy after the 1949 change in the political regime. The embargo on China that was imposed by the United Nations as a result of the Korean War did not result in the severing of these linkages. In fact, Hong Kong filled a major gap in China's trade with the Eastern Bloc by bringing China those essential goods, such as pharmaceuticals and machinery, that it needed (Schenk 2001: 41). In this regard, Hong Kong had become a more important trading partner to China after the embargo.

Indeed, agencies having direct links with the state trading authorities of the People's Republic of China were established in Hong Kong after 1949 to ensure the maintenance of contacts with markets in the West. Hong Kong continued to play this role in the following decades. Equally significant was Hong Kong's dependence on imports from China, partly for local consumption and partly for re-export. Hong Kong's entrepot trade with China did not disappear after 1951 (Schenk 2001: 12). In fact, Hong Kong's economic linkage with communist China in that period was not confined to trade. Hong Kong was an important financial intermediary for transferring remittances from overseas Chinese to their families on the mainland. In sum, Hong Kong did not distance itself from mainland China as it underwent drastic economic and political changes but, in fact, strengthened its position as a commercial and financial 'window' for its neighbour in that critical period when China was increasingly segregated from the non-Soviet blocs of the world economy. This China connection was essential, as we shall see in the subsequent discussion, to Hong Kong's success in capturing the new opportunities opened by China's re-entry into the world economy since 1978.

Second, in the period of post-war economic recovery and the rebuilding of world economic order, and in the context of Cold War politics and political tensions within the region, Hong Kong occupied a unique position in the international monetary system. Given its colonial status, Hong Kong benefited from its affiliation with the sterling area. It enjoyed the privileges of preferred access to goods markets and was free from exchange controls on capital flows between Hong Kong and other members of the sterling area. At the same time, to meet the needs of entrepot trade, the US dollar could be freely exchanged in Hong Kong. While the Hong Kong dollar was pegged to sterling and the US dollar, it could also be freely exchanged at a rate set by supply and demand. This free market for currency exchange facilitated capital flows in and out of Hong Kong:

> During the crucial period from 1945 to 1965, when Hong Kong was rocked by a succession of political and economic shocks, Hong Kong's regulatory system fell into the cracks between the tightly controlled sterling area arrangements and the free markets which persisted in Asian trade. The result was that Hong Kong attracted customers from the West as well as elsewhere in Asia. These investors and merchants sought to maximise their profits by exploiting the opportunities for trade and arbitrage which were offered by the free markets in Hong Kong. It was this combination of being a British colony and an Asian entrepot that was the foundation for Hong Kong's emergence as an international financial centre in these early decades.
>
> (Schenk 2001: 9–10)

At a time when a number of countries in the region suffered from political instability, such a flexible arrangement made Hong Kong 'a stable target for flight capital' (Schenk 2001: 10). More importantly,

> the Hong Kong Gap (as it became known) allowed Americans and Europeans to sell sterling securities for dollars, which they could not do in London or New York or any other financial centre. Australians, British and other residents of the sterling area could use the market to convert their sterling to US dollar securities within the rules of the exchange control. Again, this was a transaction that was not possible in the usual international financial centres.
>
> (Schenk 2001: 82)

Such security switches grew in volume in the 1950s as Hong Kong's unique position in the international monetary system attracted the inflow of money from various parts of the world and made the colony an important foreign exchange marketplace.

Third, geo-politics also impacted on Hong Kong's involvement in the gold trade in a different way. With the free market for exchanging US dollars, Hong Kong gold dealers could handle gold imports in US dollars and exports in the local currency. In the context of global controls on capital flows and the gold trade, Hong Kong, despite officially closing down the gold market in 1949, continued to do well in the gold trade.

While it was not legal to trade in gold of a quality of 0.99 fine, the market continued to operate legally in 0.945 fine gold. External trade in 0.945 gold was still illegal but once on Hong Kong shores, it could be bought and sold openly. This involved smelting 0.99 fine gold temporarily in nearby Macao or smuggling it into Hong Kong to be smelted before reaching the market.

(Schenk 1995: 391)

Largely because of restrictions on the gold trade in other countries in the region, Hong Kong was an important gold market serving Southeast Asia (even after the opening of the Bangkok gold market), and played the role of 'crucial link between international gold suppliers in South Africa, Australia and Canada, the Western gold markets in Europe, and the Southeast Asian gold purchasers' (Schenk 1995: 395).

In short, Schenk cogently argues that the early post-war years were by no means insignificant in the shaping of Hong Kong's subsequent development into an international financial centre. Its unique position in the international monetary system, its close connection with China, and its connectivity with the global flows of money and capital and regional markets involving various kinds of financial transactions were crucial factors behind Hong Kong's success in advancing its status as a regional and international financial centre when new opportunities opened from the late 1960s. That said, by the mid-1960s, the Hong Kong Stock Exchange was still small compared to others in the region, and its turnover was low relative to what it would later become.

From local to regional

Jao and Schenk argue, though in different ways, that Hong Kong's emergence as one of the global centres of commerce, finance and business services cannot be viewed as just another page in the long history of its engagement in trade and finance since 1841. While historical legacies count, they tell us very little about the course of development in Hong Kong's rise to the status of international financial centre and, particularly relevant to this book's main theme, that of global city. In this regard, the debate about the timing of Hong Kong's becoming an international financial centre is not trivial. It reminds us at least of the substantial changes that Hong Kong has undergone in the past few decades.

The years immediately following the end of the Japanese occupation witnessed a rapid growth of banks and companies offering banking and related services in Hong Kong: 'By mid-1947 about 250 institutions offered banking services in the colony, including 14 European/American banks, 32 Chinese commercial banks, 120 native banks, 76 exchange shops and 20 others including insurance companies' (Schenk 2003: 141). This drastic increase in the number of banks became a matter of concern to both the colonial government and the Chinese government, as some of those banks were 'engaged in speculation or in the infringement of trade or exchange control regulations of the Chinese Government and of this colony' (quoted in Ghose 1987: 63).

It was against this background that the first Banking Ordinance was passed in 1948. By present standards, the regulatory arrangements under this ordinance were 'extremely liberal' (Jao 1974: 17), if not primitive. But its enactment did show a departure from the Hong Kong colonial government's *laissez-faire* policy tradition. Indeed, one of the reasons why the agency houses were able to take up banking business as an ancillary to their trading business was that there were no specific regulations governing banking and finance in the colony. The issuing of bank notes was governed by the Colonial Banking Regulations, which were applicable to all colonies in the British Empire. A Company Ordinance was passed in Hong Kong in 1865 and the Hong Kong and Shanghai Banking Company Limited was the first company to register under this Ordinance (Ghose 1987: 18). However, many native banks were still unincorporated firms.

Under the 1948 Banking Ordinance, the business of a bank was, for the first time, given an official definition as

> in the receipt of money on current or deposit account or in payment and collection of cheques drawn by or paid in by a customer or in the making or receipt of remittances or in the purchase and sale of gold or silver coin or bullion.
>
> (quoted in Ghose 1987: 64)

This was a rather broad definition of a banking business. Under this umbrella we could find remittance houses, goldsmiths and even travel agencies registered as banks (Jao 1974: 17). That said, with the enactment of this new Ordinance, companies providing banking services were required to obtain a licence and pay an annual fee. The licensed banks also had to submit their annual balance sheets to the Financial Secretary. A Banking Advisory Committee was also set up by the government to oversee the licensing and regulation of companies providing banking services.

A large amount of capital flowed into the banking sector following the civil war in China and political unrest in Southeast Asian countries in the period 1948–54 (Jao 1974: 18). Since most official banking statistics date from 1954, it is difficult to know precisely the conditions of the colony's banking business before then (such as why the number of banks fell from 143 in 1948 to 94 in 1954, as suggested by Jao (1974: 18)). Table 3.1 shows the number of licensed banks and their branches in Hong Kong since 1954. The development of the banking business in the 1950s and 1960s was driven by four main factors (Jao 1974). First of all, Hong Kong's institutional environment (a stable currency and free exchange market) was attractive to capital funds from outside Hong Kong. Second, international banks established their representative offices in Hong Kong. According to Jao (1974: 21), their numbers grew 'from a mere handful in the early sixties to forty-four at the end of 1972'. Third, and more importantly, the process of industrialization created a growing demand for banking services. Last but not least, as a result of industrialization and economic growth, together with the local population's relatively high propensity to save, there was an expansion of deposits. The sharp increase in the number of branches shows the fierce competition in the banking industry during that period for the growing consumer segment of the market.

Table 3.1 Number of licensed banks and local branches, 1954–2004

Year	Licensed banks	Local branches
1954	94	3
1959	82	13
1964	88	204
1969	73	289
1974	74	557
1979	105	906
1984	140	1,407
1989	165	1,377
1994	176	1,464
1999	156	1,490
2004	133	1,221

Sources: adapted from Tai (1986:2); *Hong Kong Annual Digest of Statistics* (Census and Statistics Department, various years)

The expansion of the banking industry, and the resulting fierce competition among the banks, sowed the seeds for the 1961 banking crisis. In order to attract deposits, many banks began to offer more lucrative interest rates to depositors. At the same time, the booming real estate market and share markets exposed the banking industry to unanticipated risks. Many banks' active engagement in property financing, whether for home purchases or larger commercial and industrial land development, led to their overexposure, with their business depending heavily on the conditions of the property market. The roaring stock market, with many speculators reaping short-term profits from new flotations and rights issues, created a liquidity squeeze and put those banks that had overly committed their funds to real estate under enormous pressure. A crisis was sparked by a bank run on the Liu Chong Hing Bank in June 1961.

As a consequence of the bank run, a review of the regulatory framework for the banking industry was carried out by H.J. Tomkins, an expert from the Bank of England. The so-called Tomkins Report, published in 1962, highlighted the negative effects of 'cut-throat' competition as well as the banks' over-commitment in the real estate and share markets, and problems stemming from the close connections between banking activities and directors' family businesses (see Ghose 1987: 69). However, the Report's recommendations and proposals placed more emphasis on 'the need for prudential financial management rather than on any crucial dysfunction in the banking structure of the territory' (Ghose 1987: 69–70). Before the new Banking Ordinance, based upon the Tomkins Report, was enacted in 1966, Hong Kong experienced yet another banking crisis, in 1965. Once again, it was bubbles in real estate and share markets, together with imprudent financial management, that led to bank runs on local banks. The basic problems, as shown in the earlier crisis, were 'the lack of prudential supervision and poor corporate governance' (Schenk 2003: 150). In the 1967 amendments to the Banking Ordinance, the minimum capital required for establishing a bank was doubled and the supervisory power of the Banking Commissioner was strengthened. But the most crucial move was a ban on the issuing of new bank licences. The purpose of this ban was to consolidate the banking industry and to protect it from 'cut-throat' competition.

As a result of this moratorium on the issuing of new bank licences, foreign banking institutions entering the market had to operate under the names of finance companies or deposit-taking companies (DTCs). Under a different format, when Barclays Bank International Limited launched its business in Hong Kong in 1972, it was granted a single-unit bank licence that restricted its activity to only one operational office in the colony.

The 1970s witnessed a dramatic increase in the number of finance companies or DTCs in the territory. One source estimates that there were some 2,000 finance companies in 1973 (Hsu 1986: 20; also see Ghose 1987: 80). This phenomenal growth of DTCs was driven by three factors: (1) the boom in 1971–3; (2) their competitiveness in attracting public deposits by offering higher interest rates for deposits than the traditional banking business (possible because their activities fell outside the orbit of the Banking Ordinance); and (3) their functioning as a 'back door' for overseas banks to gain access to Hong Kong's market (Jao 1997: 144). The rapid growth of DTCs eventually led to the enactment of the Deposit-taking Companies Ordinance in 1976.

The banking sector was further reconstructed into a three-tier financial system in 1981, comprising banks, licensed DTCs and registered DTCs. Also in 1981, the moratorium on the issue of new bank licences was lifted and foreign institutions were granted full banking licences. Foreign banking institutions quickly responded by establishing 'themselves in Hong Kong in the form of branches, rather than as foreign subsidiaries incorporated in Hong Kong' (Jao 1997: 145; also see Ghose 1987: 84). Meanwhile, stock market speculation in the early 1970s (which ended in a crash in 1973) and growing securities activity led to new opportunities for merchant banks (Fell 1992: 43). Schroders launched its business in partnership with the Chartered Bank and the Kadoories. Jardine Fleming was formed by Robert Fleming and Jardines. The Hong Kong Bank also formed Wardley Limited.

The changing structure of the banking sector is best shown in the changing distributions of bank assets and bank liabilities (see Tables 3.2 and 3.3). Statistics on the 'amount due from banks abroad', 'reflecting the banking system's increasing use of foreign balances both as earning assets and as liquid assets' (Tai 1986: 2), and on the 'amount due to banks abroad' show the sophistication of fund management and the growing significance of Hong Kong as a financial centre. Li (2004: 239) observes that:

Even before 1969, of course, Hong Kong could boast of a fairly cosmopolitan banking system, in which the banks of the principal industrial and commercial nations were all represented. However, in those days such banks were primarily interested in financing bilateral trade and investment between Hong Kong and the countries they represented; there was little thought that Hong Kong would be used as a headquarters to service the whole Aspac [Asia-Pacific] region. Things then began to change in about 1969. The first salient feature is

Table 3.2 Distribution of bank assets, 1961–1984

| Year | Items of bank assets (% per annum) | | | | |
	Cash	Amount due from banks abroad	Loans and advances	Investments	Other assets
1961	2.4	23.1	39.3	3.9	31.3
1965	2.0	26.3	45.5	4.8	21.4
1969	2.0	32.1	47.7	4.0	14.2
1973	1.4	26.9	57.8	4.9	9.0
1977	0.9	34.0	55.5	3.9	5.7
1981	0.7	34.9	47.6	8.8	8.0
1984	0.3	46.4	40.4	7.0	5.9

Sources: adapted from Tai (1986: 2)

Table 3.3 Distribution of bank liabilities, 1961–1984

| Year | Items of bank liabilities (% per annum) | | |
	Deposits	Amount due to banks abroad	Other liabilities
1961	56.3	6.2	37.5
1965	65.2	7.5	27.3
1969	74.4	11.2	14.4
1973	65.1	22.1	12.8
1977	52.8	36.7	10.5
1981	32.0	52.2	15.8
1984	39.9	50.3	9.8

Sources: adapted from Tai (1986: 4)

the growing number of international banking institutions and other financial intermediaries set up in Hong Kong.

Indeed, a key feature of a regional financial centre is that the scope and geographical spread of financial activity extend beyond the local level. A regional financial centre functions as an intermediary of financial flows. Hong Kong assumed such a role in the 1970s:

During the early 1970s, Hong Kong generated surplus capital for use abroad, but after 1974 the inflow of deposits ('amount due to banks abroad') always exceeded outflows ('amount due from banks abroad'), although the two came relatively close to balancing from the late 1970s to the mid 1980s. This shift from exporter to importer of capital during the 1970s suggests that the start of export industrialization in Asia and the growth of regional trade may have motivated this net transfer of capital to Hong Kong for redistribution, and after 1978, the reforms of Deng Xiaoping and the start of investment in China, especially Guangdong Province, impelled global banks to augment their net inflow of capital.

(Meyer 2000: 203)

Meyer (2000: 203–4) further relates such changes in financial services offered by Hong Kong to important developments in the regional economy in the late 1970s:

> Prior to the mid 1980s, the majority of loans financed business inside Hong Kong; loans for use outside jumped from a small base, yet the small amounts emphasize the meagre economic development in Asia through the early 1980s. Loan volume grew both inside and outside Hong Kong after the start of the reforms of Deng Xiaoping in 1978, and loans for use outside rose faster than for use inside after 1985. Economic growth in the Nanyang countries and the pell-mell rush of Hong Kong industrialists to Guangdong Province prompted a surge of loans for outside use in 1990, vaulting them past the loans for use inside.

In short, Hong Kong had assumed a regional profile in terms of the financial services it provided.

Crises and institutional reconfigurations

We have discussed so far Hong Kong's rise to the status of regional financial centre. As noted above, the path to attaining this status was not a smooth one as it was characterized by 'the strong lead of the private sector, with regulatory institutions playing catch-up; and the rapid growth punctuated by systemic crises' (Montes 1999: 160). The crises that cropped up from time to time played a critical role in facilitating the Hong Kong government's revisions to the regulatory framework.[1] Institution building in the financial sector was largely a response to such crises. In this brief section we review how these crises have brought about institutional reconfigurations since the 1970s in three major domains of the field of finance in Hong Kong: the stock market, banking and currency.

The stock market

Stock trading has a long history in Hong Kong, with its first stock exchange (the Hong Kong Stock Exchange) dating back to 1891. The market developed slowly in the early post-war years in terms of growth in both the volume of turnover and the number of listed companies:

> Although the sustained growth of the Hong Kong economy, as measured by stock turnover, began in 1959, following the heavy industrialization of the previous years, few companies were added to the stock exchange list in the period 1957–67. During these years, the number of companies listed on the Hong Kong Stock Exchange fluctuated between 50 and 70, but active dealings were confined to the shares of fewer than 25 of these companies. Of the most active stocks, 8 were the stocks of utility companies.
>
> (Wong, K.A. 1986: 60)

Table 3.4, which reports the number of listed companies by industry group for the

Table 3.4 Number of listed companies by industry group, 1957–1977

Industry group	*1957*	*1967*	*1977*
Banking and finance	5	4	16
Utilities	9	12	8
Land and construction	3	4	113
Commercial and industrial	5	9	44
Docks, wharves and godowns	4	6	4
Hotels	2	4	9
Investments	3	4	10
Shipping	4	5	18
Textiles	2	4	20
Miscellaneous	14	17	16
Total	51	69	258

Source: Adapted from Wong, K. (1986: 60)

period 1957–77, shows how narrow the composition of the stock market was before 1969. In the period 1959–68 the stock exchange helped to raise capital amounting to less than 1 per cent of Hong Kong's GDP, and played a relatively insignificant role in supplying capital to the then growing manufacturing sector (Schenk 2004b: 143).

In the early 1970s, however, a major boom in the stock market led to a rapid increase in trading volume and number of listed firms (also see Table 3.4). A total of 251 new companies were listed between 1969 and 1973. The total value of turnover also increased from HK$5,989 million in 1970 to HK$95,684 million in 1980 (Table 3.5). Because of the rather stringent requirements for listing on the Hong Kong Stock Exchange, three new stock exchanges (Far East, Kam Ngan and Kowloon) were established during this period to enable smaller companies to become listed. The establishment of these new stock exchanges posed a challenge to the 'gentleman's club atmosphere' (Schenk 2004b: 148) of the Hong Kong Stock Exchange by facilitating the popularization of stock trading among small investors.

Schenk (2004b: 154) suggests that the stock market boom of the early 1970s 'transformed the nature of the equity market':

> The proliferation of exchanges took place in a rapidly rising market and itself contributed to the new issue boom. Unlike the 1960s, the exchanges aimed

Table 3.5 Value in stock turnover, 1948–1980 (HK$ million)

Year	Turnover	Year	Turnover
1948	159	1967	305
1950	60	1970	5,989
1955	333	1973	48,217
1958	150	1975	10,335
1960	876	1977	6,127
1961	1,414	1980	95,684
1965	389		

Source: Adapted from Wong, K. (1986: 59)

new issues at the small investor and the phenomenal rise in prices drew a wide spectrum of the population into the market. The government made a variety of efforts to stem the boom both directly and through the banking system, but its most decisive legal intervention was to introduce a moratorium on new exchanges. ... The end of the exchange as a gentleman's club also opened the case for government intervention to protect the public from the widely publicised abuses of the system such as spurious floatations and fraudulent shares.

(Schenk 2004b: 154–5)

The 1970s witnessed the establishment of a Securities Advisory Committee in 1973, the introduction of the Ordinance for the Protection of Investors and the setting up of the Securities Commission in 1974, and the publication of the Code on Takeovers and Mergers in 1975.

The periodic stock market crashes during the 1970s and 1980s left their marks. The Hang Seng Index surged 5.3 times between December 1971 and March 1973. Then it fell by 91.5 per cent towards the end of 1974 (Wong, K.A. 1986: 61–2). As noted previously, the government introduced new regulatory measures as a result of this 1972–3 boom and bust. In 1981, the market lost 38 per cent of its value. Each successive crisis prompted the government to tighten the regulatory system for the stock market, but it was not until the mid-1980s that a modern institutional framework was put in place. The milestone was the unification of the four stock exchanges. After the formation of the four stock exchanges, the government passed the Stock Exchange Control Ordinance of 1973 to impose heavy penalties on anyone operating a stock exchange that was not recognized under the Ordinance. Since then no new stock exchange has been established. When the four bourses coexisted, not only did the dispersal of trading into four different localities put a brake on the further growth of stock transactions, it also had the consequence of inhibiting effective screening of the quality of companies seeking to be listed, due to differences among the four exchanges on listing requirements. Multiple listing in more than one exchange also led to confusion from time to time because of the differences in stock prices across the exchanges. A number of studies in the early 1980s concluded on these grounds that the Hong Kong stock market was inefficient (Wong, K.A. 1986).

In 1977 the government formed a working party to draw up a plan to merge the four exchanges. Although the working party recommended a gradual process of unification from four to two and then finally to a single exchange, the government enacted the Stock Exchange Unification Ordinance in 1980 to create a unified stock exchange, the Stock Exchange of Hong Kong (SEHK), in 1986. Unifying all trading under one roof had the advantage not only of enhancing economies of scale but also of enabling the implementation of computerized trading. Prior to the unification, foreign brokerage firms were excluded from direct involvement in trading, but the new stock exchange now allowed locally incorporated brokerages of foreign origin to become members. This also speeded up the globalization of the stock market and facilitated the inflow of foreign capital into it. As Wong (Wong, K.A. 1991: 222) observes, since the unification, the market has quickly transformed from an essentially domestic market into one assuming international attributes. Corporate brokers, who were for the first time formally admitted as members of the Exchange, increased their share of turnover from about 20 per cent to over 60 per cent in a period of three years.

Further regulatory changes were introduced following the market crash of 1987. Before that the Exchange was basically a private company with limited liability incorporated under the Companies Ordinance and its management was dominated by a small group of directors. After the reform, the Exchange operated more along the lines of a public utility. Following the 1987 Crash that was induced by a similar Wall Street crash, the government appointed the Securities Review Committee to review the constitution, management and operations of the stock and futures exchanges and their regulatory bodies. The Committee eventually recommended an overhauling of the regulatory and management arrangements of the stock and futures exchanges as follows. First, the governing body of the SEHK should be reformed to give proper representation to both individual and corporate members. Second, the daily management and operation of the SEHK should be delegated to a professional staff and an independent Chief Executive. Third, a single independent statutory body outside the Civil Service should be established to replace the two Commissions that previously separately supervised the stock and futures markets.

The Securities and Futures Commission was established in 1989 to perform the regulatory functions. Since then, successive regulations have tightened rules on listing, takeovers and mergers and insider trading so as to impose discipline on the market and to protect investors. After the stock market unification in 1986, stock market growth accelerated in all measures of performance (Table 3.6). By 1995, Hong Kong ranked ninth globally in terms of market capitalization, eleventh in trading volume, and sixteenth in the number of listed domestic companies (Table 3.7).

Banking

Another set of institutional changes conducive to the development of the tertiary sector occurred in the banking industry. As discussed earlier, Hong Kong's banking industry had been subject to periodic crises in the post-war years. This led to the progressive tightening of banking regulations. In the 1980s a number of cracks were evident in Hong Kong's financial system, leading to more forceful interventions by the government. In 1982, a local bank, the Hang Lung Bank, became insolvent in the face of a bank run. In 1985, the Overseas Trust Bank and its subsidiary, the Hong Kong Industrial and Commercial Bank, also collapsed. In each of these cases, the government moved in and took over the failed banks. In 1983, seven second-tier financial institutions (i.e. deposit-taking companies) also failed, causing severe losses to depositors. During the mid-1980s, the banking crisis reverberated and four smaller banks were acquired by larger counterparts. In addition to short-term measures in the form of the 'nationalization' of the collapsed banks, the Hong Kong government also revamped banking regulations by enacting the Banking

Table 3.6 Value in stock turnover volume and market capitalization, 1986–2000

Year	Total turnover (HK$ million)	Hang Seng Index (31 July 1964 = 100)	Hang Seng sectoral sub-indices (31 July 1964 = 100)				Total market capitalization (HK$ million)
			Finance	Utilities	Properties	Commerce and industry	
1986	123,128	1,960.06	1,379.74	2,659.87	2,435.92	1,759.33	—
1987	371,406	2,884.88	1,933.37	3,594.42	4,257.11	2,536.89	419,612
1988	199,481	2,556.72	1,625.69	3,486.63	3,847.90	2,317.96	—
1989	299,147	2,781.04	1,808.10	3,198.71	4,535.15	2,686.98	—
1990	288,715	3,027.47	1,906.92	3,840.58	4,874.47	2,797.00	650,410
1991	334,104	3,471.54	2,304.06	4,448.91	5,843.30	2,981.10	949,172
1992	700,578	5,545.97	4,643.61	6,689.14	9,215.66	4,379.31	1,332,184
1993	1,217,213	7,695.99	6,282.81	8,993.74	12,362.49	5,733.18	2,975,379
1994	1,137,414	9,453.52	7,988.80	10,708.04	16,556.57	7,331.10	2,085,182
1995	826,801	9,098.47	8,381.38	10,323.01	15,550.75	6,719.82	2,348,310
1996	1,412,242	11,646.55	11,411.80	10,243.35	21,925.96	8,647.50	3,475,965
1997	3,788,960	13,294.70	16,039.15	11,722.60	22,495.26	8,857.60	3,202,630
1998	1,701,112	9,484.47	13,383.24	11,868.83	11,713.44	5,421.48	2,661,713
1999	1,915,941	12,859.93	18,736.10	14,877.75	15,676.95	7,589.14	4,727,527
2000	3,047,565	15,838.33	20,229.51	18,896.90	16,558.25	10,640.86	4,795,150

Source: *Hong Kong Annual Digest of Statistics* (Hong Kong Census and Statistics Department, various years)

Table 3.7 World ranking of equity market capitalization, turnover volume and number of listed domestic companies, 1995

Rank	Total market capitalization (US$ million)		Total turnover (US$ millions)		Listed domestic companies	
	Market	Value	Market	Value	Market	no.
1	US	6,857,622	US	5,108,591	India	7,985
2	Japan	3,667,292	Japan	1,231,552	US	7,671
3	UK	1,407,737	Germany	1,147,097	Japan	2,263
4	Germany	577,365	UK	1,020,262	UK	2,078
5	France	522,053	France	729,099	Czech Republic	1,635
6	Switzerland	433,621	Taiwan	383,099	Canada	1,196
7	Canada	366,344	Switzerland	310,928	Australia	1,178
8	Netherlands	356,481	Netherlands	248,606	Pakistan	764
9	Hong Kong	303,705	Korea	185,197	Egypt	746
10	South Africa	280,526	Canada	183,686	Korea	721
11	Australia	245,218	Hong Kong	106,888	Germany	648
12	Malaysia	222,729	Australia	97,884	Israel	654
13	Italy	209,522	Sweden	93,197	South Africa	640
14	Spain	197,788	Italy	86,904	Brazil	543
15	Taiwan	187,206	Brazil	79,186	Malaysia	529
16	Korea	181,955	Malaysia	76,822	Hong Kong	518
17	Sweden	178,049	Singapore	60,461	France	450
18	Singapore	148,004	Spain	59,791	Thailand	416
19	Brazil	147,636	Thailand	57,000	Netherlands	387
20	Thailand	141,507	Turkey	51,392	Spain	362

Source: Adapted from Jao (1997: 42)

Ordinance in 1986. Ho (1991: 98) summarizes the main features of the new regulations as follows:

a   The Ordinance governs both banks and DTCs and the Commissioner of Banking supervises both types of institution.

b   The power and the duty of the Commissioner of Banking is enhanced.

c   A ratio constraint, the minimum capital to risk assets ratio requirement, is instituted.

d   A new liquidity requirement is imposed.

e   The Commissioner is also empowered to issue guide-lines for banking operations from time to time.

It is suggested by Hsu (1998: 161) that the Banking Ordinance enacted in 1986 was a significant step in bringing the regulatory framework of banking in Hong Kong closer to international standards. The Ordinance has certainly fostered better governance on the part of the banks, but perhaps more important was the government's takeover of collapsed banks. By doing so, although costly, it restored public confidence in the banking system, thus forestalling possible chain reactions.

Money

Behind the remarkable expansion in trade and finance, however, was an institutional innovation in Hong Kong's monetary system: the HK–US dollar peg (for a detailed discussion, see Latter 2007a). The foreign exchange rate system constitutes a crucial institutional interface between the Hong Kong economy and the global economy, and also mediates (but does not necessarily mitigate) the impact of external turbulence on domestic economic activities. For a small developing economy like that of Hong Kong, it also signals the particular forms of its dependency to the core countries and the international regime they forged. International trade, capital flows and other transactions are also conditioned by this institutional arrangement.

Before 1972, the Hong Kong dollar was pegged to sterling in line with Hong Kong's status as a British colony. In addition to the fixed exchange rate at around £1 = HK$14.55 in the late 1960s, an exchange control system was also maintained to prevent a reserve drain from the sterling area. In July 1972, severe pressure on sterling forced the British government to float its currency, and Hong Kong dollar was then pegged to the US dollar instead. From 1974 the Hong Kong government had to float the Hong Kong dollar because of a wave of speculative attacks on the US dollar. In the mid-1970s, Hong Kong's large trade surpluses exerted upward pressure on the exchange rate. From the late 1970s, however, the US dollar was subject to downward pressure due to a combination of the trade deficit and domestic expansion in the money supply. By the early 1980s, a currency crisis was in the making. And it was finally triggered by the crisis of confidence sparked off by negotiations between China and the United Kingdom over the future of Hong Kong, and the continuous appreciation of the US dollar. According to Joseph Yam, the head of the Hong Kong Monetary Authority (HKMA), the crisis had deep roots:

> Despite the obvious role of the political situation in acting as the catalyst for the HK dollar currency crisis in 1983, the origins of the crisis in fact went deeper and beyond the uncertainties over Hong Kong's future. The credit explosion made possible by the lack of effective monetary management and loose supervisory environment had fuelled an asset price bubble that by 1981 was being kept alive largely by inflows on the capital account. When the economic fundamentals deteriorated sharply in 1982, the bubble burst, and the overlent position of the banking system to the property sector set the scene for a major liquidity squeeze. The political shock then came at the worst possible moment when the financial system was already very fragile and under pressure.
>
> (Hong Kong Monetary Authority 1995: 15–16)

By the end of 1982, the Hong Kong dollar stood at HK$6.48 per US dollar. In September 1983, when the crisis broke out, the Hong Kong dollar slumped to HK$9.6 per US dollar. In October 1983, the government introduced a currency peg with the US dollar at HK$7.8 per US dollar, effectively returning Hong Kong to the currency board system practised before the floating system (Table 3.8). This

Table 3.8 Exchange rate regime for the Hong Kong dollar

Date	Exchange rate regime	Reference rate
Until 4 November 1935	Silver standard	—
6 December 1935	Pegged to sterling	£1 = HK$16
23 November 1967	Fixed to US dollar within	£1 = HK$14.55
6 July 1972	±2.25% intervention	US$1 = HK$5.65
14 February 1973	bands around a central rate	US$1 = HK$5.085
25 November 1974	Free float	—
17 October 1983	Link system to US dollar	US$1 = HK$7.80

Source: Adapted from HKMA (1995: 11)

measure proved to be effective since the exchange rate has stabilized around the pegged rate ever since.

Supporters of the linked exchange rate system note that it has been successful in stabilizing the exchange rate even during a number of domestic and international economic and political crises. In the 1980s and 1990s, the exchange rate between the HK and US dollars never exceeded 2 per cent of the official rate. Even the 1989 crisis of confidence sparked off by the Tiananmen incident in Beijing only pushed the exchange rate down by about a mere 0.34 per cent (Jao 1993: 72). The remarkable stability of the exchange rate has contributed to rapid growth in trade in commodities and services. Hong Kong also accumulated international balance of payment surpluses on a regular basis during the final decades of the twentieth century. By the 1990s, Hong Kong's foreign reserves were the third highest in the world. Furthermore, the economy registered considerable growth in GDP. In the first decade after the implementation of the linked exchange rate system, the average annual growth rate of GDP was about six per cent.

Critics argue that the linked exchange rate system has three major disadvantages (for a review, see Jao 1993: 142). First, under the currency peg Hong Kong's interest rate is basically determined by American interest rate movements. Hong Kong could not implement its own independent monetary policy through the interest rate instrument. Second, the linked exchange rate makes Hong Kong particularly dependent on the American economy so that it is very vulnerable to the effects of business cycles and economic disturbances in the United States. Third, the weak American economy and its consequent low interest rate policy forced Hong Kong to follow suit. By the early 1990s, the saving rate in Hong Kong was less than 1 per cent. This aggravated the problem of inflation. As the real interest rate was actually negative, the money supply was chasing after assets like stocks and properties, driving their prices up. We shall return to this connection later.

Following the establishment of the linked exchange rate system, the Hong Kong government also sought to strengthen its tools for influencing the money supply. Hong Kong has never had a fully fledged central bank, but the Exchange Fund performed the function of regulating Hong Kong's currency in the earlier decades. This Fund was established in 1935 to serve as the ultimate backing for notes issued by all note-issuing commercial banks. During the sterling period, banks had to deposit sterling with the Exchange Fund before they could issue more bank notes.

In return they received Certificates of Indebtedness, which enabled the banks to issue Hong Kong bank notes of an equal amount. When turbulence has occurred in the foreign exchange market, the Fund has intervened to stabilize the exchange rate. It has achieved this objective mainly by direct intervention through buying or selling Hong Kong dollars or foreign currencies on the foreign exchange markets.

The introduction of the exchange rate link with the US dollar effectively stabilized the currency, but the periodic crises in the local banking system have also led to government interventions. In particular, the Exchange Fund was used in the rescue of several banks that became insolvent. Neither the colonial government's *laissez-faire* ideology nor its lack of an appropriate policy tool in the form of a central bank appear to have deterred it from intervening when this type of market failure occurred. And a creative interpretation of the role of the Exchange Fund sufficed to confer on the Fund the role of banker of last resort:

> This use of the Fund, which was still technically confined by the Exchange Fund Ordinance to the regulation of the value of the currency, was justified on the grounds that the collapse of a major local bank would have had unacceptable effects on the inter-bank market and the banking system as a whole, and hence on the exchange value of the HK dollar.
>
> (Hong Kong Monetary Authority 1995: 17)

Under the linked system, the Fund was also used to intervene in the foreign exchange markets to defend the link rate. In addition, it served as a tool of monetary policy by influencing inter-bank liquidity and thus short-term inter-bank interest rates. With the Federal Reserve Bank-style open market operations, its main instrument was by the placement or withdrawal of Exchange Fund deposits from the inter-bank market. In 1988, the government introduced the Accounting Arrangements that require the Hong Kong Bank, the clearing house for all banks in Hong Kong, to open an account with the Exchange Fund. The balance in the account then represents the net amount of liquidity that can only be altered by the government. Any excess liquidity in the banking system over the balance of the account is penalized by the Fund through the levy of a 'penal rate' of interest. The Arrangements allowed the government to exert control over the level of inter-bank liquidity, making the Fund in effect the banker of last resort.

The Fund also issued Exchange Fund Bills and Notes respectively in 1990 and 1993, providing the banking system with a highly liquid asset but also the Fund with an instrument to conduct open market operations. When the Fund wanted to reduce the level of liquidity, it could issue Exchange Fund paper to mop up excess liquidity. If extra liquidity was needed, it could also buy back Exchange Fund paper. This came to be called the Liquidity Adjustment Facility (LAF) in 1992 (a Hong Kong version of the discount window), under which banks could borrow overnight funds from the HKMA through repurchase agreements of eligible securities at the offer rate set by the HKMA. They could also place surplus funds overnight with the HKMA at the bid rate. For some observers, such as John Greenwood who first proposed the link system, the new arrangements since 1988 effectively established a central bank in Hong Kong to regulate the money supply and interest rate (see Jao 1991: 30).

As the Fund gradually acquired central bank functions and enhanced the government's capacity to intervene in the financial markets, the government moved to consolidate its interventionist capacities by establishing the Monetary Authority in 1993 to assume the central bank functions from the Exchange Fund and the Commissioner of Banking. In addition to regulating the exchange rate, the Authority was also empowered to maintain the stability and integrity of the monetary and financial systems of Hong Kong. The HKMA still does not issue bank notes except for the HK$10 bills that are being used to replace the coins of the same denomination. It still delegates the clearing house function to the Association of Banks. Yet it has come to play an increasingly important role in stabilizing Hong Kong's financial system. Through its open market operations, the HKMA now frequently intervenes in the inter-bank market to adjust the inter-bank rates, and targets the level of inter-bank interest rates rather than the level of inter-bank liquidity. It also supervises the operation of commercial banks under the Banking Ordinance and the operation of the government debt market. As in the Exchange Fund era, the Authority also acts as the lender of last resort and organizes emergency support for banks in trouble (Hong Kong Monetary Authority 1994, 1995).

Concluding remarks: a centre of financial and commercial services

By 1995, Hong Kong had indisputably become a centre of regional and international finance. Table 3.9 shows that it was among the top five on most ranking lists measuring financial development in the Asia-Pacific region, and was among the top ten worldwide. The net result is the rising share of business services in GDP at the expense of manufacturing, as well as the growing prominence of financial services, trade and commerce (Figure 3.1). We shall return to recent developments in Hong Kong's financial services in a later chapter. Hong Kong has thus followed a course of restructuring that enabled it to develop into a global city.

We have focused on the course of Hong Kong's development into an international financial centre. However, given our concern with Hong Kong's rise to the status of global city, we also need to show how this transformation process has brought about the vibrant development of various kinds of commercial services. Table 3.10 provides basic information on the development of Hong Kong's service sector for the period 1991–2004. It is evident that Hong Kong has experienced growth not only in banking and finance, but also in the areas of professional services, trading and re-exports.

Hong Kong's status as a regional and international financial centre was put to the ultimate test by the Asian financial crisis. In 1997, following events in other parts of Asia, primarily Indonesia, Thailand and South Korea and finally the devaluation of Taiwanese dollar by late October, Hong Kong's pegged exchange rate came under attack as speculators launched a two-pronged attack on the Hong Kong dollar. On the one hand, they sold and took short positions in the Hong Kong dollar, betting the government would eventually devaluate the Hong Kong dollar or even

Table 3.9 Ranking of Hong Kong as an international financial centre

Categories	Asia-Pacific ranking	World ranking
Banking (1996):		
No. of foreign banks	1	2
Banks' foreign assets	2	5
Banks' foreign liabilities	2	5
Cross-border inter-bank claims	3	8
Cross-border inter-bank liabilities	2	4
Cross-border credit to non-banks	2	3
Syndicated credits by volume	2	8
Signed project finance deals	1	2
Forex market (1995):		
Net daily turnover	3	5
Derivatives market (1995):		
Net daily forex contract turnover	3	5
Net interest rate contract turnover	4	8
Overall	3	7
Stock market (1996):		
Market capitalization	2	7
Value traded	6	14
No. of listed domestic companies	7	17
Value of new equity issues	1	Not available
Bond market (1995)	8	Not available
Gold market (1996)	1	4
Insurance (1995):		
No. of authorized insurance companies	1	Not available
Premium income	5	27
Qualified actuaries	1	Not available
Fund management (1996)	2	Not available
Source of foreign direct investment (1996)	2	5

Source: Adapted from Jao (2001: 46)

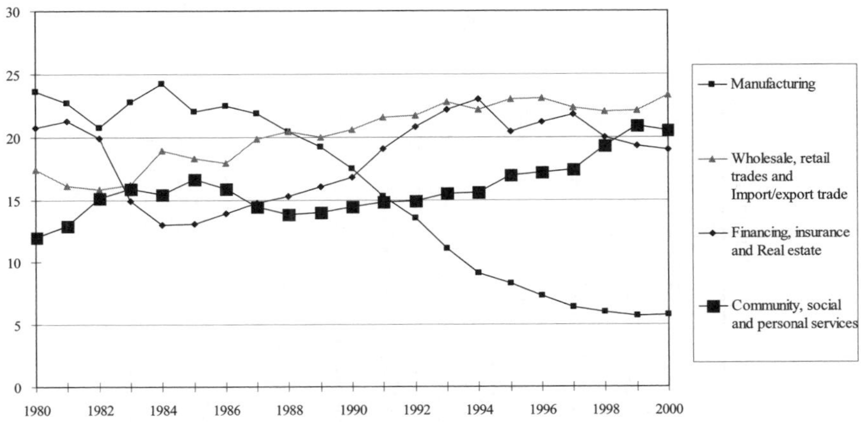

Figure 3.1 Sectoral share in GDP of manufacturing and major service sectors (%)

Table 3.10 Major statistics on Hong Kong's service sector, 1991–2004

	1991	1996	1997	1998	1999	2000	2001	2002	2003	2004
Banking industry:										
No. of establishments	1,972	1,954	1,936	1,962	1,922	1,837	1,798	1,688	1,588	1,529
Business receipts index (1996 = 100)	—	100.0	103.9	97.6	104.0	104.8	107.6	106.7	106.7	111.2
Presence of world's largest 500 banks in HK	206	213	215	213	186	186	176	168	170	157
Financial markets and fund management services industry:										
No. of establishments	1,802	2,402	2,321	2,200	2,361	2,464	2,523	2,545	2,368	2,354
Business receipts index (1996 = 100)	—	100.0	165.2	93.3	98.4	132.9	106.4	91.3	114.0	154.4
No. of listed companies (main board)	357	583	658	680	701	736	756	812	852	892
No. of Chinese state-owned companies listed in HK	—	23	39	41	44	47	50	54	64	72
Professional services industry:										
No. of establishments	5,713	9,199	10,003	9,058	9,686	9,893	10,350	10,723	11,190	11,656
Import and export industry:										
No. of establishments	69,066	104,076	101,324	92,604	98,714	104,455	100,438	102,902	97,977	95,451
No. of import/export firms with manufacturing related functions	—	25,530	25,980	21,640	22,330	19,000	15,647	16,378	15,231	—
Re-exports of the mainland of China origin to other places (HK$ million)	221,450	552,822	595,511	559,726	570,126	647,338	578,329	594,708	603,592	684,888

Source: *Statistical Digest of the Service Sector* (Census and Statistics Department, various years)

abandon the dollar peg so that the HK–US dollar exchange rate would plummet. On the other, they shorted future contracts to bet simultaneously against the Hang Seng Index.

As the sell positions mounted in the market, under the 'normal' operation of the currency board discipline, the HKMA passively sold amounts of US dollars on 21 and 22 October to defend the link rate.

> As the banks collectively had sold more Hong Kong dollars to the HKMA than they could settle by using their credit balances in their clearing accounts with the HKMA, there was an acute shortage of inter-bank liquidity when these foreign exchange transactions were settled on 23 October.
>
> (Hong Kong Monetary Authority 1998: Ch. 5)

The result was that inter-bank interest rates shot up and the overnight HIBOR (Hong Kong's inter-bank rate) briefly touched 280 per cent. This successfully stemmed the speculative outflow of US dollars. In response, overnight HIBOR eased to around 100 per cent by the close of 23 October, and quickly dropped to around 5 per cent on the following day (Hong Kong Monetary Authority 1998).

The HKMA also sought to discourage the use by licensed banks of the LAF to lend to speculators who took short positions on the Hong Kong dollar. The HKMA clarified the definition of 'repeated borrowers' in respect of LAF borrowing on 12 November. If a bank had borrowed through LAF on eight occasions in any period of 25 days or on four consecutive days, it was then defined as a 'repeated borrower'. If a repeated borrower failed to provide a satisfactory explanation of his repeated use of LAF and continued to borrow, a punitive rate may be charged on his future borrowing. By the end of November, inter-bank term rates had started to come down.

In the following year, the speculative actions escalated from the attack on the exchange rate to a coordinated 'double market play' by attacking the money and stock markets at the same time. As the HKMA defended the dollar peg by pushing the interest rate up to discourage forward selling, the speculators used future contracts to bet against the Hang Seng Index. On the one hand, speculative funds borrowed a sizeable amount of Hong Kong dollars to make forward sales in the market. This jacked up the interest rate and it follows that asset prices would fall because of this interest hike. Hence speculators built up substantial short positions in the stock and futures markets so that they could profit from the fall in stock prices when interest rates rose in response to selling pressures on the Hong Kong dollar. By August 1998,

> the selling pressure on the Hong Kong dollar was far greater than in earlier episodes. Trading in stock index futures grew sharply and disproportionately. Gross Open Interest in spot Hang Seng Index futures rose from 70,000 contracts in June to some 92,000 contracts in early August.
>
> (Hong Kong Monetary Authority 1999: 37)

To counteract the selling pressures on the Hong Kong dollar, the HKMA sold some of its foreign currency reserves and switched into Hong Kong dollars. By buying back the sell positions on Hong Kong dollars in the market, the HKMA stabilized the inter-bank liquidity. Inter-bank interest rates firmed slightly only in early August, with overnight and one-month inter-bank interest rates moving to around 6–7 per cent and 10–11 per cent respectively. By mid-August, to frustrate the double market play, the government decided to use the Exchange Fund to mount operations in the stock and futures markets, purchasing the constituent stocks of the Hang Seng Index and acquiring Hang Seng Index futures contracts to counteract market manipulation. By using its sizeable reserves to 'bet against' the speculators in both the money and stock markets, the government successfully defended the currency peg and stabilized the market. In the last two weeks of August, the HKMA bought almost US$15 billion worth of local stocks in order to ward off the speculators, emerging in the process as the biggest shareholder of many blue-chip companies in Hong Kong (Clifford and Engardio 2000: 227).

Critics pointed out that the government's interventions in the market were unprecedented and unjustified, yet it could not be denied that the Hong Kong SAR government's efforts proved successful in stabilizing the economy amid the turbulence created by the Asian financial crisis. Much of the credit for this success can be traced to the institution-building processes in the decades preceding 1997. In particular, the strengthened capacity of the HKMA proved instrumental in enabling it to defend the currency peg from efforts by the speculators to undermine it. Although there have been debates over whether abandoning the peg would have been a wiser decision, the LAF and the quasi-central bank functions of the HKMA had contributed to the reduction of volatility of the interest rate, and forestalled the collapse of the peg and the stock market (Tse and Yip 2003). The tightened grip on the banking industry also made it easier to restore order in the financial markets. The Hong Kong case thus testifies to what Steven Vogel observes, that globalization does not always lead to freer markets with fewer rules. In

> most cases of 'deregulation', governments have combined liberalization with *reregulation*, the reformulation of old rules and the creation of new ones. Hence we have wound up with freer markets and *more* rules. In fact, there is often a logical link: liberalization requires reregulation.
>
> (Vogel 1996: 3; original emphasis)

4 A divided city?

Spatial polarization arises from class polarization. And in world cities, class polarization has three principal facets: huge income gaps between transnational elites and low-skilled workers, large-scale immigration from rural areas or from abroad and structural trends in the evolution of jobs.

(Friedmann 1986: 76)

There is now greater inequality in earnings distribution and in household income, a greater prevalence of poverty, and a massive increase in foreign and domestic investment in luxury commercial and residential construction. Do these merely represent changes in magnitude along an upward or downward gradient, or are they ruptures and discontinuities in the social fabric of these cities?

(Sassen 2001: 323)

In the early years of this century, more than a decade after Hong Kong's structural transformation from an industrial colony to a global city, the public suddenly was made aware of the problem of rising social inequality in its midst. Indeed, it has become the kind of social issue reported as newspapers' headline stories. The public was alerted to the fact that Hong Kong's Gini Coefficient was now higher than that of Brazil and many less developed countries. The news media also drew public attention to reports concerning the living conditions of poor families (e.g. underage scavengers who collected scrap paper for sale) and they elicited a sympathetic response from the public. In recognition of the growing seriousness of the problem and the public's concern about it, the Hong Kong SAR government established the Commission on Poverty in 2005, whose primary task is to formulate proposals to alleviate poverty. The government also included social inequality as an issue worthy of discussion by its Strategic Development Commission, a forum of social notables and academics appointed to deliberate on the long-term development of Hong Kong.[1] The issue of the causes of and the solutions to poverty remain highly contentious. Grassroots groups lament that the free market is creating a huge rift between the social underclass and the nouveau riche, and demand a heavier dose of social intervention by the government to alleviate poverty. Conservatives retort that inequality in Hong Kong is neither a new phenomenon nor is it intolerable since the availability of plentiful opportunities for substantial upward mobility make a certain level of inequality bearable.

The claim that there is a strong relationship between global city development and social polarization is one of the major theses of global city studies (see the above quotations from Friedmann and Sassen) and has generated a rich literature both debating and testing its validity. Most of this literature focuses on global cities in advanced Western societies such as London and New York, or regions like the Randstad cities in the Netherlands (Sassen 1991, 2001; Hamnett 1994). Baum (1997, 1999) is one of the few that extend analysis to cities other than those in North America and Continental Europe.[2] This chapter follows on from this discussion by examining the case of Hong Kong, another widely acknowledged global city out-side the primary axes of London, New York and Tokyo. Hong Kong is an ideal site for testing this so-called 'dual city thesis' (Mollenkopf and Castells 1991) because it has undergone the critical transformation postulated in the global city literature in the most striking manner: the rapid decline of secondary production and the expansion of services, especially producer services. If social polarization is in fact an inevitable outcome associated with the development of global cities, then Hong Kong should prove to be no exception. In what follows, we will document various dimensions of the linkage between the global city development and indications of social polarization in Hong Kong. We will then move beyond the analysis of the effects of the structural changes in the economy from manufacturing to services on social polarization to a discussion of the socio-demographic changes associated with global city development. We aim to shed light in particular on the role of immigration and guest workers in shaping the social structure of Hong Kong as it has in the classic cases of London and New York. By using the population census micro-data rather than published aggregate data, we can conduct a more direct test of the polarization thesis by examining the relationship between structural and occupational changes in global cities and social polarization.

Global city development and employment changes

Hong Kong's recent development clearly merits its inclusion among a small number of global cities standing at the apex of the contemporary global economy. As documented in previous chapters, the structural change in the economy since the 1980s has also been mirrored in employment trends. Manufacturing's share of employment plummeted from 41.2 per cent in 1981 to a meagre 12.3 per cent in 2001 as this sector lost close to half of its working population over the decade, falling from 990,365 to 400,952. Commerce (wholesale, retail, import, export and hotels) emerged as the largest employing sector, accounting for more than a quarter of total employment in 2001, followed by community services, and business services (financing, insurance, real estate and business services). The largest proportionate employment gain was, however, recorded in business services. Between 1981 and 2001, the working population in this sector increased by 233.5 per cent, followed by community services (63.2 per cent), and transport, storage and communications (49.3 per cent) (Census and Statistics Department 1982, 2002a).

Analyses of the de-industrialization process in the advanced economies find that the decline of manufacturing does not necessarily lead to rising levels of unemployment since new jobs are created for those without higher-level educational credentials in the expanding market for private consumer services. The conditions of these new jobs are however typically inferior in a number of respects to those lost in manufacturing:

> Jobs in growing sectors have thus become polarized between the financial and business service sectors, which traditionally offer secure jobs to workers with some form of qualification, and the private consumer services, including the burgeoning hotels and catering sector, where jobs are highly unstable and opportunities for training or advancement limited, but which do take largely unqualified workers.
>
> (Gordon and Harloe 1991: 386–7)

In Hong Kong the number of skilled and semi-skilled manual workers in the 'craft and related' and 'plant and machine operators' categories has plummeted (Table 4.1). Between 1991 and 2001, the number of craft and related workers dropped by 19.3 per cent, while 'plant and machine operators' fell by 34.8 per cent even as the total labour force grew by 19.8 per cent (from 2.72 million to 3.25 million). While the number of production workers (craftsmen and operatives) fell substantially, the ranks of managerial and professional employees actually expanded during this period. The number of managers, for example, grew by 40.3 per cent from 1991 to 2001. Professionals and associate professionals also increased substantially, by 81.0 per cent and 78.2 per cent respectively over the decade. This signifies the growing importance of professional workers in the provision of specialized producer services in finance, real estate and insurance. Clerks and service and sales

Table 4.1 Working population by occupation, 1991 and 2001

Occupation	1991		2001		1991–2001	
	no.	*%*	*no.*	*%*	*Absolute change*	*% change*
Managers and administrators	249,247	9.2	349,637	10.7	100,390	40.3
Professionals	99,331	3.7	179,825	5.5	80,494	81.0
Associate professionals	279,909	10.3	498,671	15.3	218,762	78.2
Clerks	431,651	15.9	529,992	16.3	98,341	22.8
Service workers and shop sales workers	359,319	13.2	488,961	15.0	129,642	36.1
Craft and related workers	397,992	14.7	321,000	9.9	−76,992	−19.3
Plant and machine operators and assemblers	365,826	13.5	238,666	7.3	−127,160	−34.8
Elementary occupations	503,832	18.5	635,393	19.5	131,561	26.1
Others*	27,996	1.0	10,561	0.3	−17,435	−62.3
Total	2,715,103	100.0	3,252,706	100.0	537,603	19.8

Sources: Census and Statistics Department (2002a: 135)

Notes: 'Others' refer to 'skilled agricultural and fishery workers and occupations not classifiable'

workers also experienced major increases. In fact, in terms of absolute numbers, the magnitude of the growth in these two occupational groups far exceeded the growth in managerial and professional occupations.

The most dramatic growth for a specific occupational group, however, was registered in the elementary occupations. Over the decade 1991–2001, this group added 131,561 persons, the largest among the nine major occupational categories, although their number swelled in relative terms by only 26.1 per cent because it was already the largest occupational group in 1991 (see Table 4.1). As we shall see later, this dramatic expansion is largely a result of the inflow of foreign domestic helpers, which highlights the importance of migrant workers in the emergent global cities. In any case, the rapid expansion of sales and service workers, and of the various unskilled elementary occupations is consistent with the polarization thesis. That is, social polarization is clearly reflected in Hong Kong in the changes in the occupational structure. And this polarization is *both relative and absolute*. Following the changes in the sectoral distribution of the labour force as a result of global city development, both the relative share of, and absolute numbers in, occupational groups at both the top and the bottom have increased.

Further support for the occupational polarization thesis comes from data on the relative income differentials among the various occupational groups. Ignoring agricultural and fishery workers (a negligible group in any case), the elementary occupations had the lowest median monthly income among the other eight major occupational groups. This group of workers earned an average of HK$3,500 (at current price) per month in 1991 and HK$5,300 in 2001, a 51.4 per cent increase. During the same period, however, the median income of the labour force as a whole almost doubled (by 93.4 per cent to be precise) from HK$5,170 to HK$10,000. The other occupational group that experienced lower than average income growth was service and sales workers, whose average income grew by only 82.2 per cent during this period. In 2001, these two occupational (elementary and sales and services) groups had the lowest monthly median income and were the only two groups whose median income fell below the overall median income of HK$10,000 (see Table 4.2). The gap between these two groups and the highest income group, the professionals, also widened. The median income of the professionals was 4.3 times that of the elementary occupations in 1991 but had risen to 5.7 times in 2001. The comparable ratio for professionals versus service and sales workers was 3.0 and 3.3 in 1991 and 2001 respectively. And, to re-emphasize the fact documented earlier, these groups (elementary occupations and service and sales workers) experienced the largest numerical growth during the 1990s. Although there are signs of professionalization occurring since the higher income groups experienced the largest relative growth, the overall thrust of the changes in Hong Kong's occupational structure appears to fit the social polarization thesis.

Widening income disparities

According to its proponents, occupational polarization is but one facet of the constellation of social impacts unleashed by global city development. The other

Table 4.2 Median monthly income from main employment of working population by occupation, 1991 and 2001

| Occupation | Median monthly income from main employment (HK$ at current price) | | % change |
	1991	2001	1991–2001
Managers and administrators	12,000	26,000	116.7
Professionals	15,000	30,000	100.0
Associate professionals	8,000	16,000	100.0
Clerks	5,000	10,000	100.0
Service workers and shop sales workers	5,000	9,110	82.2
Craft and related workers	5,000	10,000	100.0
Plant and machine operators and assemblers	4,500	10,000	122.2
Elementary occupations	3,500	5,300	51.4
Others*	3,500	7,000	100.0
Overall	5,170	10,000	93.4

* 'Others' refers to 'skilled agricultural and fishery workers and occupations not classifiable'

Source: Census and Statistics Department (2002a: 138)

dimension, income polarization, is also important. As a result of the changing conditions of growth in the global cities:

> The occupational structure of major growth industries characterized by the locational concentration of major growth sectors in global cities in combination with the polarized occupational structure of these sectors has created and contributed to growth of a high-income stratum and a low-income stratum of workers. It has done so directly through the organization of work and occupational structure of major growth sectors. And it has done so indirectly through the jobs needed to service the new high-income workers, both at work and at home, as well as the needs of the expanded low-wage work force.
>
> (Sassen 1991: 13)

Widening income disparities are a direct result of the variations in earning abilities and rates of growth of firms in different sectors in global cities. Occupational polarization in the form of the dual expansion of employment at both the top and the bottom of the occupational hierarchy is therefore the driver behind growing income inequality. While there are disputes over whether occupational polarization is occurring and, if so, to what degree, there is general agreement in the global city polarization literature that income inequality has widened (Hamnett 1994, 1996; Baum 1997; Wessel 2000). The only exception appears to be Baum's (1999) study of Singapore, in which he finds a shift in income distribution towards middle- and high-income groups.[3]

In the case of Hong Kong, available data show that income *inequality* is clearly widening but the data are more ambivalent on whether income *polarization* is occurring. Our analysis is based on the two population censuses conducted in 1991 and

2001. Instead of simply using the published information, however, we have also analysed the public use data files generated by the Hong Kong Census and Statistics Department.[4] While published statistics show the relative income changes of different occupations and households, official publications provide little information on the distribution of individual incomes.[5] The polarization thesis is also primarily about earnings from main employment rather than total income, which includes income from investments or other sources. As Baum (1999: 1109) reminds us:

> The household is important in a discussion of social polarization due to its position as a consumption unit and the association between this role and the allocation of scarce resources in the wider social structure. Yet a discussion of global cities and social polarization is, in the first instance, structured around individual-level incomes. The flow of reasoning is from changes in individual-level occupations to changes in the distribution of individual-level incomes.

To analyse this, we need to use individual-level information taken from the raw data of the two censuses. We take the monthly income of the working population (therefore excluding those who were economically inactive or unemployed at the time of the census) but exclude those who had no income because they were unpaid family workers. We also include only the earnings from main employment and exclude those derived from a second job or other sources because we want to know more primarily about the consequences of the changes in the occupational structure and labour market. The results show that, for the whole working population, the rate of growth in income for those at the top was much faster than for those at the bottom (see Table 4.3). The ratio between the median of the lower income group and that of the highest income group declined significantly (see Table 4.4). This testifies clearly to the worsening income inequality, but it does not necessarily show polarization in the sense that people at the top are becoming better off while those at the bottom are becoming worse off in absolute terms. Although income growth in the lowest decile (4.31 per cent) was sluggish over the decade and very low relative to the highest decile (55.65 per cent), there was still a net gain (Table 4.3). The only exception was in community, social and personal services, where income in the bottom decile declined absolutely as income increased substantially in the upper deciles. This decline is linked to the expanding numbers of foreign domestic helpers in the personal services sector. Therefore evidence for income polarization appears to be weaker than that for occupational polarization. The absence of a clear trend of income polarization is perhaps a result of the strong growth in overall income over the period, which was in turn a product of the finance-driven economic growth, at least prior to the 1997 Asian financial crisis. A full analysis of the consequences of the crisis is beyond our scope here, but it suggests that the speed of economic growth in the context of global city development is still important in determining the social consequences, especially at the individual income level. In other words, a rising tide did raise most (if not all) boats in a growing economy. This suggests that Sassen's hypothesis of the determinant relationship between growth and polarization needs some qualification.

Table 4.3 Percentage change in decile points of median monthly income from main employment of working population by industry, 1991–2001

| | | % change in income decile point, 1991–2001 | | | | | |
Income deciles	Manufacturing	Construction	Wholesale, retail and import/export trades, restaurants and hotels	Transport, storage, and communications	Financing, insurance, real estate and business services	Community, social and personal services	Overall
1st (the lowest)	62.13	80.15	6.12	22.36	14.88	−4.80	4.31
2nd	47.00	51.32	11.18	13.49	23.53	−20.01	21.60
3rd	48.23	29.71	13.49	13.32	29.71	−22.18	21.60
4th	54.03	23.22	15.29	24.52	30.41	6.65	29.71
5th	51.32	17.91	27.11	19.47	39.68	17.91	29.71
6th	63.42	29.71	13.49	19.73	41.35	20.56	35.11
7th	62.13	29.71	27.74	38.97	36.53	33.52	38.97
8th	85.29	29.71	29.71	42.23	55.65	31.02	44.12
9th (the highest)	86.45	29.71	24.30	41.50	45.92	37.81	55.65
median income in 2001 (HK$)	10,500	10,000	9,800	10,500	14,000	10,000	10,000

Source: Tabulations from Hong Kong Population Census public use data files (1991, 2001)

Notes: Unpaid family workers were excluded from our analysis; income data are converted into constant price February 2001

The global city polarization thesis also posits a direct relationship between sectoral change and worsening income inequality. Was therefore the widening income inequality over the 1990s a result of structural changes following from Hong Kong's development as a global city? In what ways have sectoral changes contributed to the income polarization? To obtain an intuitive measure of the extent of the inequality, we obtained the decile points (i.e. the cut-off points of the decile income groups) of monthly earnings from the main employment of the working population classified by industry in 1991 and 2001. Then we calculated, as shown in Table 4.3, the percentage change from 1991 to 2001 in the decile points in different industries, along with the median income in each industry. It is clear that there are substantial differences in the *levels* of earnings across industries. Financing, insurance, real estate and business services in general have the highest income in all decile groups. The broad sector comprising wholesale, retail and import/export trades, restaurants and hotels, on the other hand, has a consistently low level of earnings across income levels except at the highest decile. In terms of the median (5th decile point), financing, insurance, real estate and business services was highest in 2001, with transport, storage and communications, and manufacturing tied at second. The industry with the lowest median income was wholesale, retail and import/export trades, restaurants and hotels. In terms of the relative fortunes of different industries, the general pattern is lower rates of growth in the bottom deciles than in the higher decile groups. Surprisingly, manufacturing workers saw a consistent and significant improvement in earnings at all levels, although this was still much higher for those at the top than for those at the bottom. As noted earlier, community, social and personal services is the exception in that the bottom three deciles experienced a decline in real income over the decade.

Table 4.4 Ratio of selected monthly income deciles of working population by industry, 1991 and 2001

Industry	1991			2001		
	1st/9th	*3rd/9th*	*5th/9th*	*1st/9th*	*3rd/9th*	*5th/9th*
Manufacturing	0.20	0.35	0.45	0.17	0.28	0.37
Construction	0.18	0.40	0.55	0.25	0.40	0.50
Wholesale, retail and import/export trades, restaurants and hotels	0.23	0.33	0.42	0.20	0.30	0.43
Transport, storage and communications	0.29	0.43	0.52	0.25	0.35	0.44
Financing, insurance, real estate and business services	0.18	0.25	0.33	0.14	0.22	0.31
Community, social and personal services	0.16	0.23	0.34	0.11	0.13	0.29
Overall	0.19	0.32	0.40	0.13	0.25	0.33

Source: Tabulations from Hong Kong Population Census public use data files (1991, 2001)

Notes: Unpaid family workers were excluded from our analysis; income data are converted into constant price February 2001

In Table 4.4 we compute the ratios of selected decile points – the first, third and fifth – to the highest decile across different industries in 1991 and 2001. The results show that financing, insurance, real estate and business, as well as community, social and personal services, were already the sectors with the highest income inequality in 1991, with the lowest inter-decile ratios. Still, in both industries, income inequality further increased during the 1990s. And in all other industries (wholesale, retail, restaurants and hotels, and transport, storage and communications) that experienced substantial growth between 1991 and 2001, the inter-decile ratio rose during the period. Only in construction did the inter-decile ratio remain more or less constant during the 1990s. The dramatic downsizing of manufacturing should also have contributed to increasing overall inequality because income distribution *within* the industry was relatively equal in 1991, especially in the middle deciles. Not only did the inter-decile ratios drop in manufacturing over the 1990s, but the sectoral shift from manufacturing to services also contributed to the overall polarization. Thus the increase in observed overall inequality has been the result of the combined effect of a widening gap between the top and the bottom, and the redistribution of the labour force from the manufacturing sector with lower inequality to sectors with significantly higher inequality ('finance, insurance, real estate and business services' and 'community, social and personal services'). Indeed we can trace the widening income disparity in Hong Kong to the structural changes brought about by its transformation towards a global city. De-industrialization and the rise of producer services, as well as various personal and consumer services supporting these changes, all contributed to the worsening income inequality.

Gendering the polarization thesis

There are frequent calls in the global city polarization debate to bring the gender dimension to the centre of analysis. As Bruegel (1996: 1434) notes, 'income or status differentials between occupational groups are likely to be influenced by changes in the gender composition of different occupations'. We turn in this section to the evidence on how the gender factor shaped the polarization process in Hong Kong. As the labour force participation rate for males dropped from 78.7 per cent in 1991 to 71.9 per cent in 2001 as a result of a longer education period and earlier retirement, the participation rate for women increased moderately from 49.5 per cent to 51.6 per cent (Census and Statistics Department 2002a: 130). We have already documented the overall changes in the occupational structure between 1991 and 2001, and noted the signs of occupational polarization. Yet if we re-analyse the data by gender, a more nuanced picture emerges.

In 1991 women accounted for 44.3 per cent and 68.6 per cent of elementary occupations and clerks respectively. The corresponding figures for 2001 were 59.0 per cent and 72.0 per cent (Census and Statistics Department 2002a: 135). Together they accounted for over half of all women in the working population in both years. Since these occupations, as noted earlier, are at the bottom of the job hierarchy in Hong Kong, it suggests that the occupational polarization over the last decade was

Table 4.5 Working population by occupation and sex, 1991–2001

Occupation	No. in whole population		
	1991	*2001*	*% change, 1991–2001*
Managers and administrators	50,390	92,614	83.8
Professionals	30,815	65,485	112.5
Associate professionals	115,788	232,842	101.1
Clerks	295,986	381,346	28.8
Service workers and shop sales workers	128,496	224,495	74.7
Craft and related workers	45,728	26,964	−41.0
Plant and machine operators and assemblers	130,897	31,665	−75.8
Elementary occupations	223,398	375,056	67.9
Others*	7,239	2,836	−60.8
Overall	1,028,737	1,433,303	39.3

Occupation	% of women workers		% of women workers in occupational groups	
	1991	*2001*	*1991*	*2001*
Managers and administrators	4.9	6.5	20.2	26.5
Professionals	3.0	4.6	31.0	36.4
Associate professionals	11.3	16.2	41.4	46.7
Clerks	28.8	26.6	68.6	72.0
Service workers and shop sales workers	12.5	15.7	35.8	45.9
Craft and related workers	4.4	1.9	11.5	8.4
Plant and machine operators and assemblers	12.7	2.2	35.8	13.3
Elementary occupations	21.7	26.2	44.3	59.0
Others*	0.7	0.2	25.9	26.9
Overall	100.0	100.0	37.9	44.1

* 'Others' refer to 'skilled agricultural and fishery workers and occupations not classifiable'

Source: Census and Statistics Department (2002a: 135)

clearly gendered. Changes at the top of the job hierarchy also had a gender dimension. The number of women managers, professionals and associate professionals registered the largest relative increase between 1991 and 2001. The numbers of female professionals and associate professionals more than doubled, while managers and administrators increased by 83.8 per cent. These data suggest that women have increased their presence at both the top and the bottom, but obviously they are *overrepresented* at the bottom. The overall share of women workers in the labour force increased from 37.9 per cent to 44.1 per cent between 1991 and 2001. Women gained percentage share in most occupations except the two directly related to manufacturing, craft and related workers, and plant and machine operators, and especially in the latter group (Table 4.5). By 2001, clerks, elementary occupations, associate professionals, and service and sales workers could be regarded as 'feminized' occupations, as women accounted for over or close to half the occupational totals. Their most notable gains, as measured by the increase in percentage share, are found in service workers and shop sales, and elementary occupations.

Next we examine the trends in the gender gap in income for the 1990s. For the entire working population, the gender gap as measured by the ratio of men's median monthly income from main employment to that of women dropped from 1.41 to 1.35 between 1991 and 2001 (see Table 4.6). This is largely a result of gains at the top of the job hierarchy, with women gaining relative to their male counterparts as the gender gap narrowed for managers, professionals and associate professionals. Nevertheless, the same polarization tendency could be observed as the gender gap actually widened at the bottom. The gender gap for elementary occupations increased from 1.33 in 1991 to 1.94 in 2001, the highest among the occupational groups in 2001. The gender gap for service and sales workers also showed a

Table 4.6 Gender gap in income by occupation, age group and educational attainment, 1991 and 2001

	Male to female median income ratio	
	1991	*2001*
Occupation		
Managers and administrators	1.20	1.10
Professionals	1.28	1.14
Associate professionals	1.06	1.03
Clerks	1.10	1.00
Service workers and shop sales workers	1.50	1.51
Craft and related workers	1.53	1.43
Plant and machine operators and assemblers	1.83	1.67
Elementary occupations	1.33	1.94
Others*	2.00	1.78
Age group		
15–19	0.95	1.02
20–24	1.11	1.13
25–34	1.30	1.24
35–44	1.75	1.50
45–54	1.69	1.71
55–64	1.50	1.50
65+	1.65	1.55
Educational attainment		
No schooling/kindergarten	1.45	1.74
Primary	1.56	1.73
Lower secondary	1.47	1.54
Upper secondary	1.20	1.20
Matriculation	1.33	1.65
Tertiary (non-degree course)	1.27	1.31
Tertiary (degree course)	1.65	1.46
Overall	1.41	1.35

* 'Others' refers to 'skilled agricultural and fishery workers and occupations not classifiable'

Source: Census and Statistics Department (2002a: 137–9)

moderate increase from 1.50 in 1991 to 1.51 in 2001. Similar differentiations in the relative positions of women are found when we calculate the gender gap across different levels of education and age groups (Table 4.6). Again, we see that the overall narrowing of the gender gap is the result of the gains made by women with tertiary education as most other educational categories actually witnessed a widening gender gap. The increase in the gap was most notable for those workers with low educational standards. The gender gap also increased significantly for the younger and hence inexperienced women, but has improved for those with more experience. For middle-aged women workers between the ages of 45 and 54, however, the gender gap shot up again. The stable and narrowing gender gap for those workers over age 54 can be explained by the significant drop in the female labour force participation rate in this age category.

The role of migration

Our analysis has highlighted thus far three critical trends contributing to occupational and income polarization in Hong Kong: the expansion of the service sector (financial and business services, and community and personal services), the absolute and relative increase in the low-skilled and low-paid elementary occupations, and to a lesser extent sales and services workers, and the over-representation of women in these occupations. The global city thesis also predicts, however, not only the transnationalization of business and economic activities but the occurrence of a comparable transformation in the urban labour market. Sassen (2001: 321) argues that

> immigration can be seen as providing labor for the low-wage service and manufacturing jobs that service both the expanding, highly specialized service sector and the high-income lifestyles of those employed in the specialized, expanding service sector. … The expansion in the supply of low-wage jobs generated by major growth sectors is one of the key factors in the continuation of ever-higher levels of the current immigration.

Global city development therefore strengthens on the one hand an expanding demand for low-wage service jobs that support the transnational producers' services. This in turn amplifies the demand for more migrant workers to fill those low-wage jobs that locals shun. The critics claim this two-step argument restricts the generalizability of Sassen's thesis because the massive immigration found in New York and London is not a universal phenomenon but clearly depends on local factors beyond the global trend of economic restructuring (Hamnett 1994).

Yet Sassen's observation is highly relevant to the Hong Kong case and greatly enhances our understanding of the polarization process. While we cannot give a detailed exposition of the trends and patterns of immigration here, what is most important for our discussion is that Hong Kong witnessed rapid growth during the 1990s in three types of migrant worker: those from mainland China, highly skilled workers with employment visas, and those who came as foreign domestic helpers (for an overview see Chiu 2003). In 2000, for example, the total inflow of legal migrants (excluding those from the mainland) into Hong Kong was 98,648, or 1.47 per cent of the total population. Of this inflow, 19,432 entered with employment visas and another 62,619 were foreign domestic helpers (Chiu 2003).

Migrants from the mainland have always been considered a special category. Some 33.7 per cent of Hong Kong's population in 2001 was born in mainland China (including Macao and Taiwan) and another 6.6 per cent elsewhere (Census and Statistics Department 2002a: 39). Before October 1980, under immigration control maintained between the border of China and Hong Kong, a 'touch-base' policy was adopted such that illegal immigrants from China were allowed to stay if they reached the urban areas without being caught. From October 1980, this 'touch-base' policy was abolished. Since then only legal immigrants from China have been granted the right to stay, and an informal agreement was reached between Hong Kong and China that set a maximum of 75 mainlanders allowed to migrate to Hong Kong per day. With 1997 drawing closer, the daily quota was lifted to 105 and then further to 150 in July 1995. The number of legal entrants from mainland China for residence in Hong Kong therefore rose steadily, from 38,218 in 1994 to 61,179 in 1996 (Chiu 2003: 11). Apart from Chinese immigrants, people of other nationalities can also be granted residence visas. In 2000–2001, a total of 13,967 non-Chinese were granted residence visas, mostly on the grounds of family reunion (Hong Kong Immigration Department 2001).

As a result of these recent changes in immigration policy, the number and relative size of recent arrivals from the mainland have swelled. In 1991, a total of 143,944 men and women had arrived for less than seven years (the legal requirement for naturalization), or 2.6 per cent of the total population. The figure almost doubled in 2001 to 266,577 persons, or 4.0 per cent of the population. Some 66.9 per cent of these recent arrivals (for less than seven years) in 2001 were female (Census and Statistics Department 2002b: 16). They were also younger on average than the local population – for instance, with a median age of 25 versus 36 for the whole population in 2001 (Census and Statistics Department 2002b: 16). This is because the majority came for family reunions, and many were spouses and dependants of local men who married on the mainland. As a result, recent arrivals (that is, those from the mainland) also had a lower labour force participation rate (44.2 per cent) than that for the whole population (61.4 per cent) in 2001 (Census and Statistics Department 2002b: 30).

Because of their lack of locally recognized credentials, local knowledge and sometimes language barriers (some do not speak the local dialect of Cantonese), recent arrivals are obviously in a disadvantaged position in the labour market. Their presence means that the expanding low-skill and low-wage service jobs have a ready supply of willing takers. If we compare these migrants' labour market profiles with the entire population, a striking feature is how their occupational distributions dovetail with the polarization we discussed previously. Population census statistics for 1991 and 2001 show that recent arrivals are overrepresented relative to the whole population in wholesale, retail, and import/export trades, restaurants and hotels (Census and Statistics Department 2002b: 34). Another noticeable trend is in community, social and personal services. Some 7.6 per cent of recent arrivals were found working in this sector in 1991 but the corresponding figure in 2001 had increased to 16.2 per cent (Census and Statistics Department 2002b: 34). As noted earlier, both industries had low average income relative to the other industries. The de-industrialization process hit new migrants particularly hard because manufacturing used to offer a supply of manual jobs that were less likely to require local credentials and knowledge. One result is the sharp decline in the share of new migrants working in manufacturing, from 48.0 per cent in 1991 to a mere 10.4 per cent in 2001 (Census and Statistics Department 2002b: 34).

Occupational distribution tells a similar story (see Table 4.7). New migrants are significantly overrepresented in two occupational groups: service and sales workers, and elementary occupations. Service and sales workers accounted for only 15.0 per cent of the whole working population in 2001, but 30.7 per cent of working recent arrivals were located in this occupational category. The proportion of new migrants entering the elementary occupations also increased, from 25.4 per cent of all recent arrivals in 1991 to 34.9 per cent in 2001. In 2001, by contrast, only 19.5 per cent of the whole working population was in this occupational group. As a result of de-industrialization, plant and machine operators ceased to be a major occupational category for recent arrivals as the share of recent arrivals in these jobs plummeted from a sizeable 24.0 per cent in 1991 to a mere 4.1 per cent in 2001. During the same period, as the share of operatives shrunk, the corresponding percentage of the whole Hong Kong population in this group also fell from 13.5 per cent in 1991 to 7.3 per cent in 2001.

The end result of the skewed labour market profiles of recent arrivals is a skewed income distribution. In 1991, the median monthly income from main employment

Table 4.7 Proportion of working new migrants from the mainland China by occupation, 1991 and 2001

| Occupation | % of working population | | | |
| | 1991 | | 2001 | |
	New migrants	Whole population	New migrants	Whole population
Managers and administrators	4.9	9.2	3.0	10.7
Professionals	0.9	3.7	0.9	5.5
Associate professionals	3.2	10.3	4.1	15.3
Clerks	10.3	15.9	10.9	16.3
Service workers and shop sales workers	15.2	13.2	30.7	15.0
Craft and related workers	15.7	14.7	11.0	9.9
Plant and machine operators and assemblers	24.0	13.5	4.1	7.3
Elementary occupations	25.4	18.6	34.9	19.5
Others*	0.5	1.0	0.3	0.3

Source: Census and Statistics Department (2002b: 33)

* 'Others' refers to 'skilled agricultural and fishery workers and occupations not classifiable'

Table 4.8 Distribution of new migrants from the mainland China in income deciles, 1991 and 2001

Income deciles	% of migrant across decile group without FDHs		% of migrant in decile group without FDHs		% of migrant across decile group with FDHs		% of migrant in decile group with FDHs	
	1991	2001	1991	2001	1991	2001	1991	2001
1st (the lowest)	19.32	29.90	4.53	6.83	19.58	13.41	4.50	2.89
2nd	22.75	29.75	5.33	6.80	19.70	34.47	4.52	7.44
3rd	18.02	15.46	4.22	3.53	19.88	22.05	4.57	4.76
4th	13.58	8.59	3.18	1.96	12.81	11.57	2.94	2.50
5th	8.98	5.94	2.11	1.36	9.96	6.61	2.29	1.43
6th	6.30	3.83	1.48	0.88	6.55	4.48	1.51	0.97
7th	4.31	2.33	1.01	0.53	4.51	2.84	1.04	0.61
8th	3.35	1.50	0.79	0.34	3.47	1.70	0.80	0.37
9th	2.08	1.27	0.49	0.29	2.13	1.37	0.49	0.30
10th (the highest)	1.32	1.43	0.31	0.33	1.41	1.50	0.32	0.32
Overall	100.00	100.00	2.35	2.29	100.00	100.00	2.30	2.16

Source: Tabulations from Hong Kong Population Census public use data files (1991, 2001)

Notes: Unpaid family workers were excluded from our analysis; income data are converted into constant price February 2001

(at current prices) for recent arrivals was 69.6 per cent of the median for the whole working population (HK\$3,600 versus HK\$5,170). In 2001, however, recent arrivals earned on average only 60.0 per cent of the average monthly income of the entire working population (HK\$6,000 versus HK\$10,000) (Census and Statistics Department 2002b: 35). Despite the overall increase in the median income of recent migrants, it is clear that the income gap between them and the rest of the working population has widened. When we classify the monthly income from main employment of the whole working population – excluding the foreign domestic helpers (FDHs) – into decile groups, we find that the proportion of recent migrants in the lowest income deciles had actually increased during the 1990s. In 1991, about 42.07 per cent of the new migrants were in the two lowest income deciles, but in 2001, close to 60 per cent fell within the two lowest deciles (Table 4.8). If we include the FDHs, the percentage of new migrants in the lowest income decile drops between 1991 and 2001. Yet it is clear that the massive increase in the number of foreign domestic helpers (who have an administratively fixed salary much lower than the local median) 'pushed' the new migrants slightly up the income hierarchy. It remains the case, however, that the relative position of new migrants in Hong Kong's income distribution deteriorated over the last decade.

Another category of people who are allowed to take up residence in Hong Kong are highly skilled workers with an employment visa. British citizens used to be an exception because they were allowed to stay for a 12-month period and were free to take up employment during their stay. This privilege was removed after Hong Kong's return to Chinese sovereignty. People of other nationalities, if they are highly skilled or have professional qualifications, can apply for an employment visa with guarantees of employment from their company or employer. What constitutes 'skilled and professional' often has to be judged on a case-by-case basis, but the general rule is that the granting of such employment visas will be limited to professionals, specialists, administrators and managerial personnel who possess skills, knowledge or experience that are of value to and are not readily available in Hong Kong. The number of employment visas approved increased steadily from the late 1980s, probably due to the local shortage of managerial and professional personnel, especially those with proficiency in English. Since 1995 the total number of employment visas approved has been declining, largely as a result of the slowing down in the local economy. From 2000, however, the government began to step up its efforts to attract mainland professionals to Hong Kong. The arrival of those with employment visas, therefore, had the opposite effect from the case of migrants from China by making available a new source of labour supply to staff the ever expanding need for professionals and managers in producer services. Table 4.9, which reports the distribution of 'ethnic minorities' (meaning non-Chinese ethnicity) in different occupations, highlights the overrepresentation of foreign nationals from certain advanced countries (Japan, South Korea, European countries, the USA, Canada, Australia and New Zealand) in managerial and professional occupations.[6] Conversely, migrant workers from developing regions (the Philippines, Indonesia, Thailand and South Asia) were predominantly concentrated in elementary occupations. This shows clearly how migration has accentuated occupational polarization

Table 4.9 Proportion of working ethnic minorities by ethnicity and occupation, 2001

Ethnicity	Proportion of working population in occupation (%)					
	Managers and administrators	Professionals/ associate professionals	Clerks/service workers and shop sales workers	Crafts and related workers/plant and machine operators and assemblers	Elementary occupations	Others*
Developing Countries						
Filipino	0.7	1.7	2.8	0.4	94.5	0.0
Indonesian	0.4	0.3	1.1	0.4	97.8	—
Indian	31.2	22.3	18.1	4.9	23.2	0.3
Thai	2.0	2.2	25.4	1.6	68.8	—
Nepalese	1.1	4.3	20.7	29.2	44.6	—
Pakistani	9.2	6.9	14.2	24.4	45.2	—
Developed Countries						
Japanese	65.5	23.7	10.4	—	0.5	—
Korean	59.9	21.9	17.1	0.4	0.7	—
British	39.2	53.2	5.6	0.5	1.3	0.2
Other European	56.2	34.4	6.8	0.8	1.8	—
American/Canadian	48.1	46.9	3.5	0.4	1.1	—
Australian/New Zealander	39.4	54.3	3.6	0.7	1.5	0.5
Total ethnic minorities	9.5	8.8	6.0	2.2	73.4	0.0
Whole population	10.7	20.9	31.3	17.2	19.5	0.3

Source: Census and Statistics Department (2002d: 60)

Notes: 'Others' refer to 'skilled agricultural and fishery workers and occupations not classifiable'

Table 4.10 Number of foreign domestic helpers (FDHs) in Hong Kong, 1987–2006 (year-end figures)

	Total FDHs		FDHs' nationality (% to all FDHs)			
	No.	Annual growth rate (%)	Philippines	Thailand	Indonesia	Others
1987	36,831					
1988	45,154	22.6	92.4			
1989	57,971	28.4	91.2			
1990	70,335	21.3	90.5			
1991	84,619	20.3	89.4			
1992	101,182	19.6	88.1	6.6	3.5	1.8
1993	120,604	19.2	87.4	5.8	5.1	1.7
1994	141,368	17.2	85.7	5.0	7.6	1.7
1995	157,026	11.1	83.5	4.3	10.4	1.8
1996	164,299	4.6	82.0	3.5	12.8	1.7
1997	170,971	4.1	80.8	3.0	14.5	1.8
1998	180,604	5.6	77.7	3.0	17.6	1.7
1999	193,700	7.3	73.9	3.0	21.4	1.7
2000	216,790	11.9	69.9	3.0	25.5	1.7
2001	235,274	8.5	66.1	3.0	29.3	1.7
2002	237,104	0.8	62.6	2.8	33.0	1.6
2003	216,863	−8.5	58.4	2.5	37.4	1.7
2004	218,430	0.7	54.8	2.3	41.2	1.7
2005	223,204	2.2	52.9	2.0	43.4	1.7
2006	232,781	4.3	51.9	1.8	44.7	1.5

Sources: *Hong Kong Annual Digest of Statistics* (Census and Statistics Department, various years); *Hong Kong Yearbook* (Hong Kong Government Information Services, various years)

since the 1990s by fuelling the expansion both at the top and the bottom of the job hierarchy.

The majority of migrant workers in 'elementary occupations' are foreign domestic helpers (FDHs). There is no quota for them, so any family with a need for a domestic helper can apply for a permit to hire one from overseas, mainly from the Philippines but also Thailand and Indonesia. The number of FDHs in Hong Kong increased steadily over the 1990s. Even the onset of the Asian financial crisis had no significant impact on the demand for FDHs as their numbers continued to grow during 1998. In 2001, the total rose further to 235,274, or by 8.5 per cent over the previous year (Table 4.10). In terms of national origin, the largest group of FDHs in Hong Kong continues to be those from the Philippines but the number of Indonesian FDHs grew rapidly in the second half of the 1990s. They accounted for 10.4 per cent of all FDHs in 1995 but close to 30 per cent of the total in 2001 (see Table 4.10).

The 179,005 female FDHs recorded in the 2001 Population Census accounted for 12.0 per cent of the female working population (Census and Statistics Department 2002a: 126). Female FDHs constituted 47.7 per cent of all women workers in elementary occupations, and 33.8 per cent of women workers in community, social and personal services in 2001 (Census and Statistics

Department 2002a: 135–6). They thus basically fed into the rapidly expanding service sector and the elementary occupations. The government has set a minimum monthly salary (HK$3,670 in 2001) for them, but employers have to provide accommodation and medical benefits. This means that most FDHs are live-in servants, unlike the arrangement in other global cities where the nannies do not usually live in. Since their minimum salary is significantly lower than the median salary for the whole population (HK$10,000 for both sexes and HK$8,900 for women in 2001 (Census and Statistics Department 2002a: 138)), the FDHs have thus swelled the ranks of the low-income groups. Their minimum salary places them into the lowest income decile. In 2001, they therefore accounted for 45.0 per cent (using the number of FDHs recorded by the census) of the lowest income decile (10 per cent of the total working population) if we compare their number to the number of people in the lowest income decile.

As Bruegel observes, the gist of Sassen's argument is that

> it is possible to see the increasing concentration of women in high-level jobs as having fuelled demand for labour-intensive services, which employ *other* women, often from migrant/ethnic minority communities in increasingly precious jobs. Income for such jobs will only decline relatively where there is a sufficient supply of labour ready and willing to take such jobs at the levels of pay offered.
>
> (Bruegel 1996: 1434; original emphasis)

The remarkable increase in the number of foreign domestic helpers in Hong Kong offers striking support for this argument. The expansion of producer services and transnational commerce fuelled the rapidly growing demand for managers and professionals. The increasing opportunities for higher educational attainment for women, and the increased supply of local university graduates, in general partially satisfied this demand (the other source being the arrival of highly skilled migrant workers).

The Hong Kong case is in this respect but a variation on a story happening in many global cities. Susser's study of New York highlights the trend towards the separation of children from their mothers in childcare arrangements.

> Among the professional, educated households of New York City there has also been a progressive separation of children from maternal supervision. In contrast to the poorer groups, children may stay in their own households. Fathers, if present, may increase their input. However, in general, highly educated, well-paid mothers hire poor women to replace themselves in the household.
>
> (Susser 1991: 220)

In the conclusion to the new edition of *The Global City*, Sassen (2001: 322) reiterates this point:

> This is a type of household [in global cities] that could be described as the 'professional household without a 'wife'' regardless of the demography, i.e., sex

composition, of that household, if both members are in demanding jobs. As a consequence we are seeing the return of the so-called 'services classes' in all the global cities around the world, made up largely of immigrant men and women.

Of course, in the case of Hong Kong, members of these services classes are mainly women from the Philippines, Indonesia or Thailand who 'live in' with the employing family, instead of coming mainly from Mexico and Central and South America (as in the USA) and providing only daytime care.

Between 1991 and 2001, the number of women with a university degree increased rapidly from 95,209 (4.4 per cent of all women aged 15 and over) to 330,919 (11.5 per cent) (Census and Statistics Department 2002c: 28). Their continuing participation in the labour market is conditional, however, on strategies that resolve their 'double burden' of work and family responsibilities. Hiring a foreign domestic helper therefore becomes the solution for the majority of middle-class families with both marital partners in the labour force. As a result, some 75.7 per cent of all women with a university degree were in the labour force in 2001 (Census and Statistics Department 2002c: 40). While the labour force participation rate for university-educated women remained largely stable over the 1990s, the rapid expansion of university education for women (and men alike) therefore contributed substantially to the more than three-fold increase in the number of foreign domestic helpers between 1990 and 2001.

Conclusion: globalization and the local institutional context

In this chapter, we have used data generated from the population censuses to document the process of social polarization that has accompanied Hong Kong's globalization. By the early 1990s, Hong Kong obviously qualified as a global city based on the criteria found in the relevant literature. Since the 1990s, as predicted by this literature, Hong Kong has experienced a process of occupational polarization and growing income inequality as a result of its transformation from an industrial colony to a producer service-driven global city. We have also outlined the gender dimension in this polarization process and how the forces of migration have altered the social stratification system so that the social structure now resembles more closely the shape of an 'hourglass'. Save in the dimension of absolute income polarization, our findings largely support Sassen's hypotheses regarding the social consequences of global city development. We have also sought to highlight the mediating effect of local institutional contexts in shaping these consequences, as we have done so far throughout this book.

A number of critics have pointed out that the analysis of the process of urban restructuring tends to overemphasize the role of global and economic determinants at the expense of local and institutional factors. Burgers and Musterd, for example, suggest a three-layer model for analysing and explaining urban inequality: 'The global level relates to economic restructuring, the emergence of international consumer markets, increasing mobility of capital, people, commodities and information' (Burgers and Musterd 2002: 406). The second level is the national institutional differences that mediate between global restructuring and local consequences. The local level refers to the particular social and economic history of individual cities. As Hong Kong has been a city-state (as a colony before 1997 but currently as a self-governing special administrative region in China), the national level and the urban level are synonymous. While we do not think Sassen has overlooked completely the significance of local institutional configurations (see particularly her discussion of the place-ness and embeddedness of the global city (Sassen 2001: 350)), we do agree with Hamnett that 'the forces driving polarization in different cities differ or are mediated in various ways' (1996: 1408). In other words, how local institutional contexts mediate between the global forces and local consequences needs to be analysed explicitly.

One crucial aspect of the occupational changes in Hong Kong during the last decade was the shrinkage in manufacturing employment and the resulting disappearance of many middle-income manual production jobs. The local institutional context and policy framework are important in this respect since Hong Kong is considered as the archetypical *laissez-faire* economy because of minimal government intervention in the economy. Although we have reservations about this characterization since the Hong Kong government has an extensive record of intervention in the sphere of collective consumption (housing, education and medical services) in the urban economy, we do agree that the non-intervention was critical to the process of industrial restructuring. In particular, it resulted in an experience of de-industrialization that has been faster and more extensive than that seen in most other East Asian economies (Chiu, Ho and Lui 1997).

The global city literature also considers the mediating effect of local welfare regimes on polarization (Wong 2000). In contrast to Sassen's argument regarding a generalized dismantling of the welfare state, Esping-Anderson's (1990) distinction among three enduring types of welfare regime is useful for highlighting another critical context shaping social polarization in different urban settings (also Esping-Anderson 1993). Hong Kong fits squarely in his typology within the North American model of residual welfare states characterized by a low social wage guarantee and by a passive approach to full employment policy (McLaughlin 1993).

Another good example of how the local institutional context mediates the impacts of globalization is migration. As critics of Sassen's model of the global city have pointed out, the presence of a large number of migrant workers that serves as the reserve army of labour in the urban labour market cannot be taken for granted since the local political economy can always create very different regimes for regulating immigration. Hong Kong has generally welcomed the immigration of highly skilled and professional personnel from abroad in order to satisfy the almost insatiable demand for high-level employees in the context of high economic growth. The coming of foreign domestic helpers is also non-controversial because of the difficulty in the 1970s and 1980s in hiring local domestic helpers due to a tight labour market and the reluctance of locals to enter this occupation. By contrast, another aspect of labour migration into Hong Kong, namely the importation of non-professional workers at the craftsmen, operatives and technician levels, has stirred up a highly divisive political debate between labour and capital, with the government stuck in the middle trying to balance conflicting demands.[7] In the end, only a limited number of 'imported' workers have been admitted under the various schemes of labour importation since the 1980s.[8] A review of the policy changes over the importation of semi-skilled labour into Hong Kong suggests that while Hong Kong has been relatively liberal in allowing the entry of highly skilled and professional workers as well as the FDHs, this dual policy has again mirrored the occupational polarization over the last decade. We have seen a sizeable increase at both the top and the bottom of the occupational hierarchy, and both these trends were related to the inflow of migrant workers. Had there been an unrestricted supply of foreign workers for all types of jobs, Hong Kong's development as a global city would have been very different.

This chapter has been exploratory in that it has taken just the first step in fully delineating the process and social impacts of Hong Kong's transformation into a global city. More work needs to be done on explicating the mechanisms of income and occupational polarization in the urban labour market. More fine-grained studies of occupational changes need to be conducted. We also need to further examine how individual-level polarization has affected household level inequality. This is because, ultimately, we do not live as isolated individuals in the global city but as members of families. To understand how globalization has changed our lives we need to know how these individual-level processes add up at the household level. The spatial consequences of global city development also need to be spelled out.[9] That said, this chapter has clearly alerted us to the social consequences of becoming a global city. In the case of Hong Kong, it is social polarization, with a social structure taking the archetypical shape of an 'hourglass'.

5 Decolonization, political restructuring and post-colonial governance crisis

In their original formulation, Friedmann and Wolff recognized the highly political nature of global city formation. ... However, neither these authors nor most other early contributors to world cities research engaged systematically with the politics of the global city. Although Friedmann and Wolff insisted on the strategic importance of sociopolitical struggles within global city-regions, the question of how political institutions structure, and are in turn structured by, processes of global city formation, was left largely open during the decade following the publication of their classic article in 1982.

(Brenner and Keil 2006: 249)

Introduction

We have discussed in previous chapters the nature of Hong Kong's economic restructuring in the changing contexts of its own internal business structure and the broader world economic environment, and how this restructuring process impacted on the economy of the city itself. In this chapter we focus on the process of political restructuring triggered by the decolonization of Hong Kong. Our discussion of global city politics is intended to serve two purposes. The first relates to our criticism of the global city literature for neglecting the political issues underlying global city formation (see the above quotation). It is interesting to observe that many local governments in the periphery and semi-periphery take very seriously the project of becoming a global city. Their political rhetoric of climbing up the urban hierarchy in the world economy and strengthening global links and connections in order to join the ranks of other major global cities clearly entails more than political symbolism since it often involves substantive policy deliverables. Local governments' pronouncements that they seek to become global cities often quickly materialize in the form of active support for their participation in ambitious projects ranging from massive infrastructural construction (e.g. the building of a new airport) to heavy investments in culture (e.g. place marketing and promoting urban cultural tourism). Setting a goal of becoming a first-class global city is seldom challenged even if there is much contention over the best way to achieve this goal.

While there are numerous discussions of the active role that local governments play in the context of intense inter-city competition to become recognized as a globalizing city (see, for example, on Seoul, Hill and Kim 2000; on Shanghai, Yusuf and Wu 2002), the political dimension has by contrast been largely neglected in the global city literature that focuses primarily on New York, London, Tokyo and other North American and European cities (a notable exception is Le Gales (2002)). It is our contention that this under-emphasis of the political in global city research is an issue that needs to be addressed. We attempt to redress the balance in this chapter. We argue that, in order to understand the rise and fall of a global city in the world economy, we need to probe the processes of global city formation that explain *why* and *how* some cities are successful in upgrading their ranking in the global 'urban hierarchy' in the context of fierce competition among cities for this status. More specifically, we shall argue that while the mapping of the global urban network and hierarchy is important for understanding the context in which the global cities compete with each other, such macro-analysis does not explain how individual cities are able to secure the opportunities opened to them to pursue effectively their continuous development in a stratified world economy. The key to success appears to be the ability of these cities to develop a growth coalition or hegemonic bloc in order to ensure that they have the capacity and supporting conditions for the pursuit of a global city strategy. For this reason, we need to pay close attention to the nature of governance of the global or globalizing city itself as a key variable affecting the outcomes of a globalizing city strategy.

The second purpose of our discussion in this chapter is to probe the political dynamics underlying Hong Kong's current impasse in maintaining its competitiveness in the global hierarchy of urban centres. It is our contention that this impasse is not simply a matter of tweaking economic policy. Nor will the changing global and regional environment automatically provide Hong Kong with the panacea for dealing with the pains of restructuring. Local institutions become pertinent in these circumstances to the structuring of a social, economic and political setting that is conducive to advancing up the stratified system of global cities. Opportunities come and go. How a city prepares itself to capture such opportunities, or its failure to do so, determines its long-term prospects for success in the inter-global-city competition for status advancement in the world economy.

What follows is a discussion of the origin of the present governance crisis in Hong Kong. It is our contention that the post-1997 governance crisis in Hong Kong – most evident in growing social and political conflicts, the premature departure of the Chief Executive of the Hong Kong Special Administrative Region (SAR) government, and the government's failure in implementing major restructuring projects – is an outcome of institutional breakdown brought about by the process of decolonization. Through a review of the literature on political governance in Hong Kong, we argue that the crux of the matter lies in the failure of the post-colonial government in rebuilding its ruling alliance. The ruling strategy of non-interventionism under the colonial regime was built upon an allocation of interests and the resultant tacit understanding between the government and organized business interests. The changing configuration of business interests (particularly the rise of Chinese business and the decline of British companies), together with the decolonization process, have called for a new state–business relationship that has failed to materialize since 1997. The new government is trapped in a political impasse, and this has significant implications for Hong Kong's response to new socio-economic challenges posed by globalization and its own economic restructuring.

The making of a political impasse

Post-1997 Hong Kong appeared to be falling into disarray as social tensions mounted and political conflicts increased in volume and intensity (Mitchell 2000; Lee 2001; Lau 2002; Wan and Wong 2005). On 1 July 2003, the sixth anniversary of Hong Kong's return to China, an estimated half a million citizens from all walks of life, including many from the middle class, joined a mass protest. Fuelling their participation in this mass protest was a diverse set of accumulating social, economic and political grievances (Lui 2005). The protest showed the dissatisfaction of the public with the performance of the government of the Hong Kong Special Administrative Region (SAR) under the leadership of the Chief Executive Mr Tung Chee-hwa. Similar mass mobilizations, though on a smaller scale, were staged on 1 January and 1 July 2004. Largely due to this growing public discontent, Mr Tung Chee-hwa resigned as the Chief Executive of the Hong Kong SAR government in March 2005 without completing his term of office.

The mass protests had diverse origins (Lui 2005). Some were protesting because they believed the methods of governance of the Tung administration undermined Hong Kong society's core values.[1] Others, motivated by political and economic concerns, were critical of the Hong Kong SAR government's initiatives in these policy domains (the most notable examples were Tung's attempt to regulate the housing market and to propose enacting laws to prohibit any act of subversion against the central government). But what ultimately united critical voices from different corners of Hong Kong society was the perceived failure of the Tung administration to govern effectively. Its policies swung from one extreme to another as compromises or major revisions were made in the face of fierce opposition before the impacts of those policy initiatives could be tested (Chan and So 2002). More interestingly, critics of the Hong Kong SAR government were not confined to the middle class and the grassroots who suffered considerably from the economic downturn, rising unemployment and the collapse of the property market. Even the business sector expressed its discontent. The government found itself repeatedly in the crossfire of contentious political actions because it had failed to build a consensus and thus faced great difficulties in governing proactively. Arguments and conflicts continued to plague the Hong Kong SAR government even after Tung's resignation. The government, by then under the leadership of the new Chief Executive, Mr Donald Tsang, was forced to shelve (but officially to relaunch) the heatedly debated West Kowloon Cultural District project (a mega project for building a new landmark for Hong Kong and symbolizing the city's cultural turn to creative industries) in February 2006 after almost six years' planning and discussion. The continuation of political conflicts suggests that the problem of governance did not stem from the qualities of the leaders concerned. Rather, it is a strong indication that the Hong Kong SAR government had become trapped in an impasse.

While there have always been those sceptical about the workability of integrating capitalist Hong Kong into socialist China, few observers predicted the dramatic development of social tensions and conflicts after the handover. The 1997 handover was generally conceived to entail merely a change of flags since the arrangements for post-handover Hong Kong and the accompanying rhetoric emphasized the maintenance of continuity: Hong Kong would continue to be a place for making money, whether for compensating individuals' hard work and/or risky investments or for supporting projects of modernization on the mainland. Although the handover would have a huge symbolic significance as a marker of an end to national humiliation arising from the defeat by the British in the Opium War, the lives of ordinary people were expected to carry on as usual. The locals were told that they could continue to bet on horse racing and to go dancing in nightclubs. The 1997 change in political sovereignty was not supposed to bring disruption to their everyday way of life. The year 1997 eventually proved, however, to be a year of great significance for most Hong Kong people. It was not just the year that marked the end to more than 150 years of British colonial rule in Hong Kong; it was also the year in which the Asian financial crisis impacted on the region, without exception. Hong Kong experienced a sudden change in its economic climate followed by a loss of economic confidence. The collapse of the bubble economy, with a dramatic fall in stock and property prices, and a sharp rise in the unemployment rate, precipitated popular discontent. People became restless and increasingly unhappy with the way the newly established SAR government was handling the situation. Indeed, one of the most striking features of the social and political landscape of Hong Kong society immediately after the 1997 transition was the evaporation of popular support for the established social and political order. The old magic of Hong Kong seemed to have dissipated after its return to China.

The political settlement reached between the British and Chinese governments in the 1980s concerning Hong Kong's future was, on the surface, an ideal political compromise that would serve the interests of all the parties concerned. China would resume its sovereignty over Hong Kong, a city that has long been its 'window to the world', a source of foreign exchange and overseas investment, a springboard for acquiring modern business and management know-how, and most important of all a prosperous economy in its own right. Hong Kong was expected to be highly instrumental to China's development, both economically and politically. Britain would maintain its effective governance of Hong Kong before 1997 (so that the colony would not become a source of political embarrassment). It would give up its colonial rule gracefully and in the most dignified manner without having to curtail substantively its informal influence (ranging from the investments of British capital to cultural influence) in Hong Kong. Local citizens were promised by Chinese leaders that the status quo would be preserved for 50 years – that is, until 2047. The institutional arrangements of the colony, which were believed to contain all the basic ingredients contributing to its past economic success, would be 'frozen' (i.e. remain intact) and the mainland's system of state socialism would be tightly segregated from capitalist Hong Kong.

That set of institutional arrangements turned out, however, to be the main source of problems facing the post-colonial polity. It brought about the subsequent structural and institutional incongruity underlying the Tung Chee-hwa administration's (1997–2005) failure to build its hegemonic rule in the post-colonial environment. The idea of preserving an executive-led, bureaucratic and benevolent authoritarian rule after decolonization, then seen as a continuation of the basic elements of colonial governance that had proved to be effective and efficient in bringing Hong Kong to economic prosperity and social stability, turned out to be very problematic. The process of decolonization has restructured the state–society relationship. Contrary to the Tung administration's expectation that it could continue to keep Hong Kong committed to an orientation as an 'economic city' by the strategy of de-politicization employed by the previous colonial administration, the SAR government soon found itself caught in the crossfire of contending interests. The economic downturn since late 1997 made the situation even more difficult to handle. The mass demonstration on 1 July 2003, mentioned earlier, best illustrates the ongoing crisis of governance.

The major objective of the Basic Law, the mini-constitution of the Hong Kong Special Administrative Region, is to ensure continuity in Hong Kong's social, economic and political systems. 'Freezing' the existing systems was intended on the one hand to meet China's expectations that Hong Kong should continue to serve the economic interests of China without posing new threats (say, a political challenge to the authoritarian rule on the mainland) and/or triggering undesirable changes to the socialist system under reform. This was to be achieved by controlling Hong Kong's pace and extent of democratization before and after 1997. The post-1997 SAR polity would not include a fully popularly elected legislature despite the expectation that decolonization would give the locals the opportunity to become the masters of their own society. Nor would the Chief Executive of the SAR government be popularly elected. This institutional design was also aimed, on the other hand, at easing the anxiety of the local population. Continuity in institutional arrangements would help to convince local people that the Hong Kong way of life would remain unchanged for at least 50 years.

Immediately after 1997, however, the institutional arrangements comprising the Hong Kong system were challenged on all fronts (Lui 1999). The three pillars of the Hong Kong system – rule of law, personal freedom and an efficient bureaucracy – came under growing pressure. First, the promise of the continuation of the rule of law was undermined by the controversy concerning the right of abode issue. Second, the maintenance of existing freedoms – of speech, worship and association – is an issue that cuts to the core of the existing system. Such freedoms are highly valued by Hong Kong people so that any perceived threat to them raises the level of anxiety. This is reflected in concerns over the possibility that the media are exercising self-censorship. It is also reflected in the controversy over the status of the *Falun Gung*, which became a source of political embarrassment to the SAR government. Third, the fiasco of the hasty opening of the new international airport and the government's clumsiness in handling the outbreak of bird flu in the first year of Tung's administration fully exposed the sluggishness of the administrative bureaucracy and raised questions about its presumed competence. To further complicate matters, the leadership of the SAR government itself openly criticized the inefficiency and inflexibility of the bureaucracy in dealing with issues arising from the changing social and economic environment, and called for and initiated civil service reforms. In brief, the once promised continuity in institutional arrangements that was intended to ensure continuation of Hong Kong's stability and prosperity was now becoming a problem in itself.

Falling apart

Observers of Hong Kong politics are well aware of the environmental and institutional changes triggered by the political transition. Lau (e.g. 1999) has long called for the formation of a strategic governing alliance for the purpose of maintaining effective governance after the 1997 handover. In his more recent analysis of the institutional foundation of an executive-led polity, Lau again underlines the importance of building a strategic governing alliance (Lau 2000, 2002). He argues that the Chief Executive and his administration must secure meta-constitutional political power and authority. The viability of such an executive-led polity depends on obtaining reliable and steady support from a powerful and influential strategic governing alliance. Lau envisions this strategic governing alliance to include leading and influential political, economic and social leaders, as well as the groups and organizations under their leadership. This alliance would be an organized force, with a certain degree of stability and continuity. Also, members of this alliance must be willing to negotiate with each other and be able to reach compromises. This alliance is also expected to be able to reach out and secure grassroots support. Lau contends that the absence of support from a powerful strategic governing alliance will in the long run not only jeopardize the effectiveness of the SAR government's rule, but will also undermine the rationality and legitimacy of the entire political system.

Lau has raised an important question about the social basis for the political support of the authoritarian and executive-led SAR government. While Lau is of course right to say that the Chief Executive and his administration need to develop their mechanisms for interest articulation and political integration vis-à-vis the dominant leaders, it is not clear whether and how the formation of a strategic governing alliance is a viable political project. What is to guarantee, for example, that local political, economic and social elites who are key players in the political and social arena will necessarily be able and willing to make compromises to reach a consensus regarding the best way forward for the long-term development of Hong Kong society? Lau's argument begs questions about the formation and workability of a strategic governing alliance. He underestimates the diverse economic and political interests among the local elites, and their significance.[2] Without taking into account the impact of the interests of class fractions, which are diverse and sometimes conflicting, one is left puzzled about the social basis upon which the members of the strategic governing alliance are supposed to develop their consensus concerning the long-term development of Hong Kong.

Lee (1999) relates this issue of the effectiveness of the post-colonial SAR governance to a wider context. She argues that 'the governance crisis in Hong Kong is the result of institutional incongruity' (Lee 1999: 941). More specifically, she claims that the political and administrative institutions that functioned rather effectively under the colonial setting, which paradoxically served as the blueprint for the institutional arrangements of post-colonial Hong Kong and are deliberately preserved in the Basic Law, are no longer capable of meeting the needs of the new era due to changes in the broader socio-economic and political environment. While the bureaucratic colonial state fared reasonably well in an environment of continuous economic growth, a weak civil society and steady improvements in the standard of living, the effective functioning of the institutional arrangements transferred to the post-colonial regime is becoming problematic in the context of economic restructuring, the slowing down of economic growth and a more vocal civil society. These changes in the socio-economic and political environment call for a different form of political governance but the Chief Executive and the SAR government have been incapable of providing the political leadership required to revamp the institutional framework of governance or of maintaining the political legitimacy to placate rising expectations.

Lee's analysis of the governance crisis in post-colonial Hong Kong is both perceptive and pertinent. We largely agree that institutional incongruity is a critical factor in bringing about the governance crisis in post-colonial Hong Kong. We argue, however, that her analysis can be further strengthened by developing a more sophisticated analysis of the changing state–society relations. In particular, we believe that Lee's depiction of the changing state–society relations in terms of the strength of the civil society is overly simplistic. She is correct in pointing out that the period since the 1970s has witnessed rising popular demands for policy outputs and political participation, but the problem encountered by the SAR government is not simply that of demand overload from below. As we shall argue in a later section, and as was also evident in the controversies arising from the Cyberport project and the housing strategy announced by Mr Tung Chee-hwa in his first policy speech, the SAR government was not quite capable of maintaining hegemony over both the dominant class and the dominated classes. Actually, the process of decolonization has posed more problems for the SAR government than was envisaged by those who drafted the Basic Law. Lee has rightly pointed to the institutional incongruity in the design of 'one country, two systems'. However, in our view, the problem is not confined to the incompatibility between institutional arrangements and environmental changes. Equally significant is the political restructuring triggered by the longer-term emergence of local Chinese capitals and the more immediate process of decolonization. The resulting constitution and re-constitution of the dominant class has wider repercussions for state–society relations and the capacity of the SAR government to govern. Failing to take note of how the Tung administration proved unsuccessful in developing its hegemonic dominance on the basis of a new alliance with the various capitalist fractions significantly weakens any analysis of the origins of the governance crisis in post-colonial Hong Kong. In other words, the SAR government faced a challenge not only in meeting popular demands from below. It also faced a challenge in gaining the cooperation of resourceful and influential capitalists, who were uncertain whether and how their interests would be protected in the post-colonial era. As Lau (2000) has noted, the formation of a strategic governing alliance is still wanting. And the failure to build a hegemonic bloc has weakened the basis of political support for, as well as the ruling capacity of, the new government.

The commentaries on post-colonial politics in Hong Kong discussed above share the same weakness of neglecting to buttress their political analysis by linking it to the nature of Hong Kong's political economy.[3] Their analyses all imply certain interpretations (largely similar, though) of government–business relations. Their understanding and analysis of the dominant class assume that its members share a common orientation, but this may not be warranted. Few have tried to spell out clearly who constitutes the dominant class and how different fractions within that class may pose problems for the articulation of a hegemonic class project. Hegemony is formed, constituted and constantly negotiated. The existence of a dominant class is a necessary but not sufficient condition for the formation of political hegemony. We argue that the unity within the dominant class cannot simply be assumed but should be further investigated. Our analysis takes the formation of the dominant class as our starting point and proceeds to investigate how this formation process impacts on government–business and state–society relations.

The political order under colonial rule

As noted above, one of the major considerations underlying the political blueprint proposed in the drafting of the Basic Law for Hong Kong was to preserve after 1997 the proven stable political order that had existed under British colonial rule. It was expected that by including those institutional arrangements of the colonial system that were conductive to political stability and effective governance – an executive-led polity, an emphasis on the administrative capability of the politically neutral civil service and a partially democratized legislature – a highly autonomous post-colonial state could continue to command respect and compliance from various social sectors, play the role of referee in regulating competition among different interests and concerned parties, and keep political contention within acceptable limits. It should be noted that the colonial government's effectiveness in maintaining stability had nothing to do with complacency of older generations of capitalists. Indeed, British merchants' arrogance and their attempts to undermine the authority of the governors have been well documented (see, for example, Crisswell 1991). As Ngo notes (2002: 112), the colonial government's maintenance of order entailed a complicated juggling of 'contradictory tasks': 'the colonial system was maintained by the painstaking upholding of a delicate policy consent among the ruling elite. Like the SAR government, the colonial government was torn between the contradictory tasks of offering privileges to business in exchange for political support, assuming an arbiter role among competing business interests, and acting as a watchdog against rent seeking to prevent widespread discontent.'

The colonial system worked under certain premises (also see Ngo 1999b, 2000). The first was the inclusion of major business interests into a political oligarchy. From the very first days of the British colonization of Hong Kong, business interests have been an important part of political life in the colony: 'the colony existed primarily to magnify the profits of the British trading companies and to promote British influence in China' (Miners 1996: 246). Indeed, the dominance of business interests in Hong Kong politics is best captured by the popular saying that 'Power in Hong Kong ... resides in the Jockey Club, Jardine and Matheson, the Hong Kong and Shanghai Bank, and the Governor – in that order' (Hughes 1976: 23). Studying the political representation of socio-economic interests in the major channels of political participation in the 1960s, Rear (1971: 72) argued that:

> ... all the evidence suggests that the persons appointed by the Governor do in practice represent only limited interests and that (inevitably, given the system) they are not fully capable of representing the points of view of those whose interests conflict with their own or whose experience of life in the Colony is quite different from their own. ... 99% of the population of Hong Kong is Chinese but only fourteen of the twenty-one unofficials on the two central Councils are Chinese. These twenty-one are with very few exceptions the representatives of big business and banking and, without exception, the representatives of wealth. Thus in a system where the chief policy-makers are chosen from a narrow social class, so also are their advisers.

Rear's criticism of the narrow social basis of colonial governance was raised in the days when the colonial political system was essentially closed and undemocratic. The colonial government justified such undemocratic governance by its claim that it governed by consent (Endacott 1964b). It was able to maintain effective governance by being responsive to public opinion. The colonial government in Hong Kong before the institutionalization of political representation in the 1980s was, however, basically elitist. Based upon his study of the social background of top government officials and the councillors of the Executive and Legislative Councils, Davies (1977) elaborated on Rear's notion of 'one brand of politics in Hong Kong'. He claimed that 'there is a relatively small and homogenous elite, that this elite is socially and economically isolated from the lives of the ordinary people of Hong Kong, and that it has a commanding voice in the government of Hong Kong' (Davies 1977: 71).

Those appointed to positions in the Executive and Legislative Councils and other less important advisory bodies came primarily from a restricted socio-economic circle. Most were from the business community. Davies's empirical study (Davies 1977: 70) of the power elite in Hong Kong estimated that 'there are some one hundred to two hundred people who can be found with a dominant voice in all the parts of the policy process'. The dominance of the elite was due not only to tightly restricted entry into the key decision-making processes but also to the dominance of certain business groups and networks in the economy. Davies observed that 'the commanding heights of the Hong Kong economy are controlled by remarkably few interests. Although the total number of directorships is quite large, many of the directors are members of the families which in effect own the largest Chinese concerns' (Davies 1977: 66). He further elaborated on the nature of the business community as follows:

The business community in Hong Kong is dominated by relatively few large concerns with which its larger and wealthier members have directorial and financial links. These same few large concerns also dominate the banking system of Hong Kong and the essential public utilities. The concerns themselves are closely linked at the directorial level. However, these links are not only links of the boardroom. The directors meet also in two other places. First, there is the common round of clubs, major and minor, to which so many of them belong. They may not be close personal friends but they share an atmosphere, an ambience, a social nexus. Secondly, there is the shared membership of government councils, committees and boards as well as membership of many of the charitable organisations. The same major names recur in the patrons and boards of directors of these organisations as recur in the commercial directorships and the government committees. ... The sense of separateness that such predominance must inculcate over a period of time is important, for, given that these are the people who have to make the decisions for the lesser mortals, how much of the life of the lesser mortals can they understand and who is beside them to tell them of it?

(Davies 1977: 69)

Based upon data on company profiles and directorship, Leung (1990) later observed that the business community continued to be dominated by a handful of key players in the early 1980s:

In 1982, there were 456 people who held one directorship in the top 100 public companies. Five per cent of them were co-opted into the above-mentioned Councils and public interest bodies. Ninety-four people held two directorships, 19 per cent of whom were co-opted. Eighty people held three or more directorships, 35 per cent of whom were co-opted.

(Leung 1990: 21)

And business interests were well catered to in the political domain under the colonial bureaucratic administration:

In 1982, the Hong Kong Bank was linked to 22 of the top 50 public companies in Hong Kong through interlocking directorships. Thus nearly half of the top 50 public companies had, via the board of directors of the Hong Kong Bank, an official channel through which to communicate their views. If we confine our investigation to the top ten public companies, the data show that the Hong Kong Bank had interlocks with seven of the remaining nine, six of which had their chairman on the Hong Kong Bank's board of directors. ... The Hong Kong Bank alone accounted for two of the nine Unofficials [of the Executive Council in 1982], while the eight interlocking companies among the top ten together had four Unofficial seats. If private companies and the smaller public companies are included, then the total number of directorships in the Executive Council amounted to an impressive 71. In this light, the highest policy-making body in Hong Kong appeared like a meeting ground between top government bureaucrats and the major resource controllers.

(Leung 1990: 21–2)

In short, up to the early 1980s, prior to the introduction of the idea of widening the scope of political representation in the major decision-making bodies, politics in Hong Kong was largely in the hands of the government bureaucrats and a powerful economic elite.[4]

The above quotations should give us a clear picture of the composition of the ruling elite in the colonial system before the gradual move towards partial democratization in the 1980s. What is intriguing, however, is not economic and political elitism as such. A selectively inclusive ruling strategy is not in itself a guarantee of consensus building. What is more intriguing is how the formation of the ruling elite mirrors Hong Kong's economic power structure. In this regard, Wong's study of interlocking directorates in Hong Kong is valuable for revealing the nature of this economic power structure (Wong 1996). He focused on a sample of business groups that included 'the top 100 largest publicly listed non-financial companies ranked by annual turnover and the top 25 largest local banks ... ranked by their assets in the 1976, 1981, and 1986' (Wong 1996: 93). He identifies business groups by detecting 'a minimum of three companies linked together with each other directly or indirectly by 3-graphs or 4-graphs' (Wong 1996: 94). Wong observed that, over the period 1976–86 there had been a shift from the dominance by the British hongs to the emergence of Chinese business groups:

In the 1976 network, except for two small groups, the major business groups are made up of and controlled by non-Chinese business families or organizations. Most of the groups are controlled by a single business family. ... The network is clearly dominated by the Jardine groups of companies.

(Wong 1996: 96–7)

In terms of centrality, Hong Kong Bank was still dominant [in 1981]. ... The Bank together with the Cantonese group constituted the center of the network in 1981. The 1976 network center based on the Jardine group had disappeared. ... A new feature in the network is the rise of new multi-company Chinese business groups.

(Wong 1996: 103–4)

The network in 1986 is much more differentiated into separate business groups. ... The rise of separate multi-company Chinese business groups has become much more prominent. This was coupled with a corresponding decrease in the number of non-Chinese business groups. The importance of the Jardine group further declined. ... Compared with the relatively high group centralities of the 1976 and 1981 business groups, the inter-connections among the business groups had decreased. As a whole, we can describe the network as loosely connected and multi-centered.

(Wong 1996: 106–8)

Cheung (1994) provides an updated analysis of the interlocking directorship of the large corporations in Hong Kong for 1990. Based upon data from 33 listed corporations, which were selected as the constituent stocks of the Hang Seng Index, Cheung probes Hong Kong's economic power structure through interlocking directorate analysis. He observes that there are six significant clusters among his sampled corporations, three of which are well-known British families and the other three prominent Chinese family groups. Family control was very significant. In terms of centrality scores, the Jardine group under the Keswick family continued to exert its strategic influence in Hong Kong's business world in 1990, though Chinese family groups had emerged and become prominent.

In short, until the late 1980s, the British hongs continued to assume a dominant position in the economic structure. Not only did the British hongs occupy a central position among the major business groups, some of them, particularly the Hongkong and Shanghai Banking Corporation, operated as 'play makers' by serving as intermediaries among clusters of business interests. Equally significant was that each of these major business groups had its own turf – that is, each had carved out specific domains of business interests under its control. While some competition was inevitable, a delicate equilibrium had been maintained among competing interests, with the overarching colonial government overseeing the overall situation. In other words, the economic power structure and its corresponding representation of interests in the formal political structure allowed the colonial government to maintain effective control over the coordination of action and regulation of conflict among the major vested interests.

It was on this basis that the colonial government was able to forge what Ngo (2000) calls a 'substantive consent' among the ruling elite:

> This substantive consent involved the inseparable components of allowing business domination in the power oligarchy while upholding a policy against preferential treatment for selected business interests. Under this consent, besides the privilege of sharing policy-making power, the oligarchical interests were guaranteed that their profit making would be protected and facilitated by the government. This was realized by a range of pro-business policy measures, including low profits tax, limited social welfare provisions, minimal labour protection, free enterprise, and free capital inflow and outflow. All worked to facilitate profit maximization – a policy goal that was proudly admitted by the government. At the same time, the ruling elite agreed to constrain their privileges by accepting a policy of non-selective intervention. This meant that the government refrained from using public resources to assist or protect individual business sectors and enterprises. This avoided rent-seeking by individual elite groups, ensuring that policy outcomes were acceptable to the less powerful and to the wider population of players.
>
> (Ngo 2000: 32)

The so-called positive non-interventionism practised by the colonial government was an outcome of this compromise between the economically powerful and the colonial state as both sides accepted certain limits on their actions (also see Chiu 1996). As long as the economic outcomes were found acceptable by the two major parties concerned, this pact would allow the colonial state to enjoy a high degree of autonomy in its management of social, economic and political affairs.

Changing state–business relations

The aforementioned studies of business groups by Wong (1996) and Cheung (1994) pointed to signs of a change in the status quo within the economic power structure during the 1980s. The rise of local Chinese business groups since the 1970s, and the consolidation of their economic power in the 1980s through various acquisitions by taking over or merging with declining British companies, began to upset the status quo, create a new balance of power and gradually restructure inter-group relations among the economically powerful. Informed by the Wong and Cheung studies, we have carried out an interlocking directorate analysis of the top 250 listed corporations (including banks) in 1982, 1997 and 2004 (see Appendix). Our sample is not strictly comparable to those of Wong and Cheung as our sample size is much larger. Nor is our interlocking directorate analysis a replication of their exercises.[5] In other words, a rigorous comparison of our findings with theirs is not warranted. What we intend to do here is to describe the changing configuration of the economic power structure in Hong Kong while using the other studies as a relevant backdrop for a rough understanding of the direction of change since the 1970s. In Wong's depiction, British business groups occupied a strategic and commanding position in 1976, with the Jardine group assuming a dominating status. Since then, as a result of various business mergers, the balance of power between the British and the Chinese business groups had begun to shift in the latter's favour.

Findings from our interlocking directorate analysis are summarized in Tables 5.1 and 5.2. When we take the company as a unit of analysis, we find that relatively few firms (31 to 40 in the three panels) had no interlock with other companies in the samples. There were eight companies in 1982 with interlocks with 50 or more companies (e.g. a company that shared one or more common directors with two other companies is counted as two interlocks) but none in 1997 and only one in 2004. At other levels of multiple interlocks, we find that 1982 had the densest set of interlocking networks (37 corporations had 30–49 interlocks), while 1997 and 2004 were relatively constant (ten corporations in 1997 and only eight in 2004 having similar levels of interlocking). We also find that the percentage of firms with 5 to 29 interlocks dropped slightly between 1997 and 2004. In 1982, Sun Hung Kai Properties Ltd could be regarded as the 'executive committee' of the business community as it had the most interlocks with 67, while Hongkong and Shanghai Banking Corporation had 64. In 1997, the most interlocked company was Hutchison Whampoa (32 interlocks), and in 2004 Cheung Kong Infrastructure Holdings (35 interlocks), with both companies interestingly a member of the Li Ka Shing business empire.

Taking the individual director as a unit of analysis, we discern a similar trend. In 1982, 81 directors held four or more positions but in 1997 only 27 did so. The

Table 5.1 Number of interlocks per company, 1982–2004

	No. of companies			% to all companies		
	1982	1997	2004	1982	1997	2004
No. of interlocks per company 50 or more	8	0	1	3.2	0.0	30.4
40–49	17	1	4	6.8	0.4	1.6
30–39	20	9	4	8.0	3.6	1.6
20–29	27	22	18	10.8	8.8	7.2
15–19	27	16	30	10.8	6.4	12.0
10–14	29	42	31	11.6	16.8	12.4
5–9	31	62	49	12.4	24.8	19.6
3–4	27	35	42	10.8	14.0	16.8
1–2	29	32	31	11.6	12.8	12.4
No. of company with interlocks	215	219	210	86.0	87.6	84.0
No. of company without interlocks	35	31	40	14.0	12.4	16.0

Source: Author research

Table 5.2 Multiple directorships held by individual directors, 1982–2004

No. of multiple directorships	No. of individuals held		
	1982	1997	2004
7 or more positions	22	3	2
6 or more positions	30	5	4
5 or more positions	48	9	10
4 or more positions	81	27	19
Most positions individually held	22	7	7

Sources: Author research

figure dropped further to 19 in 2004. What this suggests is that a small group of individual directors used to link up a large number of firms but this group had clearly dwindled by the late 1990s and into the twenty-first century. For example, in 1982, 22 individuals had seven or more board memberships, but only two did in 2004. In 1982, Charles Lee Yeh Kwong was the 'director of directors', holding 22 board memberships concurrently. In 2004, Fok Kin Ning Canning and Sixt Frank John were the leaders with a relatively 'meagre' seven board memberships.

It is thus evident that there was a drop between the 1980s and the early 2000s in the 'density' of business networks as measured by interlocking directorships. A cohesive business elite in the early 1980s had become much looser two decades later as a result of decolonization and deregulation. Following Wong's study, we also analysed the network by means of components. A component is a sub-set of companies connected by a specific number of common ties, direct and indirect. For example, two companies will be regarded as in the same component even though they have no common directors if they are connected by a common director with a third company. A k-component (or component by k-graph) means the presence of k common directors between the companies within the components. Figures 5.1, 5.2 and 5.3 summarize the results of the component analysis for 1982, 1997 and 2004. They give us a rough idea of the changing economic power structure in Hong Kong in 1982, 1997 and 2004. In the figures, each circle (with different perimeters) represents a component as measured by 1 to 4-graph respectively. The letters (A to K) represent the broadest 1-graph component, whereas the two digit circles are the 2-graph components within the 1-graph ones. The 3-digit and 4-digit circles are the 3-graph and 4-graph components respectively. The size of the circles was drawn roughly in proportion to the capitalization and assets of the group.

In 1982, a total of 199 companies were found in the largest 1-graph component, meaning they were connected with one common director directly or indirectly through another company – a reflection of the dense inter-corporate network during that period; only two smaller components (Bank of Communications group and Tak Wing Investment group) were found outside it. In 1997, the 1-graph component had already shrunk to 111 firms, and dwindled further, to 78, in 2004. Further evidence for the greater cohesion of the 1982 business network is that within the large 1-graph component, 82 companies belonged to a 2-graph component, with the Hong Kong and Shanghai Bank the largest company within it. By 1997, only 13 companies were found in the largest 2-graph component, but only nine companies in 2004. Instead of one big, densely connected network, the 2004 business network had fragmented into a large number of 1-graph components with little connection between them. A peculiar feature in 2004 is that the Hang Seng Bank, which was found within the largest 1- and 2-graph components, had actually became detached from the largest 1-graph component.

Two features stand out in Figures 5.1–5.3. First, they show clearly the rise of Chinese business groups and the decline of the British hongs compared to their previous dominant and central positions. Second, unlike the pattern noted by Wong for the 1970s and found in Figure 5.1, which shows closer interconnectedness among business groups and to an extent the centrality occupied by the major British hongs, the structure has become increasingly nucleated and cellular. Each of the Chinese business groups has become, in fact, a conglomeration of economic activities run by a family. At the centre of each of these family businesses are family-based interests and concerns. These conglomerates grow and evolve around such family interests and concerns. They branch out into different areas of investment and diversify their business without creating inter-familial alliances. Instead of specializing in certain areas of business, each of these family business groups tends largely to spread out and, in doing so, crosses onto the turf of other groups. The rise of business groups with mainland connections (but not H-shares themselves) also contributed to the fragmentation of the business network. The China Resources group and the Guangzhou Investment group are prime examples. It is also interesting to note that those groups with mainland backgrounds are not connected to one another so that each formed its own 1-graph component.

So whereas the earlier structure of business groups in Hong Kong gave rise to dominant and central players like the HSBC and the Jardine Group, the structure

Components	The firm with largest total in market capitalization and assets in the component	
A1	Hongkong & Shanghai Banking Corporation	(199)
A21	Hongkong & Shanghai Banking Corporation	(82)
A311	Hongkong & Shanghai Banking Corporation	(31)
A4111	Hongkong & Shanghai Banking Corporation	(11)
A4112	Sun Hung Kai Properties Limited	(7)
A4113	Swire Pacific Limited	(3)
A312	World International (Holdings) Limited	(9)
A4121	World International (Holdings) Limited	(3)
A4122	China Light & Power Company	(3)
A4123	Nanyang Cotton Mill Limited	(3)
A313/ A4131	Wheelock Marden and Company Limited	(8)
A314	Eda Investments Limited	(5)
A4141	Associated Hotels Limited	(3)
A315/ A4151	Carrian Investments Limited	(3)
A316	Bank of East Asia	(3)
A317	Liu Chong Hing Investment Limited	(3)
A22	Overseas Trust Bank	(25)
A321	Overseas Trust Bank	(7)
A4211	Overseas Trust Bank	(5)
A322	Far East Consortium Limited	(5)
A4221	Far East Consortium Limited	(4)
A23/ A331	Federal Amalgamated Corporation Limited	(5)
A4311	Federal Amalgamated Corporation Limited	(3)
A24/ A341/ A4411	Wing On (Holdings) Limited	(4)
A25/ A351/ A4511	Regal Hotels (Holdings) Limited	(3)
A26	Nan Fung Textiles Consolidated Limited	(3)
A27	Lee On Reality and Enterprises Limited	(3)
B1	Bank of Communications	(5)
C1	Tak Wing Investment (Holdings) Limited	(3)

Keys: 1-graph; 2-graph; 3-graph; - - - 4-graph;
( ) number of firms in the component

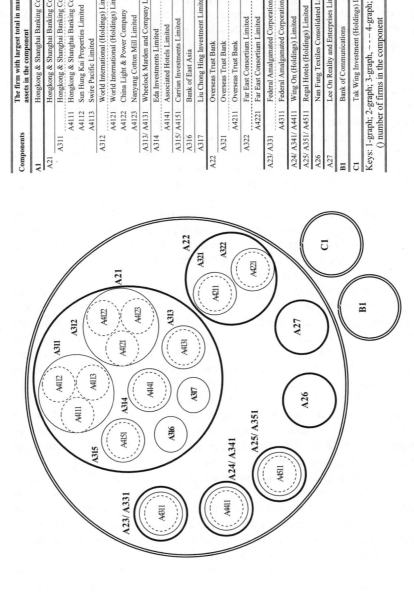

Figure 5.1 The major business groups, 1982
Source: Author research

Components		The firm with largest total in market capitalization and assets in the component	
A1		HSBC Holdings Limited	(111)
A21		Hang Seng Bank Limited	(13)
	A311	Henderson Land Development Co Limited	(8)
	A4111	Henderson Land Development Co Limited	(5)
A22		Hutchison Whampoa Limited	(7)
	A321	Hutchison Whampoa Limited	(5)
	A4211	Hutchison Whampoa Limited	(4)
A23/ A331		Swire Pacific Limited	(4)
	A4311	Swire Pacific Limited	(3)
A24		China Resources Enterprise Limited	(10)
	A341	HKCB Bank Holding Co Limited	(7)
	A4411	HKCB Bank Holding Co Limited	(3)
	A342/ A421	China Resources Enterprise Limited	(3)
A25/ A351/ A4511		Hang Lung Development Co Limited	(9)
A26		Wharf (Holdings) Limited	(3)
	A361	Wharf (Holdings) Limited	(3)
A27		Sun Hung Kai Properties Limited	(5)
	A371	SmarTone Telecommunications Holdings Limited	(3)
A28/ A381		Century City International Holdings Limited	(3)
A29		Kerry Properties Limited	(3)
B1/ B21		Guoco Group Limited	(4)
C1/ C21		Lai Sun Garment (International) Limited	(7)
	C311	Lai Sun Garment (International) Limited	(4)
	C4111	Lai Sun Garment (International) Limited	(3)
D1/ D21		Dah Sing Financial Holdings Limited	(3)
E1/ E21		Guangdong Investment Limited	(3)
F1/ F21/ F311/ F4111		Pacific Concord Holdings Limited	(3)
G1		Tsim Sha Tsui Properties Limited	(3)
H1		National Mutual Asia Limited	(4)
I1		Wing On International Holdings Limited	(3)
J1		China Travel International Investment Hong Kong Limited	(3)
K1		Tem Fat Hing Fung (Holdings) Limited	(3)

Keys: 1-graph; 2-graph; 3-graph; – – – 4-graph;
() number of firms in the component

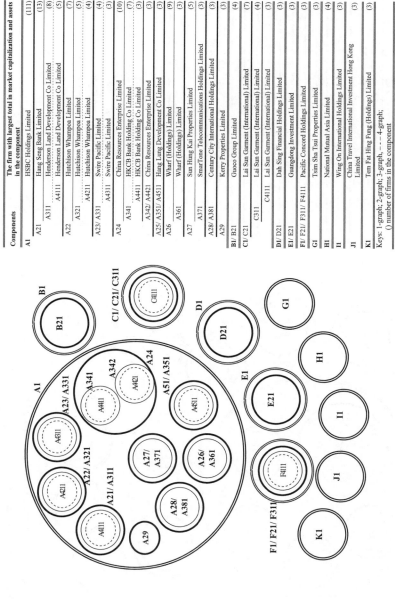

Figure 5.2 The major business groups, 1997
Source: Author research

Components			The firm with largest total in market capitalization and assets in the component
A1			HSBC Holdings (78)
A21/ A311			Hutchison Whampoa Limited (9)
	A4111		Hutchison Whampoa Limited (6)
A22			Sun Hung Kai Properties Limited (14)
A321/ A4211			Henderson Land Development Company Limited (5)
A322/ A4221			Sun Hung Kai Properties Limited (3)
A23			Swire Pacific Limited (6)
	A331		Swire Pacific Limited (4)
A24			China Netcom Group Corporation (Hong Kong) Limited (4)
	A341	A4411	PCCW Limited (3)
A25	A351	A4511	Sino Land Company Limited (3)
B1			Wharf (Holdings) Limited (10)
B21			Wharf (Holdings) Limited (5)
	B311		Wharf (Holdings) Limited (3)
C1			China Resources Enterprise Limited (4)
C21			China Resources Enterprise Limited (3)
D1			Guangzhou Investment Company Limited (5)
D21	D311	D4111	Asia Standard International Group Limited (3)
E1			COFCO International Limited (4)
E21/ E311/ E4111			Lippo China Resources Limited (3)
F1/ F21/ F311/ F4111			Regal Hotels International Holdings Limited (3)
G1			BOC Hong Kong (Holdings) Limited (3)
H1			Hang Seng Bank Limited (4)
I1			Ping An Insurance (Group) Company of China Limited (4)
J1			Guangdong Investment Limited (7)
K1			Hopewell Holdings Limited (3)

Keys: 1-graph; 2-graph; 3-graph; - - - 4-graph;
( ) number of firms in the component

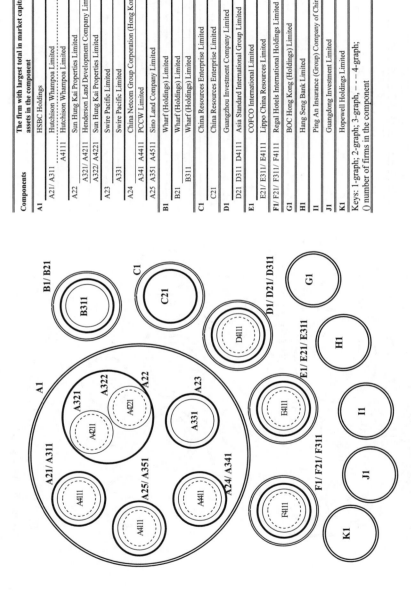

Figure 5.3 The major business groups, 2004

Source: Author research

that has emerged since the 1980s is characterized by decentring. The rising Chinese business groups have been striving to consolidate, and then to expand, their 'family kingdoms'. Table 5.3 provides a rough picture of the changing scope of activity of the Jardine Group between 1961 and 1997. While the numbers can sometimes be misleading as the coverage of activity can be affected by corporate restructuring, they do indicate a growing concentration over this period on finance, insurance and real estate, trade and shipping. The point we intend to make from this brief description of the traditional British hong's corporate activities is that for a long time these business interests have developed their own specialization. While they would also consider diversification, this is done within a selected domain of activity. A kind of tacit understanding exists, and competition and rivalry are brought under control.

Deregulation is another factor that impinged upon the Hong Kong economy during the 1990s, besides the changing internal structure of business groups with the fading out of British hongs and the rise of Chinese business groups. Under the pressures of globalization, the Hong Kong government gradually relaxed its regulations on certain monopolistic sectors. In particular, public utilities were subject to increased competition by allowing new entrants. The prime example is in telecommunications. Prior to the 1990s, there was only one service provider. The 1990s witnessed the introduction of competition in the sector first through multiple operators in mobile services and later in the provision of fixed-line services. In transport, competitors were also allowed to enter into hitherto monopolistic sectors such as ferries and bus services. The major business groups were keen to enter the rising telecommunications sector and thus came to compete head to head with their business rivals, upsetting the previous equilibrium in which each group largely avoided impinging on the informal turf of other groups. Table 5.4 presents a rough summary of the major business activities of four leading Hong Kong Chinese business groups as of the beginning of this century, indicating how much the business interests of these group overlap so that competition among them is now commonplace. It is of course quite true that the business world is always in a state of competition. In this respect, the fragmentation among business groups is not by itself an issue to be concerned about. What is of greater significance is that this fragmentation poses

Table 5.3 Jardine Matheson's scope of activity, 1961–1997

	No. of companies			
	1961–71	*1972–77*	*1977–83*	*1983–97*
Agriculture and forestry	2	3	0	1
Mining		6	6	1
Construction and engineering	7	10	3	3
Manufacturing	9	75	13	6
Shipping and transportation	22	92	44	12
Wholesale trade	18	54	13	20
Retail trade		5	9	20
Finance, insurance and real estate	19	142	111	87
Business services	6	50	24	

Sources: Adapted from Matheson Connell (2004: 61–73).

a challenge to the established order that had been worked out by the leading British hongs and the colonial government.

As noted earlier, under the colonial regime each of the leading British hongs and other major business interests had more or less secured its own turf and they were content to be left on their own to pursue their economic interests in an environment that was pro-business and entailed minimal government intervention. As long as the government remained 'neutral' (i.e. in general pro-business but without giving preferential treatment to individual groups or sectors) and refrained from becoming intrusive (so that government actions were primarily regulatory in nature), govern-ment–business relations were largely non-conflictual and collaborative. This gov-ernment–business alliance worked to secure support from the business sector for launching pro-growth strategies (mainly in the form of infrastructural construction and the facilitation of trade and commerce). Equally significant was that 'The colo-nial administration converted its non-interventionist precepts into practical protec-tion for the public interests' (Goodstadt 2005: 121). The fortunes of business appeared to be dependent on market forces rather than on a business-biased envi-ronment created by the colonial administration. Positive non-interventionism was thus perceived as an approach to economic management that would guarantee fair-ness and uphold a competitive spirit. This ruling strategy and its ideological pack-aging facilitated stability and prosperity. But the decentring, nucleating and cellular pattern of the structuring of business groups in the 1990s upset this estab-lished order. Growing inter-group competition, quite often head to head, triggered turf wars in the business world. Here it is interesting to note that the consolidation and expansion of Chinese business groups in the 1990s also coincided with, and were partly an outcome of, globalization and the resultant push for liberalization, and partly an effect triggered by advances in new technology and the deregulation of major services including telecommunications, energy and public transportation. The opening of new business opportunities intensified competition among busi-ness groups, disrupted the previous tacit understandings to 'live and let live' and posed the issue of how a new balance of economic power among the business groups should be constructed. Our discussion of the pattern of nucleation and frag-mentation in Hong Kong's economic power structure implies that once the govern-ment–business relations (and thus the tacit understanding governing the claims and allocation of economic interests) have to be restructured, the state will soon find itself swamped by new claims made by different players from the business world.

The breakdown of the established order

The decolonization process can also be viewed as a process whereby the state is re-embedded into the socio-economic structure. For most people, the matter of politi-cal legitimacy, previously rarely questioned, now became contentious. When the government failed to ensure economic prosperity and its performance was found wanting, its political authority constantly came under challenge. As the state began to rebuild its relationship with the business sector, it inadvertently kick-started competition among leading capitalists, who sought in turn to stake their claims.

Table 5.4 Composition of the four major Hong Kong Chinese business groups

Sector	Li Ka Shing Group	Lee Shau Kee Group	Kwok Family Group	Peter K.C. Woo Group
Property	Cheung Kong (Holdings) Limited (1)	Henderson Land Development Company Limited (12), Henderson Investment Limited (97), Henderson China Holdings Limited	Sun Hung Kai Properties Limited (16)	Wheelock and Company Limited (20), Wharf (Holdings) Limited (4), Wheelock Properties Limited (49), Realty Development Corporation Limited
Telecom	Hutchison Telecommunications International Limited (2332)	—	SmarTone Telecommunications Holdings Limited (315)	New T&T (Hong Kong) Limited
Infrastructure	Cheung Kong Infrastructure Holdings Limited (1038)	—	—	—
Energy	Hongkong Electric Holdings Limited (6)	Hong Kong and China Gas Company Limited (3)	—	—
Transportation	Hutchison Whampoa Limited (13)	Hong Kong Ferry (Holdings) Company Limited (50)	Airport Freight Forwarding Centre Company Limited, River Trade Terminal Company Limited, Asia Container Terminals Limited, Kowloon Motor Bus Holdings Limited (62)	Modern Terminals, Hongkong Air Cargo Terminals Limited, Cross-Harbour (Holdings) Ltd (32), Hongkong Tramways Limited, The 'Star' Ferry Company Limited
Hotel	Harbour Plaza Hotels & Resorts, Sheraton Hotel	Miramar Hotel & Investment Company Limited (71)	Royal Garden Hotel, Royal Park Hotel, Royal Plaza Hotel	Harbour Centre Development (51), Marco Polo Gateway Hong Kong Hotel, Marco Polo Prince Hotel, Marco Polo Hong Kong Hotel
Finance	Cheung Kong Bond Finance Limited, Cheung Kong Investment Company Limited	Henderson International Finance Limited, Henderson Development Limited	—	Beauforte Investors Corporation Limited (21)
Retail	PARKnSHOP, Watsons, Fortress	—	—	Lane Crawford, Joyce Boutique (647)
Technology	Tom.com (8001)	Henderson Cyber Limited	SUNeVision (8008)	I-Cable Communications (1097)

Source: Adapted from *Prime Magazine* (2005a, 2005b)

Previously the prevalence of British business interests was taken as a part of colonial rule. Furthermore, the colonial state was able to rise above diverse interests, maintaining its autonomy and thus effective governance, because it was never fully captured by the capitalists (cf. Evans 1995). We can say that decolonization has dragged the Hong Kong SAR government back into the world of real politics. The government has had to strike a new deal with the business sector by reassuring the capitalists that they would get their fair share of the pie.

This was exactly what the Tung administration struggled to achieve.[6] To do justice to the Tung administration, it must be acknowledged that it did not have much room for political manoeuvring. The growth of Chinese business groups and the fragmentation of the economic power structure had restructured the established order so that the Tung administration could no longer simply copy the winning formula adopted by the colonial state. Growing inter-group competition and the changing balance of economic power meant that the Hong Kong SAR government had to work out its alliance with the business world comprising a different set of players and within a different set of parameters. The SAR government was forced to test its relationship with the major business interests by constructing a new kind of tacit understanding as the basis for collaboration. The Tung administration encountered the almost impossible situation of having to forge an alliance without upsetting competing interests among the potential members that it was eager to co-opt.

The Cyberport incident serves as a good illustration of why and how the Tung administration came under severe criticism when it took the first step to build a new business alliance. The government's idea of building the mega Cyberport was first announced in the Financial Secretary's budget speech in March 1999. The 26-hectare project was to contain office buildings and residential developments that would serve as a base for the development of new telecommunications and media technology. It would provide space for enterprises of different sizes and for residential development, and would facilitate the creation of some 16,000 new jobs. The project was promoted in the aftermath of the 1997 Asian Financial Crisis as a way to kick-start the economy back onto a growth track. However, the government skipped the usual practice of open land auction or invitations for tender, and granted the project to the Pacific Century Group owned by Mr Richard Li, the son of business magnate Mr Li Ka-shing. This caused uproar in the business community. Ten major land developers issued a joint statement to the government offering to buy the residential land at a price higher than evaluated in the PCC offer and also promised to pay the government an additional sum (for a brief account of the series of events in the Cyberport incident see Ngo 2002: 108–9). Local newspapers reported that intense behind-the-scenes lobbying occurred to block, unsuccessfully as it turned out, the government's approval of the project.[7] This unprecedented chain of events over the Cyberport project is indicative of the underlying changes in the business network, and consequently 'the attempt of rival business interests to capture the economic rent created by government intervention and to undermine rivals by means of market protection and closure to competition' (Ngo 2002: 109). The example set by the Cyberport project prompted other business groups to push for similar projects involving the public provision of subsidized land in the guise of supporting projects designed to spearhead particular strategic sectors: bio-tech, Chinese medicine and even a shipping terminal complex.

The Cyberport incident was notable not so much because of the claims that it revealed government–business collusion but more because of the surfacing of conflicts between rival business groups in Hong Kong.[8] Another incident, in 2002, also served to illustrate such intra-class conflicts, when seven major groups (Sun Hung Kai Properties, Swire Properties, Wharf Holdings, Hongkong Land, Great Eagle Holdings, Hysan Development and Hang Lung Properties) formed a group called Electricity Consumer Concern to express dissatisfaction over allegedly excessive electricity charges: 'The group seeks to urge the government to ensure the efficient production and distribution of electricity and to establish an efficient regulatory system to enforce the scheme of control' (*South China Morning Post* 2002b). This led to a war of words between the power companies and the Concern group. Hong Kong Electric (owned by Mr Li Ka-shing) went public with a statement countering the criticisms by claiming that other public utilities, such as tram, bus, ferry, taxi and MTR, had all registered a higher increase than electricity since 1983. The fact that the tram, bus and ferry services were all owned by members of the Concern group only served to accentuate the point made by Hong Kong Electric. Even Mr Li himself publicly rebuked the critics (*Next Magazine* 2002).

Conclusion

The colonial political order was built on a solid coalition between the government and big business in the territory. This coalition developed a kind of tacit understanding about the nature of the relationship between the government and the major business interests. The government was to assume the role of a pro-growth political machine without taking up the directive functions of a developmental state. So-called 'positive non-interventionism' is more of a shorthand description for this political pact between the colonial government and major businesses than an accurate portrayal of the state's role in social and economic life. It is our contention that the pro-growth coalition between the colonial government and major business groups was made possible by a cohesive business community composed of a dense network of major corporations. The consensus of the business community (or at least among its dominant segments) on major policy issues, positive non-interventionism prominent among them, was the pillar of the colonial governance. This made it easier for the colonial government to forge social support for its policies. Since the 1990s, however, cohesion within the business community has declined, due first to the rise of the Chinese business groups (and the resultant decentring of business clustering) and, second, to the process of deregulation, which led to the incursion of business groups onto each other's turf and thus intensified competition among them. While the colonial state could appear to be an impartial arbiter of conflicts of interest between big businesses, the SAR government does not have this luxury but has been dragged into rivalries among the business groups whenever it has wished to intervene in the economic sphere.

Accusations of government–business collusion have cropped up from time to time in the SAR because whenever the government chose to place its bet on any project by assisting its development, it has inevitably aided one group to the chagrin of its rivals. The recent debate over the alleged demise of the 'positive non-interventionist' approach to economic management, a discussion initiated by the Chief Executive, was quickly brought to an end in order to avoid accusations of a major change in the government's orientation towards its role in the economy (see, for example, Friedman 2006; Tsang 2006). This perhaps illustrates the double bind that the government faces. While it has been trying its best to articulate a viable development strategy and carve out a new direction for Hong Kong's development, it has been caught in the crossfire of conflicting demands and interests. We argue that such conflicting demands do not emanate merely from the process of democratization or the popular demands for political participation or provisions of welfare, but is also symptomatic of the underlying changes in the power structure. To construct a viable governing coalition that supports the quest for strong governance, the government must seek a way to overcome the fragmentation of business interests and forge a broader base of support to strengthen the legitimacy of its major development policies.

The failure to rebuild viable state–business and state–society relations has posed serious challenges for Hong Kong after 1997. As we noted in an earlier section, Hong Kong is currently in a state of impasse. In the face of economic restructuring, regional integration and competition from other Asian globalizing cities, the government is expected to assume a new leading role in steering cross-border mega-infrastructural construction projects for the facilitation of socio-economic integration with the Pearl River Delta, in promoting culture and the creative industries for the purpose of building new forms of economic strength vis-à-vis other post-industrial cities in the region (Yusuf and Nabeshima 2006), and in creating new policy initiatives to deal with a greying population and emerging welfare needs, such as rising poverty brought about by economic restructuring and growing inequalities (see Wong 2007). Yet, the leadership of the Hong Kong SAR government is finding it increasingly difficult to take action. To be sure, the fact that it is not a popularly elected government undermines its legitimacy (Ma 2007). But equally important is that it has not yet built up its own governing coalition. As a result, it is constantly exposed to criticism from all fronts so that it finds it difficult to develop new initiatives to address issues and problems that require a longer-term framework and state commitment to solve. Nevertheless, further growth and development of Hong Kong as a global city requires innovative ideas and inputs backed by a pro-growth coalition. In this regard, the current political impasse has much wider implications. It undermines Hong Kong's ability to adjust to the changing environment and rising competition. It also weakens its capacity to innovate and make swift changes. It is under these circumstances that we find Hong Kong becoming passive in responding to the changes in the global, national and regional environment. The rise of China has brought Hong Kong closer to the national, a picture very different from that originally envisaged during negotiations over its political future in the 1980s. Instead of China one-sidedly relying on

Hong Kong for its modernization and economic reform, the latter now depends increasingly on the former's further participation in the global economy in order to find the new impetus for growth, an issue that we shall discuss in the next chapter.

Appendix

Data sources

Two kinds of public companies were analysed in our study. They are companies that are listed on the Hong Kong Hang Seng Stock Exchange and licensed banks incorporated in Hong Kong, some of which are also listed on the Hong Kong stock market. We confine ourselves to public companies incorporated in Hong Kong. By so doing, two types of public company were excluded from our study: first, the listed companies that issued H-shares, preference shares or B-shares; second, the licensed banks incorporated outside Hong Kong. Further, due to the data collection problem, we have also excluded those licensed banks even incorporated in Hong Kong if no information on the board of directors or company's financial record is available.

In our study, we have studied the board membership of public companies at three different time points: 1982, 1997 and 2004. In our study, only the top 250 public companies were studied at each time point. In 1982, there were only 238 public companies, but there were 36 non-listed licensed banks for which data are available. By 1997, the total number of listed companies reached 627, and 975 in 2004. We first entered the asset and capitalization data of all listed companies, and then the top 250 companies with the greatest total of 'assets' and 'market capitalization' would be selected in each year. As there are some non-listed licensed banks, only company assets could be counted and compared in our study, and we basically included all of them in the analysis.

Company information, such as company assets, market capitalization and composition of board of directors, came mainly from two sources. For the listed companies, their information was mainly collected from published listed company database handbooks. The databases have collected the data of all listed companies on the Hong Kong Stock Exchange at different time points. These comprehensive handbooks contain archived information on company history, company structure, financial data from previous years and share prices, and they are available in university libraries. For the licensed banks, lists of banks from different years were first collected from various Hong Kong Monetary Authority annual reports. Then, for the licensed banks that are also listed, their information would be cross-referred to the database handbooks mentioned above. For non-listed licensed banks, their company information would be traced from their company annual reports and official websites. This is why information from some licensed banks cannot be found, as some of the banks do not have official website, or their annual reports cannot be accessed by the public.

The statistical software UCINET 5 was used to generate the components.

Information sources

For 1982

DataBase Publishing (1982) *Data Base Hong Kong 1983 Public Companies. A DataBook of Public Companies Listed on the Four Stock Exchanges in Hong Kong*. Hong Kong: Printrite.

DataBase Publishing (1982) *Data Base Banks 82/83: A Directory of All Licensed Banks in Hong Kong*. Hong Kong: Printrite.

For 1997

EFP International (1999) *The Primasia Guide to the Companies of Hong Kong*. Hong Kong: EFP International.

Hong Kong Monetary Authority (1998) *Annual Report 1997*. Hong Kong: Hong Kong Monetary Authority. Available at: http://www.info.gov.hk/hkma/eng/public/ar97/toc.htm (accessed 12 May 2005).

HSBC (1999) *NetTraderCards*, September. Hong Kong: HSBC Broking (Data Services) Services.

For 2004

Hong Kong Monetary Authority (2005) *Annual Report 2004*. Hong Kong: Hong Kong Monetary Authority. Available at: http://www.info.gov.hk/hkma/eng/public/ar04/toc.htm (accessed 20 December 2006).

HSBC (2006) *NetTraderCards on CD*, February. Hong Kong: HSBC Broking (Data Services) Services.

We also consulted the annual reports and official websites of various licensed banks.

6   The return of the regional and the national

The city's force field is not a linear one, however. Rather, it stretches for a hundred miles in each direction, over towns and villages and across vast tracts of what appears to be open country, far from any existing settlement that could be conventionally be called a city. ... Cities compete with each other in a grimly determined struggle to maintain the energy that keeps them working. But the lives of their citizens take in other cities to an extent that is unparalleled in history. They move from one to another constantly, to live, to visit, to do business. ... Perhaps the hundred-mile city has already become the thousand-mile city.

(Sudjic 1992: 305, 308)

Introduction

On 20 March 2006, there were three noteworthy news items concerning Hong Kong's economic future and its competitiveness. The first reported that, according to the Chinese Academy of Social Sciences' annual report on urban competitiveness among Chinese cities for 2005, Hong Kong, which together with Macau and Taiwanese cities had not been included in earlier assessments, replaced Shanghai in occupying the very top rank on the list. More interestingly, it was noted by the team that carried out the research that Hong Kong and Shanghai do not compete at quite the same level (*South China Morning Post* 2006a). The second item referred to a speech by Mr Rafael Hui, the Chief Secretary of the Hong Kong SAR government, at a public forum on Hong Kong's position and role in China's eleventh five year plan. He warned of 'the city being marginalized by rapid development in the Pearl River Delta' (*South China Morning Post* 2006b). He based this warning on the fact that Guangzhou and surrounding cities have undergone rapid economic growth, with the former assuming the role of a transport hub of the region. Current and further developments in the areas of logistics, finance, information and business services in the Pearl River Delta under China's new five year plan means that Hong Kong will face serious challenges to its existing competitive advantages in the very near future. Reassurance about Hong Kong's 'irreplaceable position' was provided by Mr Xu Jialu, Vice-chairperson of the National People's Congress, who also spoke at the same forum. Despite this reassurance, Hong Kong could ill afford to remain complacent about its future status in a transforming China The third news item concerned another step that had been taken to strengthen Hong Kong's role as a centre for financial transactions from the mainland. The National Council for Social Security Fund opened an account in the clearing house for Hong Kong's stock market, allowing it to receive shares from the initial public offerings of state enterprises (*South China Morning Post* 2006c). This was greeted as 'a major policy shift' (*South China Morning Post* 2006c), signalling China's further liberalization of management and control of financial transactions related to the mainland's business as well as public funds via Hong Kong. Even more important is that the mainland gave the green light in April 2006 for the launching of the Qualified Domestic Institutional Investor (QDII) scheme. This would allow mainland financial institutions to invest in some overseas funds. Hong Kong is expected to reap the benefit of this policy shift as money from this new source will be pumped into its financial market, thus confirming Hong Kong's important position in the larger context of a changing interface between China's economy and the rest of the world.

These three news items highlight in a nutshell Hong Kong's current situation and its changing fortune as a global city. On the one hand, they clearly show how Hong Kong's status as a global city and financial centre continues to facilitate its economic development, particularly by tapping into the new opportunities opened by China's economic reform and its efforts to 'go global'. The global connectivity of the city is a source of strength and competitiveness, and its future development very much hinges upon the maintenance of this advantage. And, with this advantage in hand, Hong Kong's influence, in a manner best captured by Sudjic's analogy of a hundred-mile city becoming a thousand-mile city (see the above quotation), continues to expand. On the other hand, however, it is also apparent that Hong Kong needs to compete with other Chinese cities in order to maintain its competitive edge. The growth and expansion of cities, as Sudjic points out, are bringing them into head-to-head competition. This competition is partly about their nature and extent of connectivity with the world economy. It is also partly dependent on these competing cities' connectivity with the mainland. The mainland's rapid economic growth and development mean that it is now the driving force of further development. Hong Kong's economic future is increasingly dependent on China's development at the regional and the national level. As we noted in our earlier chapters, the dual economic and political restructuring that Hong Kong has undergone in the past two decades is best understood in the context of its integration into its neighbouring region and, more importantly, the national ambit of China. Instead of Hong Kong's economy becoming more deeply integrated into the global economy by a loosening of Hong Kong's attachment to the nation-state, its economic development is increasingly embedded in China's grander national marketization and 'going global' projects (which, in turn, are in many ways shaped by the forces of globalization). The upshot is that Hong Kong is, as a result, becoming a *Chinese* global city. We underline the Chinese dimension and its pertinence because we contend that the national project is increasingly impacting on Hong Kong. And Hong Kong's struggle for survival and recovery from the recession triggered by the Asian financial crisis has also brought it closer to China.

Our analysis of Hong Kong as a Chinese global city in this chapter echoes our discussion in the introductory chapter concerning the significance of place in our understanding of the development of a global city (Sassen 2001), and how it is shaped by the interactions among the global and the local, as well as the national. The impact of such interactions in shaping the restructuring of a global city is by no means confined to specific (and given its return to China in 1997, one may say special) cases like Hong Kong. The experience of Hong Kong becoming a Chinese global city has broader empirical relevance for our understanding of other Asian cities' struggle for economic recovery after the Asian financial crisis.[1] It also casts light analytically on how the national impacts on the interplay between the global and the local. We believe in this respect that it is essential to move beyond the global–local duality in order to see how both globalization and the role of the state play their part in restructuring global cities.

Bringing the mainland back into the analysis

In Chapter 2 we discussed the success of Hong Kong's export-led industrialization in the post-war decades and its industrial restructuring since the 1980s. Two main points from that discussion are worth reiterating here. First, Hong Kong's manufacturers have been quick to capitalize on the opportunities and resources made available by the opening of the Chinese economy since 1978. The relocation of manufacturing activities is best captured by the depiction of 'front shop, back factory'. This refers to the changing division of labour between Hong Kong and the Pearl River Delta with the former specializing in the higher value-added processes (such as marketing, design and coordination) and the latter in supplying the basics for production (Sit 2006). This actually marks the beginning of a very important process of building a cross-border Hong Kong–South China growth region. The subsequent development of this region has come to constitute the major driving force turning China into the world's manufacturing powerhouse. More interestingly, the dynamism of such cross-border economic activity has not only encouraged more manufacturers from Hong Kong to invest and to develop their production bases in South China, but has also facilitated the inflow of investments from Taiwan, via Hong Kong, into mainland China. To date, this cross-border growth region and its sphere of influence have been significantly expanded. Chen (2005) sees the rise of a trans-border sub-region connecting Hong Kong, Taiwan, Guangdong, Fujian and Hainan on the mainland (also see Hsing 1998; Berger and Lester 2005). Such a development has important implications for mainland China, Hong Kong and Taiwan.

Second, though largely an outcome unforeseen by the parties concerned, the economic restructuring process goes hand in hand with the process of political restructuring. With the benefit of hindsight, we are now in a better position to comprehend the significance of the socio-economic and political changes that Hong Kong society experienced in the 1980s and 1990s. But there was a time when the expiry of the lease of the New Territories, and thus the termination of Hong Kong's colonial status and the possible return to China in 1997, was never taken seriously as a looming political reality and as a challenge to the colony's future development because

Hong Kong was prosperous and China was very much in need of seeking all available support for its 'Four Modernizations' in the aftermath of the Cultural Revolution (Mathews, Ma and Lui 2008). True, diplomatic talks between Britain and China over Hong Kong's political future began in 1982. The Sino-British Agreement was signed in 1984, kicking off the work of drafting a mini-constitution for the future Special Administration Region of Hong Kong and marking the beginning of the process of political restructuring. However, underlying all the discussions about the future of Hong Kong was the assumption that China would continue to pursue her socialist industrialization and development, while Hong Kong would remain capitalist in all respects and would be untouched by socio-economic and political changes on the mainland. In other words, the prosperous capitalist Hong Kong economy would in effect be segregated from socialist China. The guarantee of no changes in Hong Kong for 50 years after 1997 was intended to allay the Hong Kong people's political anxiety in the face of an uncertain political future. All these points were rather obvious in the 1980s and early 1990s when few observers would have anticipated a change in the balance of economic power between Hong Kong and the mainland. Hong Kong was perceived at that time as 'the goose that laid the golden egg', so that mainland China simply could not afford to jeopardize Hong Kong's crucial position as China's 'window to the world'. Economic transformation on the mainland since 1978, and the resultant galloping pace of economic change as a result of deepening economic reform in the early 1990s, has not only brought the places closer together in terms of flows of population and economic activity, but has also paved the way for building new socio-economic and political as well as cultural relationships. The mainland is no longer so lopsidedly reliant upon Hong Kong for its economic services. In fact, it is Hong Kong that has become increasingly dependent on a globalizing China for finding new economic opportunities. This changing relationship between the mainland and Hong Kong constitutes an important part of the backdrop to the discussion that follows.

Building a hinterland

Hong Kong's role in turning the Pearl River Delta into a manufacturing powerhouse began with Deng Xiaoping's rise to power after the Cultural Revolution and his launching of the 'Four Modernizations'. Deng saw the need for external resources (particularly investments, technology and related know-how) to foster economic reform. One of his new initiatives, formally promulgated in 1980, was the establishment of Special Economic Zones (SEZs). Four districts – Shenzhen, Zhuhai, Shantou and Xiamen – were designated as SEZs. These SEZs were granted greater economic autonomy than other places on mainland China and preferential policies were installed to attract investments to them. These four districts were designated as SEZs because of their proximity to Hong Kong and Macau, their long and well-established connections with overseas Chinese, and their remoteness from the heartland of China's socialist economy. Proximity to Hong Kong and Macau was expected to be an advantage for securing the inflow of capital, picking up modern management methods and facilitating technology transfer. But all these were to be carried out under the control of the socialist state. Thus the remoteness of these SEZs from the heartland of the socialist economy would allow the state to maintain its firm grip on the implementation of this newly adopted export-processing strategy, and enable a functionalist and selective utilization of an experimental open policy to the outside world. Furthermore, the south and south-eastern parts of China had long been peripheral to the development of heavy industries under socialist planning, so they had a long way to go to catch up. Paradoxically, because of the launching of this new economic initiative, the southern late developer, namely Guangdong province, and particularly the Pearl River Delta region, has not only caught up with the rest of the nation in terms of economic development, it has in fact surpassed other provinces and is in the vanguard of economic reform with the average real rate of GDP growth of 16.1 per cent per year for the period 1980–2002 (Enright, Scott and Chang 2005: 39).

Hong Kong has been a critical agent of change in the economic transformation of South China since the late 1970s. As mentioned, it played the role of China's 'window to the world'. It was not only the most important trading port, it was also a conduit through which China could learn how to reform its economy. Attempts were made 'to use Hong Kong's links to the rest of the world to foster a process of step-by-step reform in which Hong Kong would learn from the world, South China would learn from Hong Kong, and the rest of China would learn from South China' (Enright, Scott and Chang 2005: 12). More importantly, Hong Kong was a source – in fact the main source – of investment for South China's industrial development. Table 6.1 summarizes the growth of foreign direct investments (FDIs) in Guangdong province and Hong Kong's contribution for the period 1985–2003. It is clear that Hong Kong was and still is the major source of external investments into both Guangdong and China as a whole. At the early stage of the opening of China's economy in the early 1980s, Hong Kong was the key supporter of such new initiatives, contributing some 90 per cent of all foreign investments in Guangdong. Investments from Hong Kong to Guangdong continued to grow and experienced very rapid growth (124.01 per cent and 114.87 per cent for 1992 and 1993 respectively) in the early 1990s but have slackened since the mid-1990s. Still, by 2002, Hong Kong accounted for more than half of all foreign direct investments in Guangdong and about 40 per cent of the FDI in the entire country.

Indeed, it is no exaggeration to suggest that Hong Kong has played a crucial, if not the most crucial, part in reshaping the socio-economic and urban landscapes of the Pearl River Delta since 1978 (see Figure 6.1). Sit and Yang (1997) argue that, whereas Chinese urbanization in the first 30 years under the rule of the People's Republic of China was driven by state initiatives in the context of a closed and centrally planned socialist economy, what has happened since the opening of the Chinese economy in 1978 has been driven by foreign investments (mostly from Hong Kong). In their terminology, this was a process of exo-urbanization. Their statistical analysis reveals that 'foreign investment is the most significant dynamic in explaining urbanization in the Delta during the period 1980–93' (Sit and Yang 1997: 667; also see Soulard 1997: 129–38).

Partly in response to changing state policy in opening up China's economy, and partly as a result of changing corporate strategy, Hong Kong investors' strategic

Table 6.1 Foreign direct investments (FDIs) in Guangdong: growth and sources

Year	FDI in Guangdong		Investments from Hong Kong				Other Sources of FDI	
Year	Total amount	% growth	Amount	% growth	% of Guangdong's FDI	% of China's FDI	% Amount	growth
1985	51,529		45,020		87.37	47.11	6,509	
1986	64,392	24.96	60,310	33.96	93.66	45.39	4,082	−37.29
1987	59.396	−7.76	50,267	−16.65	84.63	31.45	9,129	123.64
1988	91,906	54.73	80,308	59.76	87.38	38.33	11,598	27.05
1989	115,644	25.83	91,462	13.89	79.09	44.02	24,182	108.50
1990	145,984	26.24	98,501	7.70	67.47	51.48	47,483	96.36
1991	182,286	24.87	135,657	37.72	74.42	52.60	46,629	−1.80
1992	355,150	94.83	303,879	124.01	85.56	39.43	51,271	9.96
1993	749,805	111.12	652,954	114.87	87.08	37.43	96,851	88.90
1994	939,708	25.33	776,763	18.96	82.66	39.19	162,945	68.24
1995	1,018,028	8.33	797,268	2.64	78.31	39.50	220,760	35.48
1996	1,162,362	14.18	838,660	5.19	72.15	40.22	323,702	46.63
1997	1,171,083	0.75	843,192	0.54	72.00	40.87	327,891	1.29
1998	1,202,005	2.64	812,946	−3.59	67.63	43.92	389,059	18.65
1999	1,220,300	1.52	733,892	−9.72	60.14	44.85	486,408	25.02
2000	1,223,720	0.28	744,826	1.49	60.87	48.05	478,894	−1.54
2001	1,297,240	6.01	708,675	−4.85	54.63	42.39	588,565	22.90
2002	1,311,071	1.07	697,885	−1.52	53.23	39.07	613,186	4.18
2003	1,557,779	18.82	864,593	23.89	55.50	48.85	693,186	13.05
2004	1,001,158	−35.73	501,219	−42.03	50.06	26.38	499,939	−27.88
2005	1,236,391	23.50	582,361	−16.19	47.10	32.45	654,030	30.82

Sources: Li (2006: 372); Guangdong Tongjiju (2006)

moves and the resultant contributions to the development of the Pearl River Delta varied during different phases of development:

> … during 1980–84, in a matter of only four years, foreign investment into the Delta amounted to US$1380m, about 13 times the provincial accumulated total of 1980. FDI was then focused on service infrastructure such as hotels, tourist and entertainment facilities. Most of these investments were located in Guangzhou, Shenzhen, Zhuhai and Foshan, and they accounted for 87.2 per cent of the total actualized foreign investment. During 1985–89, the pace of FDI inflow further increased. The total realized foreign investment in the Delta was US$5.36bn, over four times that of the previous four years. In this latter period, a large number of small and medium-sized Hong Kong enterprises shifted their labour intensive manufacturing into the Delta, leading to a new phase of foreign investment that has had a profound impact on urbanization there. During this period, the manufacturing sector accounted for 77 per cent of the total foreign investment inflow. By the end of the 1980s, the Delta had become a large production base for Hong Kong, and Hong Kong-invested manufacturing enterprises there employed 3m people, about five times the manufacturing employment of Hong Kong itself.

(Sit and Yang 1997: 651)

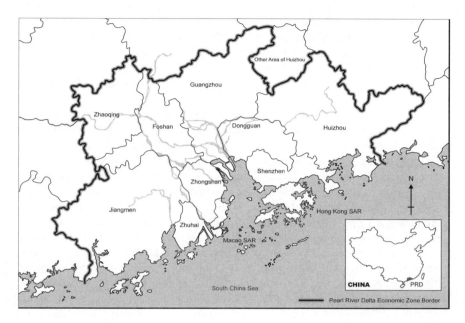

Figure 6.1 Map of the Pearl River Delta

Largely because of the driving force of foreign investment, urbanization in the Pearl River Delta did not grow and sprawl from the established centre (in this case Guangzhou) but rather was led by small cities and towns that were the targets of outside investment. The pattern of urbanization in the Delta is 'increasingly poly-centric with a number of emerging star cities, such as Shenzhen and Dongguan, which are competing fiercely with the provincial capital' (Yeh and Xu 2006: 63). More precisely, it was the location decision made by investors from Hong Kong that really mattered. And the decision was made on the basis of economic calcula-tion, strategic use of personal ties (also see Leung 1993), and capitalizing on the autonomy of local authorities. Such strategic moves, in turn, had their impacts on the pattern of development and urbanization in the region:

> More than half of the Hong Kong manufacturing joint-ventures agreements were signed with rural or township authorities [in the late 1980s]. The fact that Hong Kong managers share the same culture and language, and often the same family ascendance, made it possible for Hong Kong managers to establish operations in nearby counties, probably with the discretion of local authorities. Dongguan authorities estimated that half of the contracts signed with Hong Kong corporations involved former Dongguan residents. Furthermore, the vast majority of these contracts orchestrated through kinship ties were estab-lished in rural areas. The adaptability of numerous small-scale Hong Kong operations, the ubiquity of available labour in the Delta, and personal relations,

all reduced the degree of locational specificity of industrial development. Socially mediated arrangements, rather than bureaucratically arbitrated, promoted the diffusion of industrial activities under the oath [*sic*] of foreign capital in the Delta, hence the integration of Chinese rural areas into the world economic market.

(Soulard 1997: 137–8)

In brief, geographical analyses of economic development and urbanization in the Pearl River Delta region, whether in terms of economic growth or population mobility, have pointed to the key role played by Hong Kong in the regional socio-economic transformation (for more technical analysis of this process, see Sit and Yang 1997; Soulard 1997). Hong Kong, being the centre of this transformation process, created a wave of ripples of socio-economic change, via those townships receiving its investments, that eventually spread out to most parts of the region.

In Guangdong province alone, Hong Kong manufacturers operated 25,000 processing factories and employed three million workers in 1993 (Federation of Hong Kong Industries 1993: 3). Another estimate suggests that Hong Kong firms employed eight times as many workers in Guangdong as in Hong Kong proper in 1996, and 'its investment in Guangdong is 22 per cent as much as its domestic investment' (Berger and Lester 1997: 24). According to a survey conducted by the Federation of Hong Kong Industries, further growth of investment on the mainland had by 2002 brought more than 10 million manufacturing workers in Guangdong under Hong Kong-based companies, 3.3 times more than in 1991 (quoted in Yang 2006: 128; also see Federation of Hong Kong Industries 2003). Berger and Lester (1997), based upon their study of Hong Kong's manufacturing industries in the 1990s, thus coined the term 'made by Hong Kong' as opposed to 'made in Hong Kong' to capture the shifts in the pattern of production. Hong Kong's industrial production has gradually moved offshore, starting with selected industries and later encompassing almost the entire manufacturing sector (Lui and Chiu 1993, 1994, 2001). The location of production has long extended beyond Hong Kong's administrative boundary.

Hong Kong's changing role: from production site to operating centre

The change in Hong Kong's role from production site to an operating centre controlling a widely dispersed network of extra-territorial production locales led to other changes. First, there has been an exponential expansion of re-export trade from China. As Hong Kong manufacturers relocated their production base to China by setting up factories there or subcontracting parts of the production processes to Chinese factories, the volume of outward processing arrangements surged dramatically: 'The usual outward processing arrangement is to export raw materials or semi-manufactures from or through Hong Kong to China for processing, with a contractual arrangement for subsequent re-importation of the processed goods into Hong Kong' (Census and Statistics Department 1995: F2). Re-exports of Chinese origin involving outward processing almost doubled from HK$221 billion to HK$422 billion in 1991–4, with labour-intensive products like clothing, electrical appliances and toys among the major items. Commodities involving outward processing in China accounted for some 82 per cent of all re-exports from Hong Kong in 1994 (Census and Statistics Department 1995: F13). It is observed that:

> In a great number of other cases, essentially all manufacturing processes are moved to China, leaving only such functions as marketing, orders processing, materials sourcing, design, product development, prototype making and quality control with the local firms. ... Besides, many traditional import/export firms have also become engaged in SPAC [subcontract processing arrangements in China] to take advantage of cheap, abundant resources in China. ... Furthermore, quite a large number of new ... [trading] firms are also set up in recent years to serve as a local base for new manufacturing firms in China, operating in a way different from traditional importers/exporters.
>
> (Census and Statistics Department 1996: FA3)

Indeed, as early as 1991 when the Hong Kong Trade Development Council (1991: 13) surveyed local manufacturers and traders and asked them about their future operations in Hong Kong, 83 per cent of the respondents mentioned controlling headquarters, 81 per cent documentation, 73 per cent business negotiation and 72 per cent trade financing. In other words, Hong Kong's manufacturers have changed from being the primary production contractors for overseas buyers to being the agents of 'triangular manufacturing' (Gereffi 1994: 114), shifting towards more emphasis on linkages, coordination and management in an increasingly decentralized and sophisticated system of production. In this connection, Hong Kong is an ideal strategic base for foreign companies to develop contacts and to penetrate the regional market (also see Birnbaum 1993). It is also in the eyes of overseas buyers a highly competitive sourcing centre for China-made goods. Overseas importers 'value highly the professionalism of Hong Kong suppliers in international trade' and are impressed by their design capacity (Hong Kong Trade Development Council 2003: 17).

While the number of manufacturing establishments in Hong Kong fell from a peak of 51,671 in 1988 to 20,380 in 1999 in the course of this industrial restructuring process, the number of import/export firms with manufacturing-related activities rose from 12,580 in 1992 to 22,330 in 1999 (Census and Statistics Department 2001b: FB4). The compilation of statistics on manufacturing-related activities since 1992 actually reflects changes in the business strategy of local traders and manufacturers. In 1992 among those 12,580 import/export firms engaged in SPAC and providing technical support services, 42.3 per cent were former manufacturers. In other words, many manufacturers shifted from directly engaging in production to assuming a role in trading, marketing, and coordination and control between overseas buyers and the production plants on mainland China.

In 1999, the picture was very different. Only 26.8 per cent of the 22,330 import/export firms with manufacturing-related activities had previously undertaken production in Hong Kong. About three-quarters (73.2 per cent) of them were originally set up as importers and exporters. This observation, echoing our discussion of the market responsiveness of local manufacturers in Chapter 2, reflects the flexibility of Hong Kong business, with manufacturers taking up more commercial and trading functions, and traders integrating into production and related activities. It also shows, given the manufacturers' and traders' experience in dealing with overseas buyers, the strength of local business on the commercial side of global production. The essential components of the new prototype of successful business include the competitive advantage in handling dispersed manufacturing, skills in supply chain management, customer-sensitive marketing, and the capability of providing so-called 'one-stop-shop services' (Trade and Industry Department 2001: 2–15). More and more entrepreneurs in Hong Kong:

> have dual capacity as traders in Hong Kong and proprietors or partners of factories in the Mainland. The import and export firms in Hong Kong operated by these entrepreneurs would import goods from their factories in the Mainland and subsequently re-export those goods to the rest of the world. However, these import and export firms operate in a way somewhat different from traditional importers/exporters. Activities undertaken usually involve manufacturing-related technical support services, e.g. product design, sample and mould making and production planning.
>
> (Census and Statistics Department 2005a: FA3)

The conventional division between manufacturing production and non-production processes (such as trade-related services and marketing) has been blurred. Increasingly Hong Kong companies compete on the basis of their skills in managing dispersed manufacturing. Hong Kong manufacturers' and traders' experiences of working with global sourcing agents since the 1970s and their need to work with offshore production (particularly since the opening of the Chinese economy since 1978) have helped them pick up the skills of effectively and efficiently managing the supply chain. They can handle modularized manufacturing (i.e. the processes of the supply chain being broken up and different parts of production being farmed out to different companies across the world) and are capable of orchestrating these various processes of dispersed production carried out by a network of suppliers (Fung *et al.* 2008).

Meanwhile, the growth in cross-border trade and other transactions stimulated the growth of other producer services such as the financing of production expansion in China, trade-related services, insurance, communication, and port, transportation and logistics (Federation of Hong Kong Industries 2007: 18). What is more relevant to our discussion here is the further development of Hong Kong as a locale for coordinating and managing such transnational flows of economic activities as reflected in the regional representation of overseas companies in Hong Kong shown in Table 6.2.[2] The number of regional headquarters (RHQs) rose from 602 in 1991 to 944 in 2001, and then 1,246 in 2007, while the number of regional offices (ROs) increased from 278 in 1991 to 2,644 in 2007.

Table 6.2 Information on regional headquarters and regional offices established by overseas companies in Hong Kong, 1991–2007 (selected years)

1991

Regional headquarters   602
>   258 of US parent companies
>   43.4% of parent companies in manufacturing
>   51.7% of these RHQs engaged in wholesale/retail, import/export
>   78 and 166 responsible for HK & China and SE Asia (China inclusive) respectively

Regional offices   278
>   62 and 61 of US and Japan parent companies respectively
>   46.4% of parent companies in manufacturing
>   40.5% of these ROs engaged in wholesale/retail, import/export
>   126 and 52 responsible for HK & China and SE Asia (China inclusive) respectively

1996

Regional headquarters   816
>   188 of USA parent companies (85 from China)
>   40.4% of parent companies in manufacturing
>   50.0% of these RHQs engaged in wholesale/retail, import/export
>   314 and 172 responsible for HK & China and SE Asia (China inclusive) respectively

Regional offices   1,491
>   338 and 226 of Japan and USA parent companies respectively (128 from China)
>   39.6% of parent companies in manufacturing
>   50.8% of these ROs engaged in wholesale/retail, import/export

2001

Regional headquarters   944
>   221 of USA parent companies (70 from China)
>   27.0% of parent companies in wholesale, retail and trade-related services
>   39.7% of these RHQs engaged in wholesale/retail, import/export
>   82.8% responsible for operations/business in Mainland China*

Regional offices   2,293
>   533 and 420 of Japan and USA parent companies respectively (172 from China)
>   32.7% of parent companies in wholesale, retail and trade-related services
>   46.3% of these ROs engaged in wholesale/retail, import/export
>   78.3% responsible for operations/business in Mainland China*

2005

Regional headquarters   1,167
>   262 of USA parent companies (107 from China)
>   32.6% of parent companies in wholesale, retail and trade-related services
>   52.7% of these RHQs engaged in wholesale/retail, import/export
>   89.6% responsible for operations/business in Mainland China*

Regional offices   2,631
>   606 and 537 of USA and Japan parent companies respectively (160 from China)
>   35.7% of parent companies in wholesale, retail and trade-related services
>   52.0% of these ROs engaged in wholesale/retail, import/export
>   84.1% responsible for operations/business in Mainland China*

2007

Regional headquarters   1,246
>   298 of USA parent companies (93 from China)
>   38.6% of parent companies in manufacturing
>   55.3% of these RHQs engaged in wholesale/retail, import/export
>   1,089 of these RHQs responsible for operations/business in Mainland China*

Regional offices   2,644
    593 of USA parent companies (152 from China)
    37.1% of parent companies in manufacturing
    55.9% of these ROs engaged in wholesale/retail, import/export
    2,176 of these ROs responsible for operations/business in Mainland China*

---

* The reporting of information on the country and territory of responsibility of these RHQs and ROs since 2001 is different from those reported earlier; surveyed firms give multiple answers as their scope of activity normally covers more than one country

Sources: *Annual Survey of Regional Offices Representing Overseas Companies in Hong Kong* (Census and Statistics Department various years); *Report on 2007 Annual Survey of Companies in Hong Kong representing Parent Companies Located outside Hong Kong* (Census and Statistics Department 2007b); *Annual Survey of Regional Representation by Overseas Companies in Hong Kong* (Industry Department, various years)

Available information on overseas companies' Hong Kong-based regional representation does not allow us to discuss in greater detail the changing pattern of their activities, and the complexities of regional coordination and control. However, it should be noted that there are significant variations among MNCs of different country origins in how they use Hong Kong as a centre of regional representation, coordination and control (Thompson 2000).[3] For example, for Japanese MNCs, 'Hong Kong is most important as a location for marketing, sales and customer service functions. ... for US MNCs, Hong Kong would seem very important for coordinating, supporting and reporting on regional operations' (Thompson 2000: 182).

In 1991, the parent companies of 43.4 per cent of the RHQs engaged in manufacturing. However, upon the arrival at Hong Kong, only 11.5 per cent of all surveyed firms were in that business; the majority (51.7 per cent) were in wholesale/ retail and import/export. In the period 1991–2005, more and more RHQs (either in terms of the business of their parent companies or their Hong Kong-based activity) are found in wholesale, retail and trade-related services. Other than wholesale, retail and trade-related services, it is also found that an important line of business carried out by these RHQs in Hong Kong since 2005 was related to business services, and finance and banking. This picture is largely consistent with our earlier discussion of the restructuring of Hong Kong's manufacturing. If Hong Kong is to play a part in global production (either as a source of offshore investments, as a gateway for global outsourcing, as a hub of MNCs' global coordination and control of production, or as a platform for orchestrating dispersed production), its significance falls primarily in the areas of commerce, trading and management.

Equally significant is the rise of China as a potential market for consumer products as well as a location of production. In 2005, among the 1,167 RHQs, 1,046 were responsible for the business on mainland China, 479 indicated Taiwan and 430 Singapore. China figures prominently in the business plans of these RHQs (cf. Thompson 2000). The 2007 survey findings were largely the same but there seemed to be a change towards a broadening of the geographical spread of control by these RHQs. Many of these RHQs also had to manage offices in Korea and Thailand. At the same time, there has been an increase in the number of ROs with parent companies originating from mainland China (though there was a slight drop between 2005 and 2007). It is evident that Hong Kong constitutes an important interface between China and global business because of its strategic location together with its established business networks.[4] Indeed, it can be said that Hong Kong is a gateway (Andersson 2000) for both getting into and coming out of China.

The deepening of economic integration with mainland China, particularly with the Pearl River Delta, pushes Hong Kong further onto the path of post-industrial development. Table 6.3 shows the relevant statistics on Hong Kong's trade involving outward processing on mainland China. The most important point to note is that re-exports of mainland China origin to other places through Hong Kong amounted to some 82–6 per cent of outward processing in the mid-1990s but the proportion has dropped to less than 80 per cent since 2003. The findings of a 2004 survey of local manufacturers and traders that was conducted by the Hong Kong Trade Development Council (2004) confirms this observation. This study found that the percentage of re-exports of China-made goods via Hong Kong by local companies dropped from 78.0 per cent in 1994 to 52.3 per cent in 2003. Meanwhile, the proportion involving direct shipment rose from 10.3 per cent to 37.6 per cent in the same period (Hong Kong Trade Development Council 2004: 15). In 2003, about 50 per cent of the total export value of the respondents to that survey belonged to offshore trade (Hong Kong Trade Development Council 2004: 6). The reasons for the increase in direct shipment are diverse:

> When asked why they opt for direct shipment, 66% of the respondents give 'lower transportation cost' as their reason, followed by 'buyers' request' (46% and 'factories far away from Hong Kong' (35%) … Some overseas buyers have set up sourcing centres in China in recent years, but even if they commission the manufacturing or sourcing of goods to Hong Kong companies, they would still prefer to export the goods by direct shipment. Moreover, … since more and more Hong Kong companies, especially traders, have extended their production or sourcing activities to places further away from Hong Kong, it makes more sense to export the goods by direct shipment without touching Hong Kong.
>
> (Hong Kong Trade Development Council 2004: 17)

So, there are two sides to this phenomenon of growth of offshore trade. First, as noted above, there has been a fall in the trading of goods via Hong Kong. On the other hand, it shows that Hong Kong continues to play an important role as middleman in regional and world trade (Sung 2006). The role of middleman includes merchandising (local traders provide services to overseas buyers and suppliers in the handling of purchases and sales of goods, and the trading of such goods does not involve import and export activities via Hong Kong) and merchanting (local traders purchase goods produced overseas and such goods are forwarded directly from the suppliers for export without going through Hong Kong customs) (Sung 2006: 155). Merchanting and other trade-related services (MOTS) feature prominently in Hong Kong's exports of services, increasing from 31.0 per cent among all exported services in 2000 to 34.7 per cent in 2004 (Census and Statistics Department 2005b:

FB6). Most of these services (89.5 per cent) in 2003 were related to offshore trade (Census and Statistics Department 2005b: FB6). Moreover, the major destination of the MOTS is mainland China (around 30 per cent in 2000–4), followed by the USA (around 27.5 per cent for the same period). MOTS is an important component of Hong Kong's trade in services. In terms of exports of services, Hong Kong ranked tenth in 2004 (ninth in 2002) (Census and Statistics Department 2005b: FB12).

But equally significant is the fact that there are contending forces at work. The challenges encountered by Hong Kong are best illustrated by the studies of Japanese electronics corporations in Hong Kong (Edgington and Hayter 2006). Briefly, Japanese electronics corporations are reorganizing their Hong Kong bases in the face of a rapidly changing business environment:

> Common amongst responses was the acknowledgement that 'China is a very big country: we cannot hope to serve all parts of China from Hong Kong alone'. This points to the realization that after China's entry into the WTO is settled, part of Hong Kong's current role is slowly but surely to transfer away from being the only entry point into the PRC. Hong Kong's future role is likely to be one that pivots around being the sales and service for the southern China region.
>
> (Edgington and Hayter 2006: 186)

This is a long way from the more comprehensive set of functions performed by Hong Kong offices for Japanese corporations. Japanese business interests in post-war Hong Kong began with sales (and also after-sales service) to the local market and using local factories as suppliers of low-end OEM products. A major push to upgrade the status of the local office came with the opening up of the Chinese economy in 1978. As a result of the massive expansion of sales of household electrical appliances in China, Hong Kong offices were assigned a broader geographical coverage of business activities (in addition to the assignment of China, Taiwan and the

Table 6.3 Hong Kong companies' local and mainland operations

Type of activity	Percentage of these activities in Hong Kong or mainland China	
	Hong Kong	Mainland China
Overall management and planning	85.8	56.1
Sales and marketing	87.6	48.5
Trade documentation	95.1	71.0
Trade financing/insurance arrangement	82.7	31.4
Product design and development	69.8	62.7
Logistics, warehouse, shipping and consolidation	80.6	74.5
Quality control	64.1	84.5
Purchasing of raw materials	76.4	78.7
Management and coordination of production	55.7	77.0
Manufacturing	21.6	82.1

Source: Hong Kong Trade Development Council (2004: 43)

Philippines would quite often also be included). Also, given the increase in the volume of sales, local offices were upgraded to 'full sales office status' (Edgington and Hayter 2006: 179). The 1980s saw Hong Kong playing the role of gateway to China. Full marketing teams were established and international procurement offices (for sourcing parts and products manufactured in southern China) were also added to the local offices in Hong Kong. Japanese corporations gradually set up their plants on the mainland and correspondingly offices were established in major locations. Sales activity in Hong Kong began to decline after 1997. Japanese companies opened more factories on the mainland to cater for the growing local market. At the same time, rising competition from Chinese local manufacturers reduced sales of consumer electronics to the mainland through Hong Kong.

> By the year 2001 the only products being imported into mainland China through Hong Kong were sophisticated industrial products ... Most recently, Japanese firms have begun to manage links with those Chinese/Hong Kong/Taiwanese and Korean-based factories in China, through sub-contracting arrangements set up on an OEM basis, or even retreated from the consumer products sector completely due to increased competition from Chinese and other East Asian competitors.
>
> (Edgington and Hayter 2006: 180)

Nowadays, the most important functions of the Hong Kong offices are sales and service because financial settlements have to be conducted primarily in Hong Kong and not elsewhere on the mainland. Hong Kong's development in the function of international procurement is restricted by the fact that Taiwan is significantly more competitive in securing the supply of high-technology products. In short, Hong Kong's function as a regional office has been shaped and re-shaped by the changing regional dynamics.

The second change relating to Hong Kong's shift from a production site to an operating centre is that Hong Kong's manufacturers and traders are fully utilizing the resources and opportunities they find on mainland China. They are moving further inwards – inland – turning new towns and districts into Hong Kong's expanding hinterland. Furthermore, they are quick to make use of other resources and facilities, particularly port facilities and logistics, for the purpose of strengthening their competitiveness (such as reducing transportation and logistics costs and smoothing the supply chain interface) in the global market. This further extension of the scope and scale of Hong Kong's economic activity on the mainland is paradoxically a potential threat to the local economy, particularly in those areas where Hong Kong is becoming increasingly less cost competitive (manufacturing production is one area and logistics will soon become another). On the other hand, the relocation of production and the growth of offshore trade have pushed Hong Kong further towards the provision of specialized and professional services for local manufacturers and traders, and overseas buyers. The deepening of production relocation means that more and more production-related services, such as management and coordination of production, quality control and inventory management, are handled on the mainland. As a result, Hong Kong companies turn to focus on professional and specialized services ranging from trade financing to marketing to overall management and planning (see Table 6.3). It is evident that not only has the mainland taken up the core processes of manufacturing, but even product design as well as research and development are no longer based exclusively in Hong Kong. The changing division of labour between Hong Kong and the mainland is a dynamic interactive process. How Hong Kong will further reposition itself in the face of the turbulent global market and the changing conditions on the mainland is an open-ended question. One thing is certain: this changing division of labour will no longer be one-sidedly shaped by Hong Kong, as happened in the 1980s and to a certain extent in the 1990s as we discussed earlier. Rather, Hong Kong and the mainland, especially the Pearl River Delta region, are becoming 'competing partners' – complementary in some aspects but soon to be competing in many areas.

Changing fortunes

The changing division of labour between Hong Kong and the mainland in terms of manufacturing and production-related activities is primarily conducted at a regional level. As discussed above, Hong Kong has rediscovered its hinterland. However, in terms of financial and business services, the scale is national. Indeed, unlike most international financial centres, Hong Kong has become a national centre after attaining its status and reputation at the regional and international levels (and not the other way round). And, thanks to this return of the national, 'Hong Kong surged past New York this year [2006] to become the world's second most popular place – after London – for companies to float new stock listings' (*International Herald Tribune* 2006).

In the past, emphasis was placed upon Hong Kong's strategic role in facilitating economic reform and marketization on mainland China. However, with China experiencing rapid economic growth while Hong Kong's economy has been badly hit by the economic downturn since late 1997, the Hong Kong SAR government began to rethink its strategic role by shifting its focus to how to take better advantage of economic opportunities and resources on the mainland. Such a repositioning was noted by Mr Tung Chee-hwa, the then Chief Executive of the Hong Kong SAR government, in his 2001 Policy Address, when he stated that 'Following China's accession to the World Trade Organization [WTO], cooperation between Hong Kong and Guangdong will rise to new heights. The Government is determined to actively promote economic cooperation between Hong Kong and the PRD region with a view to achieving a "win-win" situation. This is a key element in our efforts to consolidate and enhance Hong Kong's position as an international center for finance, trade, transport and logistics, as well as a premier tourist destination' (http://www.policyaddress.gov.hk/pa01/e26.htm). In fact, even before Mr Tung had made his remark on closer cooperation, Mr Antony Leung (2002), the then Financial Secretary, drew an analogy of the China–Hong Kong boundary as a 'Goretex boundary': 'Hong Kong people and money can flow into the Mainland quite freely, but it's not the case the other way around.' Thus the government was expected to work on facilitating the 'five flows' across the boundary: people, cargo, capital, information and services. The intricate ties between the national and Hong Kong's striving to become a global city can also be seen in Hong Kong's strategy of branding itself as 'Asia's World City'. The embeddedness of the global city in the national is now highlighted in government publications: Hong Kong's position as Asia's world city rests on the foundation of being 'the gateway to the mainland of China and the hub for business in the Asia-Pacific region' (http://www.brandhk. gov.hk/brandhk/emesstop.htm).

We now discuss in more detail the key features of the flows referred to above.

Flows of people

Tourists from the mainland, particularly those from the so-called 'white-collar' stratum (i.e. the middle class), are targeted as potential spenders to boost the economy. In 2000, Hong Kong hosted some 13 million visitors, of whom 29.0 per cent were visitors from mainland China. The number of visitors shot up to more than 23 million in 2005. Over 12 million (more than three times the figure for 2000 and constituting 53.7 per cent of all visitors) were visitors from the mainland. Relaxation of restrictions on travel by mainlanders to Hong Kong facilitated this growth. In January 2002 the Hong Kong SAR government had reached an agreement with the National Tourism Administration for the abolition of the quota system for the Hong Kong Group Tour Scheme. Further relaxation was introduced in 2003 with the launching of the Individual Visit Scheme for residents in the major cities on the mainland (currently covering 44 mainland cities with potentially 220 million residents eligible to visit Hong Kong in their individual capacity). If tourism is the hallmark of a global city, then Chinese tourists appear to be the indispensable ingredient for Hong Kong's global city status.

As the mainland and Hong Kong develop closer economic ties, more business people are travelling between the two places. Previously, however, business travelling was placed under strict regulation, even during the first few years after Hong Kong's reversion. Subsequently, to further facilitate visits to Hong Kong, the mainland's public security authorities agreed in 1998 to extend the validity period for multi-entry business visas from six months to a maximum of three years, with each duration of stay extended to 14 days. Changes in Hong Kong's population policy (Government of Hong Kong Special Administrative Region 2003) have also allowed mainland investors and persons with skills and talents in demand to come and settle in Hong Kong. A so-called Quality Migrant Admission Scheme has also been established to attract highly skilled and talented persons to settle in Hong Kong, in order to enhance 'economic competitiveness in the global market' (http://www.immd.gov.hk/ehtml/QMAS_2.htm).

Capturing the opportunities opened by the maturation of the mainland's domestic market

Since China's admission to the WTO, negotiations have taken place between the central government and the HKSAR government over proposals that would grant

Hong Kong preferential treatment to enable it to take advantage of business opportunities on the mainland before similar privileges must be extended under WTO rules to other countries. Suggestions have been made to lobby for allowing mainlanders with foreign currency to transfer their funds into Hong Kong banks and/or to invest in the Hong Kong stock market (*South China Morning Post* 2002a). The most dramatic new development designed to enable Hong Kong to better capitalize on the opening of China to the world market and the hyper-growth of its domestic market was the implementation of the mainland/Hong Kong Closer Economic Partnership Arrangement (CEPA) on 1 January 2004. Lobbying by Hong Kong for preferential treatment, as noted above, had been going on for quite some time. The materialization of CEPA was largely intended as a way to help Hong Kong recover from its economic recession and mollify the growing political discontent in 2003, although this motivation was never openly acknowledged. The spread of SARS in 2003 had a dampening effect on an economy that had not yet fully recovered from its downturn following the Asian financial crisis. But Beijing probably considered the mass rally (some half a million people marched in protest against the Hong Kong SAR government) on 1 July 2003 a more alarming event. Its strategy to assuage public discontent was to help speed up economic recovery. Thus, the launching of the Individual Visit Scheme would give an immediate boost to services related to the tourist industry. The CEPA agreement would give local people a sense of reassurance, though probably more symbolic than real (SynergyNet 2007), that China would help Hong Kong by opening up access to its vibrant economy, thereby creating new business opportunities for the much troubled Hong Kong economy.

Flows of money

Previously, the 'Goretex boundary' was heavily skewed towards the northward movements of capital. Hong Kong has played a very significant role in injecting capital into restructuring the socialist economy from the late 1970s onwards. Hong Kong's well-developed capital market has served as an important conduit for those reforming Chinese enterprises to raise much needed investment funds. At first only state enterprises were allowed to be listed in Hong Kong but lately an increasing number of private enterprises are also lining up for the opportunity to do so. Bond issues, though remaining rather small in scale, have also grown in significance. As the recession hit Hong Kong, the Hong Kong and Chinese governments took steps to reverse this one-way traffic. In 2002, the People's Bank of China began a study on setting up a special financial institution to help mainland residents invest their foreign exchange holdings in the Hong Kong stock market. The QDII scheme is expected to create the impetus for at least part of the then estimated US$80 billion foreign exchange savings of mainland individuals and US$50 billion held by mainland companies to be invested in Hong Kong (*South China Morning Post* 2002a). Even though much of this money is expected to be invested only in stocks of Chinese companies listed in Hong Kong (the so-called H-shares and red chips), the scheme would still create much needed new momentum to boost the stagnant Hong Kong market. It will also stimulate more mainland companies to be listed in Hong Kong because the current undervaluation of H-shares would also be alleviated. In general, Hong Kong is expected to play a role in the gradual opening of the financial system of China.

The mainland's phenomenal economic growth and development constitute the major impetus for reshaping the landscape of Hong Kong's financial development since 2000. Jao (2006: 125) suggests that 'Hong Kong's reunification with China provides the political and legal basis for Hong Kong's role as an offshore financial centre of China.' Institutional competence, global linkages and capital mobility aside, that the Hong Kong dollar is a freely and fully convertible currency plays a significant role here: 'Through this medium, China is able to convert its huge balance of payments surplus vis-à-vis Hong Kong into international reserve currencies' (Jao 2006: 126). Over the years, China has come to occupy an important position in Hong Kong's banking sector in terms of its share of total assets, deposits from customers and loans to customers (see Table 6.4).

Equally significant is the role of Hong Kong as a fundraising centre for Chinese enterprises. Chinese state-owned enterprises were first listed on the Hong Kong stock market in 1993. 'Red chips' refers to those locally incorporated Chinese companies that float in Hong Kong, whereas H-shares are mainland firms directly listed on the Hong Kong stock market. The total amount of funds raised in 1993–2004 reached approximately US$110,200 million (Jao 2006: 130). Despite the possibilities of raising funds in the stock markets of Shanghai and Shenzhen, and in markets abroad (such as London, New York and Singapore), 'Hong Kong's remains the market of first choice' (Jao 2006: 130).

Red chips and H-shares are actively traded in the Hong Kong stock market and their significance to the market has been growing, particularly since 2005 (see Table 6.5). Growth and development at the enterprise level and the Chinese economy as a whole have generated a surge in demand for financial services. One of the financial services that mainland enterprises need is the opportunity to raise funds through an initial public offering (IPO). Indeed, Hong Kong has become a platform in this respect for mainland enterprises to reach global investors:

> In 2005, Mainland enterprises accounted for over 90% of IPO funds raised in Hong Kong; seven of the ten most actively traded stocks in Hong Kong so far

Table 6.4 China's stake in Hong Kong's banking sector (HK$ billion)

	1997	1998	1999	2000	2001	2002	2003	2004	2005
Assets	957	1,004	957	1,050	987	1,016	1,079	1,146	1,181
% of total	11.4	13.8	14.1	15.1	16.0	16.9	16.6	16.1	16.3
Deposits from customers	591	681	676	745	724	754	784	836	842
% of total	22.1	23.0	21.3	21.3	21.6	22.7	22.0	22.2	20.7
Loans to customers	436	433	405	422	418	451	453	478	510
% of total	10.6	13.1	14.4	17.1	19.1	21.7	22.3	22.2	22.1

Source: http://www.info.gov.hk/hkma/eng/public/index.htm

this year [October 2006] are Mainland companies; and of the 200 largest stocks in the Hong Kong market forming the Hang Seng Composite Indexes, 103 companies derive the majority of their revenue from the Mainland and account for about 45% of the market capitalization.

(Hang Seng Bank 2006: 2)

With the influx of mainland enterprises coming to Hong Kong to raise funds through an IPO, Hong Kong has quickly climbed to the top position in the world's top ten new issue markets (see Table 6.6).

A change in scale and perspective

This chapter has taken steps to analyse Hong Kong's changing economic position in the context of China's new national development strategy since the 1980s. The Hong Kong economy had encountered an economic bottleneck at that time, being squeezed by competitors from the region and the slowdown in the US economy. In the late 1970s, however, China shifted from self-reliance to an open-door economic policy that aimed to attract foreign capital, technology and expertise to achieve the so-called Four Modernizations. China typically used Special Economic Zones (SEZs) and joint ventures for oil field explorations to lure foreign investment. These new developments have the potential to enable China to establish a new service centre close to its territory. Consequently, borderland integration between colonial Hong Kong and mainland China is deepening. Having been involved in international trade for over a century, Hong Kong is well known for its strength in entrepot trade, financial connections and other services. Thus, Hong Kong can

Table 6.5 Market capitalization by H-shares and red chips in the Hong Kong Stock Exchange

	H Shares		Red Chips		All	
Year -end	Market capitalization (HK$mn)	% of market	Market capitalization (HK$mn)	% of market	Market capitalization (HK$mn)	H shares and red chips as % of market
1993	18,228.70	0.61%	124,129.51	4.17%	142,358.21	4.78%
1994	19,981.32	0.96%	84,279.33	4.04%	104,260.65	5.00%
1995	16,463.77	0.70%	110,701.97	4.71%	127,165.74	5.42%
1996	31,530.63	0.91%	263,330.90	7.58%	294,861.53	8.48%
1997	48,622.01	1.52%	472,970.42	14.77%	521,592.43	16.29%
1998	33,532.66	1.26%	334,966.21	12.58%	368,498.87	13.84%
1999	41,888.78	0.89%	956,942.33	20.24%	998,831.11	21.13%
2000	85,139.58	1.78%	1,203,551.95	25.10%	1,288,691.53	26.87%
2001	99,813.09	2.57%	908,854.82	23.39%	1,008,667.91	25.96%
2002	129,248.37	3.63%	806,407.41	22.66%	935,655.78	26.29%
2003	403,116.50	7.36%	1,197,770.75	21.87%	1,600,887.25	29.23%
2004	455,151.75	6.87%	1,409,357.12	21.26%	1,864,508.88	28.13%
2005	1,280,495.01	15.78%	1,709,960.75	21.08%	2,990,455.76	36.86%
2006	3,363,788.46	25.39%	2,951,581.05	22.28%	6,315,369.51	47.67%

Source: http://www.hkex.com.hk/data/factbook

Table 6.6 World top ten new issue markets (US$ billion)

Rank	2005		Dec. 2004		Dec. 2003		Dec. 2002	
	Exchange	Capital raised	Exchange	Capital raised	Exchange	Capital raised	Exchange	Capital raised
1	New York	175.0	New York	147.9	New York	83.5	New York	87.4
2	Euronext	66.0	Euronext	44.9	Euronext	51.2	Euronext	36.0
3	London	51.8	Toronto	39.1	London	30.2	London	34.4
4	Toronto	43.2	Spain	38.6	Tokyo	29.0	Spain	21.4
5	Hong Kong	38.3	Hong Kong	36.1	Hong Kong	27.5	Tokyo	15.7
6	Australia	33.2	London	32.5	Australia	22.8	Toronto	14.5
7	Tokyo	24.6	Tokyo	25.9	Toronto	17.9	Hong Kong	14.2
8	Italy	14.8	Australia	25.4	Spain	17.8	Taiwan	13.2
9	JSE	13.0	Italy	19.0	Italy	14.4	Australia	12.3
10	Nasdaq	12.2	Nasdaq	15.0	Taiwan	8.5	South Africa	9.8

Sources: Jao (2006: 135); http://www.world-exchanges.org

develop as a facilitator or intermediary for mainland trade and investment, providing valuable channels for the diffusion of information to China, serving as a contact point for China's trade, financing China's modernization, acting as a conduit for China's technology transfer, and providing a training ground for China to learn and practise capitalist skills in a market environment.

From its re-emergence as an entrepot and transhipment centre to its development as a financial hub, Hong Kong has benefited tremendously from China's new development strategy. The development of Hong Kong as a financial centre has implications, however, for the local path of restructuring because it has created path-dependent pressures. Cross-border investment and its high initial returns fuelled a local asset boom and indirectly crowded out local manufacturing production while accelerating the outward relocation of industries. Since the colonial government pursued a 'positive non-intervention' policy, and since most Hong Kong firms were small and medium sized, Hong Kong small firms found it highly attractive to relocate their labour-intensive industries to the nearby Pearl River Delta in Guangdong, which has led to a 'hollowing out' of the manufacturing sector in Hong Kong. And Hong Kong has gradually transformed itself to become an interface of production in China and the global market through its role in 'triangular manufacturing'.

So, since the early 1980s there has been a deepening of 'borderland integration' as Hong Kong firms have spread their network of operations into the South China hinterland and in the process have turned Hong Kong into the service and financial centre of mainland China. The only viable way for Hong Kong to reverse the local economy's slowdown and avoid the possibility of stagnation appears to be even deeper integration with the national economy, capitalizing on its enormous growth potential to further propel Hong Kong's development as a regional hub for high value-added financial and producer services. Furthermore, reflecting the impact of the change in sovereignty on Hong Kong's perspective, it increasingly looks upon China not only as a hinterland for expanding production but also as a neighbouring region for the expansion of its service industry, a new source of capital inflow, a potential market for consumer products and services, and a targeted population for the local tourist industry (see Chen 2005).

Such a change in understanding the economic connections between Hong Kong and the mainland has also facilitated the formation of a new perspective of contextualizing the former's economic and social development in a broader regional scale. The idea of the formation of the Pan-Pearl River Delta (Pan-PRD) region was first raised by Guangdong officials in 2003 and then an agreement was signed in June 2004 (see Figure 6.2). This new regional grouping covers one-fifth of China's land area and one-third of its population. Future development in the Pan-PRD region promises to reposition Hong Kong within a larger regional scale, with the potential to further upgrade its status of being a metropolitan economy.

This development is to some extent paradoxical. It is almost akin to the scenario projected in the early 1980s (when Hong Kong was experiencing the political uncertainties arising from the Sino-British negotiations over its future) but turned upside down. Instead of Hong Kong being the exemplar of advanced capitalism for

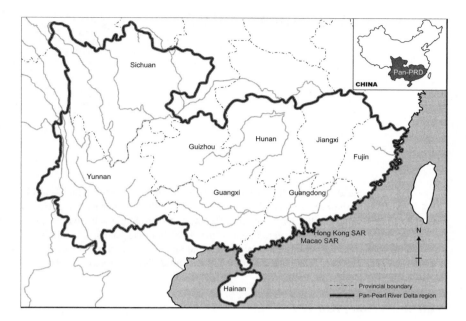

Figure 6.2: The Pan-Pearl River Delta region

steering China towards further integration with the global economy, nowadays it is Hong Kong that looks to China for new economic dynamism and resources. In other words, the economic flows between China and Hong Kong are no longer predominantly uni-directional, from the latter to the former, but increasingly flow in both directions, thus tightening the interconnections and interdependence between the two places. From the broader and longer historical perspectives of Hong Kong's integration with China (instead of seeing this as a sudden change in their fortunes after 1997) that we have highlighted here, such a development is hardly surprising. In the face of China's entry into the global market, Hong Kong's own rescaling process has increasingly involved becoming more integrated into the ambit of the larger national project. Instead of being disembedded from the larger national and regional contexts, Hong Kong is becoming a Chinese global city. While its prospects as a global city continue to hinge upon its global connections, the 'China factor' is gaining increasing prominence in structuring the flows between Hong Kong and the world economy.

7 A Chinese global city?

Looking ahead, it is worth considering whether and how Hong Kong should be involved in the preparation of the 12th Five-Year Plan (covering the period of 2011–2015) under the 'One Country, Two systems' principle. This will not only facilitate the economic development of the SAR, but also enable our timely and effective contribution to the Mainland's social and economic development during the 12th Five-Year Plan period. (Hong Kong: Central Policy Unit 2007: 29)

Who needs Hong Kong?

Our discussion in Chapter 6 points to the re-embedding of Hong Kong into China's national development. It is observed that Hong Kong continues to function as China's 'window to the outside world'. But increasingly this is less to do with China acquiring management methods or the funnelling of capital from advanced industrialized societies and Chinese overseas. It is more a matter of using Hong Kong as a springboard for Chinese enterprises, which have experienced rapid growth and development, and thus are looking for new development opportunities and means of financing further organizational growth in order to go global. Equally significant is that, nowadays, economic flows between Hong Kong and China are two-way – they are mutually dependent on one another, rather than one of them relying on the other. While Hong Kong's main function in the grand project of China's national development has changed, the saga of Hong Kong as a global city continues.

According to Hughes, 'The Hong Kong mood ... is one of masterly expedience and crisis-to-crisis adjustment and recovery' (1976: 129). How Hong Kong would make a major comeback from the post-1997 economic recession and launch a breakthrough in finding an economic future is still a question waiting for an answer. But within the post-1997 decade this global city, maintaining its economic dynamism, has proved many observers wrong. As noted in our introductory chapter, the cover of the May 2002 issue of *Fortune* ran this title: 'Who needs Hong Kong? How the city lost its lock on the China market'. Inside, it was argued:

The problem is that Hong Kong's China franchise has eroded – not, as many feared, because Beijing is keeping Hong Kong down, but because China is rising fast. … China's progress means that it just doesn't need Hong Kong as much.

(Fortune 2002: 42)

Yet, as the previous chapter showed, Hong Kong still has a lot to offer. Sassen suggests that Hong Kong 'has two specialized roles in two distinct sets of networks' (2006: 47): first, it is assuming an important role in China's building of a national capital market; second, it serves as a 'global gateway' between China and global finance. Once again, although in a different form and with a different set of functions, Hong Kong is playing a critical role of intermediation between China and the world economy.

The growing 'China factor'

So, has Hong Kong come full circle? It began as an entrepot and a centre of commercial activities bridging China and the world economy in the mid-nineteenth century. Since then, it has taken a development route of its own, flourishing as an entrepot and a centre of commerce and finance for Chinese business, then as an industrial city, and subsequently a regional and international financial centre. By the time Hong Kong was returned to China in 1997 this could be seen as part of a longer process of Hong Kong–China socio-economic integration since the 1970s so that, once again, Hong Kong holds a strategic position between China and the global economy. But epiphenomena can be misleading. It is a different China. Nor has the global economy remained unchanged. Today, Hong Kong plays this critical role of intermediation in the context of a rapidly growing and internationalizing Chinese economy in a period in which China is also changing rapidly in geo-political reach. China has become 'the factory of the world'. Equally important is that it has also become a growing centre of domestic consumption, with the world's leading chain stores and brand names staring hungrily at this very expansive consumer market. Meanwhile, the interface between China and the global economy has changed significantly in the course of its active participation in the world economy at both the global and regional levels on the one side, and the deepening of economic reform in China on the other. Interest in the Chinese economy has moved from simply taking advantage of cheap resources (namely, land, utilities and labour) to eyeing the varied potentials of the world's leading industrial export nation, and a vast and growing consumption market (especially with the arrival of a newly formed middle class (see, for example, Pearson 1997; Davis 2005; Li 2005; Goodman 2008)). The liberalization of the service and financial sectors opens new prospects for Hong Kong and global capital. At the same time, Chinese enterprises are eager to take up opportunities and resources available outside China for the purpose of raising funds, and making acquisitions and investments ranging from natural resources – above all energy – to manufactures. Our discussion in Chapter 6 underlined the importance of this changing interface between China and the world economy for the strengthening of Hong Kong's position in regional and world finance.

One eye-catching feature of the socio-economic changes in Hong Kong over the past two decades has been its important role in regional integration. This began with the relocation of Hong Kong's manufacturing to the Pearl River Delta (see Chapter 2) in the 1980s, bringing about the formation of a rediscovered hinterland and a new spatial division of labour. With manufacturing production relocated to the neighbouring region and Hong Kong specializing in design, marketing and related commercial activities, and business and financial services, Hong Kong quickly changed into a metropolitan economy (Tao and Wong 2002). By the mid-1990s, it was no longer secluded from the Pearl River Delta. Developments since 1997 have brought Hong Kong and the mainland even closer. Nowadays, Hong Kong's socio-economic integration with the mainland has long gone beyond the so-called 'front shop back factory' model (Sit 1998). In 2006, some 13.5 million mainland tourists (53.5 per cent of all visitors) visited Hong Kong. More importantly, as we have discussed in Chapter 6, mainland enterprises have actively used the Hong Kong Stock Exchange as a venue for raising funds. Almost half (47.7 per cent) of Hong Kong's market capitalization was under H-shares and red chips in 2006.

An indicator of the changing character of the 'China factor' in Hong Kong's economy is the inclusion of H-shares in the compilation of the Hang Seng Index (HSI) in 2006. Indeed, it is expected that more and more of the mainland-incorporated companies will be considered for inclusion in Hong Kong's blue-chip list. With the listing of more H-shares in the benchmark index, the HSI 'will no longer be a barometer of Hong Kong's economy, and the index's correlation with the Hong Kong economy will diminish. … This reflects the reality of the Hong Kong stock market as now over 50 per cent of the blue chips' revenue is not generated from Hong Kong' (*South China Morning Post* 2007).

The above socio-economic changes are also reflected in the number and composition of Hong Kong residents working on the mainland (Census and Statistics Department 2006).[1] The number of Hong Kong residents working on the mainland rose from slightly more than 50,000 persons in 1988 to 228,900 persons in 2005. Given the expansion and intensification of economic interflows between Hong Kong and the mainland, this is hardly a surprise. More significant is that, between 1995 and 2005, the composition of those Hong Kong residents working on the mainland changed significantly, reflecting the changing character of economic relations between the two places. First, whereas 55.9 per cent of Hong Kong residents working on the mainland were in the manufacturing sector in 1995, the percentage dropped to 20.1 per cent in 2005. The leading sector has been taken over by 'wholesale, retail and import/export trades, restaurants and hotels' (59.3 per cent). Equally important is the growth of employment in 'financing, insurance, real estate and business services', which by 2005 employed 11.0 per cent of all Hong Kong residents working on the mainland. Regarding the composition of Hong Kong residents working in China, the share of the occupation category 'managers and administrators' dropped from 42.0 per cent in 1995 to 35.6 per cent in 2005. Meanwhile, professionals (e.g. lawyers, accountants) and associated professionals (e.g. surveyors, legal clerks) rose from 22.5 per cent to 44.6 per cent. In 2005, 28.9

per cent of these Hong Kong residents (18.5 per cent in 1995) had attained tertiary education. Changes in the composition of those Hong Kong residents working on the mainland in 1995–2005 show that, following the changing pattern of economic integration, opportunities across the border are no longer confined to those closely connected to manufacturing relocation. In fact, it is not unreasonable to expect that, with more and more mainlander trainees and junior staff acquiring work experience and management knowledge, Hong Kong managerial staff in mainland production plants will be replaced by locals. Increasingly, for the people of Hong Kong, opportunities on the mainland have shifted towards the tertiary sector and professional services.

These changes suggest a potential cleavage within the professional and managerial class in Hong Kong (Lui and Wong 2003). The so-called 'China opportunity' is not open to all professionals, managers and administrators. The differences between those in private business and commercial services on the one hand, and the public sector and social and community services on the other, are rather obvious. Opportunities available in the former activities are partly driven by Hong Kong enterprises that have actively explored new business on the mainland and partly by outgoing mainland enterprises that seek commercial and financial services from Hong Kong's professionals. Those working in the public and non-profit sectors and social and community services are fully embedded in the local context. Their service recipients are primarily local residents. Of course, as Hong Kong's economy recovers from the shocks of the Asian financial crisis and a depressing business environment brought about by the SARS epidemic, with the influx of tourists from the mainland and growing demand for professional services from Chinese enterprises, the entire population stands to benefit. However, in comparison with those in private business and commercial services, the benefits that can be obtained by locally embedded professionals, managers and administrators from the booming Chinese economy are, at best, partial and indirect.

Such differences in access to the expansive 'China opportunity' remind us that further regional and national integration in Hong Kong's economic development could be contentious. We have argued (see Chapter 5) that the formation and development of a global city are shaped by its institutional responses to opportunities in a changing environment. Yet, institutional responses rest heavily on city governance. City politics is not a side issue. In fact, it is the crux of the matter: without effective governance, no successful restructuring can be implemented. That Hong Kong was at an impasse after 1997 was the result of a breakdown in state–society relations and effective governance. How Hong Kong as a global city will capitalize on the opportunities opened by China depends on the rebuilding of effective governance and a consensus between government and people. We discussed growing inequalities and social divisions within Hong Kong in Chapter 4. Here we further underline differences in access to the 'China opportunity' even among the middle class. The point we intend to highlight is that difficulties in the rebuilding of social consensus and a shared vision should not be underestimated. In this regard, the future of Hong Kong as a global city should not be understood simply in economic terms. Politics matters in determining Hong Kong's path of future development.

The inevitable question: challenge from Shanghai

Equally important would be Hong Kong's global connectivity in determining its future development (on Hong Kong global connectivity and its stable position in the league of global cities, see Taylor 2006). Discussion of Hong Kong's future development would inevitably invite sceptics to ask if fast-growing Shanghai will gradually replace its crucial position and function as a global city and international financial centre for China. Indeed, worries about Shanghai's challenge to Hong Kong's position as China's major window to global finance are not without foundation. Table 7.1 reports the market capitalization of stock markets in Hong Kong and Shanghai since 2001. It is observed that market capitalization in Shanghai's stock market was quite stable in the early years of the new century, but it has made a major leap since 2005. Very quickly, it is catching up (with an increase of 302.7 per cent in 2006–7) and surpassed Hong Kong in 2007 in terms of the amount of money raised in the market. Rapid economic growth in mainland China is the major driving force behind Shanghai's growing significance in the financial world.

The competition from Shanghai is real enough. Yet, it is still early to write off Hong Kong (Hua and Cao 2006). The long-term competitiveness of Hong Kong as a global city and an international financial centre, vis-à-vis Shanghai and other Asian global cities, rests upon its global connectivity. Table 7.2 shows world concentration of financial activities (namely the equity market, bond market, credit market, foreign exchange market and derivatives market). On the basis of an average normalized score for financial markets in the world, Hong Kong finds itself in sixth position in terms of overall concentration of financial activities. In the same 'league table', Shanghai is ranked 22nd.

This 'league table' of world financial activities prompts two interesting observations. First, there is a high level of concentration of financial activities in the USA and UK. The gap between their shares of world financial activities and those of the rest of the world is significant. One distinctive feature that divides the top two countries and the rest of the world is the structure of their financial systems. Apparently, both the USA and the UK are able to fare reasonably well across different kinds of financial activities. Those ranked between the third and tenth position may do well in one or two areas but are handicapped by their imbalanced structure. Second, there seems to be another gap between those who manage to climb up to the upper part of the table (say, on or above 15th position) and those lower down in the hierarchy. Hong Kong benefits enormously from its recent growth in IPO activities. It also does quite well in the foreign exchange market. But its equity market remains

Table 7.1 Domestic market capitalization in Hong Kong and Shanghai, 2001–2007 (US$ millions)

Exchange/year	2001	2002	2003	2004	2005	2006	2007
Hong Kong exchanges	506,072	463,054	714,597	861,462	1,054,999	1,714,953	2,654,416
Shanghai SE	333,356	306,443	360,106	314,315	286,190	917,507	3,694,348

Source: World Federation of Exchanges (http://www.world-exchanges.org/statistics/annual)

Table 7.2 World concentration of financial activities

Rank	Country/city	Financial activities concentration (average normalized score)	World share of individual markets (%)							
			Equity turnover	Fund raised through IPO	Intl bond market – amount outstanding	Domestic bond market – amount outstanding	Bank foreign assets	Bank foreign liabilities	FX turnover	FX/interest rate derivatives market turnover
1	USA	100.0	49.0	16.3	23.3	44.6	8.9	11.7	19.2	19.4
2	UK	90.6	10.9	16.9	12.6	2.4	19.8	22.5	31.3	38.1
3	Japan	32.7	8.3	3.7	0.9	18.1	7.6	3.2	8.3	6.0
4	Germany	23.0	3.9	3.6	10.6	4.4	10.6	7.3	4.9	4.1
5	France	22.1	2.8	3.8	6.2	4.4	9.1	9.3	2.6	6.6
6	Hong Kong	13.2	1.2	12.9	0.3	0.1	2.3	1.4	4.2	2.7
7	Netherlands	10.9	1.3	3.7	7.1	1.5	3.8	3.7	2.0	2.0
8	Switzerland	9.9	2.0	0.8	0.1	0.5	4.6	4.4	3.3	2.4
9	Singapore	9.9	0.3	1.5	0.3	0.2	2.4	2.6	5.2	3.2
10	Italy	9.6	2.3	1.6	4.3	5.2	1.8	2.6	0.8	1.7
20	Korea	3.5	1.9	0.8	0.5	1.5	0.3	0.6	0.8	0.4
22	Shanghai*	3.3	1.1	3.6	0.1	2.2	0.0	0.0	0.0	0.0

Source: Adapted from Cheung and Yeung (2007: 7)

Notes: Equity figures as of end-2006; international bond market figures as of Q3 2006; domestic bond market and banking figures as of Q2 2006; FX and derivative turnover figures as of 2004

* Data missing from one or more markets

relatively small in terms of its share of world market capitalization, and it still has to catch up in the bond and derivatives markets. Yet, compared with Shanghai, Hong Kong seems to be multifunctional. The competitive edge of Shanghai lies in its volume of transaction in equity market and IPO activities. Given that the RMB (renminbi) is not an internationally convertible currency, it remains rather under-developed in credit and foreign exchange markets.

So far, our discussion of Hong Kong's position as an international financial centre is based upon measurements on a national basis. Should we carry out the comparison at a city level or on the basis of measurement adjusted for GDP with other major financial centres, the outcomes of the ranking exercise would be rather different (Cheung and Yeung 2007). Indeed, with the aid of these new measurements, Cheung and Yeung (2007) find that Hong Kong is a world leader in terms of financial sector foreign direct investment. Correspondingly, according to a study carried out by the Economist Intelligence Unit in 2000, among the 8,000 multinational corporations responding to its survey, 35 per cent have established regional headquarters in Hong Kong (Cheung and Yeung 2007: 13) (compared with only 3 per cent in Shanghai). 'After [being] adjusted for GDP, Hong Kong outperforms most major financial centres to become the leading locality for international direct investment in the financial sector after Switzerland' (Cheung and Yeung 2007: 13). Regarding the export of financial services, according to the traditional measurement, Hong Kong ranked fifth in the world in 2005. Once adjusted for GDP, Hong Kong's ranking moved to third place, following the leaders of the UK and Switzerland, but occupied the same ranking as the USA (Cheung and Yeung 2007: 11).

Factors such as a sound and transparent regulatory framework, an advanced and sophisticated business infrastructure, and compatibility with world standards in professional practices are all critical to Hong Kong's success in maintaining its status as an international financial centre (Cheung and Yeung 2007: 26). In this connection, there is still plenty of room for improvement in institution building in Shanghai. In fact, as long as China's financial sector is not yet fully liberalized and its currency is not internationally convertible, Hong Kong would remain an ideal locality through which China and its corporations can prepare for further reforms in financial management. In this regard, Hong Kong functions like an offshore centre (so that China can make the best use of its institutional rules and structure) and yet it is also a part of the country. On the one hand, responding quickly to the changing needs of the Chinese economy, Hong Kong has diversified its financial services from bank syndications to IPO and asset management; on the other, China benefits from having Hong Kong as a laboratory for testing various new initiatives in the course of moving towards more active participation in world finance.

Of course, this is not to say that Hong Kong has no worries. Given the small size of its local economy, the scale of its financial markets is relatively small compared to those of other major international financial centres. More importantly, 'there is still a low degree of international element in Hong Kong's domestic stock market as measured by the number of foreign firms listed' (Cheung and Yeung 2007: 28) In other words, much remains to be done in order to strengthen Hong Kong's position as an international financial centre. It is quite true that Hong Kong will continue to benefit from the rise of mainland China. This will be a major source of demand for financial services exports from Hong Kong. But such benefits are not necessarily confined to Hong Kong and China. That Hong Kong has assumed the role of being a premier IPO centre for mainland corporations contributes to the widening and deepening of the local stock market for attracting international investors to Hong Kong (Cheung and Yeung 2007: 30). How Hong Kong is going to manage its global connectivity will be a key to its future success.

Further restructuring of the economy would also hinge upon Hong Kong's global connectivity and its services to China. It is estimated that 'if the size of the Mainland economy doubles over the next decade, Hong Kong's service exports would rise from the current 40 per cent of GDP to 50 per cent of GDP by 2016, of which half of the increase could be attributable to the Mainland factors' (Leung *et al*. 2008: 3). As noted in Chapter 6, trade-related services, mainly made up of merchanting and merchandizing activities for offshore transactions, contributed almost one-third of all service exports in 2007 (Leung *et al*. 2008: 6), the largest share among all components of exported services. It is suggested that

> One of the reasons for the rapid growth of merchanting trade is the increasingly complex global supply chain, which led to importers' demand for a broader range of services and more risk-sharing with its suppliers. For the importer, the outsourcing of such operations as sourcing, production, and logistics helps reduce the risks involved in working with different suppliers and coordinating from overseas. Some tasks are also less costly for the merchanting service provider than for the importer to do, such as ensuring compliance with relevant environmental and labour standards, where local knowledge and expertise are needed. Furthermore, given Hong Kong's robust legal system, importers may also feel more confident entering into contractual arrangements with Hong Kong service providers rather than with the manufacturers directly.
>
> (Leung *et al*. 2008: 7)

Equally important are exports of financial services. There has been a drastic increase in such exports in recent years, tripling in value over the period 2003–7 (Leung *et al*. 2008: 9). These services include asset management, securities transactions and financial intermediation, with the former two being the most important impetus to growth in exports. The USA is the largest destination for financial services exports. But information on the fee structure of financial services provided to mainland corporations suggests that about 30 per cent of financial services exports in 2006 were mainland-related services (which include the listing of mainland corporations on Hong Kong's stock market, turnover of mainland-related shares in the local market, increases in merger and acquisition activities, and inward portfolio investment from mainland investors) (Leung *et al*. 2008: 12). The important point to note is that Hong Kong has moved further towards post-industrialism. The economy is increasingly service-based and service exports have come to constitute an important source of future economic growth. Future success in these areas again hinges upon Hong Kong's connectivity not only with China but also with other leading international financial centres.

Challenges and contradictions

Given the galloping pace and momentum of China's economic growth and development, Hong Kong has been re-embedded in the national economic project of a globalizing China. As a response to the need to reposition Hong Kong's development in the broader national picture, the Chief Executive of the Hong Kong SAR government organized the Economic Summit on 'China's 11th Five Year Plan and the Development of Hong Kong' in September 2006. Prominent members of business, professional, academic and labour sectors were invited to join four focus groups to work on an action agenda in the areas of 'trade and business', 'financial services', 'maritime, logistics and infrastructure', and 'professional services, information and technology and tourism'. The agenda was published in January 2007 (see the above quotation).

The call for closer cooperation, deepening of integration and adopting an active approach was, unsurprisingly, warmly received. The spirit of this new perspective is best captured in the call for Hong Kong to 'be involved in the preparation of the 12th Five Year Plan (covering the period of 2011–2015) under the "One Country, Two Systems" principle.' In the face of a vibrant Chinese economy, becoming part of the national economy is not only a safe bet but is also probably the best opportunity for the coming decades. Yet, there has been little discussion of the implications for Hong Kong of closer cooperation and further integration. The talk of Hong Kong's involvement in the preparation of the next Five Year Plan has a certain contradictory character – this would involve strategic planning for a (at least, so defined) *laissez-faire* economy and the placement of this free market economy within the map of a planned (though increasingly market-driven) economy. Of course, one can say that, nowadays, with further marketization and liberalization, China works in fundamental ways like a market economy and the meaning of state planning has changed. So, Hong Kong's active participation need not bring about a major change in its long market-driven approach to development. While few observers of the Chinese economy would deny the significance of marketization and liberalization, it is equally important to recognize the central role played by the Beijing leadership in setting the agenda of national development, defining the parameters of reform, facilitating (or deterring) a certain course of strategic action, controlling the pace of economic growth, and defining the objectives of strategic economic action and programme. The Chinese state, whatever the label of socialism, is becoming less and less important in many domains of social life. Yet it remains the central player in directing national development. In this connection, Hong Kong's hope of closer cooperation with the mainland and assuming a more strategic role in national development depends to a significant extent on its strategic value to the Beijing leadership. Recent initiatives by the central government in making use of Hong Kong as a venue for the gradual opening of channels for individual mainland investors to invest overseas confirm the significance of Hong Kong's special status and position to China. Hong Kong continues to find its place in Beijing's strategizing and national development.

With support from the central government, the Hong Kong SAR government may find it easier to handle infrastructural projects involving cross-border coordination. Indeed, the strengthening of Hong Kong's metropolitan economy in the context of further regional integration would call for more inter-governmental collaboration at the local and regional levels. No only would this require changes in the government's role in planning and development, it would also challenge the existing framework of coordination in cross-border development. How ready is the HKSAR government, which quite consciously maintains an image of having minimal intervention in economic development, to deal with these emerging developmental issues on a larger scale? How ready is Hong Kong – both the government and the private sector – to espouse a new perspective and assume a new position in regional development?

Surely new opportunities are in sight, but it is alarming to see that Hong Kong appears willing, even eager, to submit to the grander plan of national development. The expressions of fear of being marginalized in the national project, as we noted in Chapter 6, best reflect this change in perspective and orientation. Hong Kong's opinion leaders had long believed that Hong Kong would take the lead in reforming China's economy and bringing the country to the world – both capturing the opportunities available through linkages with the outside world, and conveying to China critical information concerning world standards and practices. The active role played by Hong Kong between China and the world economy would not only be critical to China's modernization, but would also be crucial to maintaining Hong Kong's special position and status vis-à-vis China. Now the tables appear to have been turned. The mainland has become an 'economic powerhouse' and Hong Kong's role as an intermediary appears to rest on how China chooses to use it to reach the outside world. It will be the Beijing leadership that determines how to liberalize its financial market, which in turn will shape Hong Kong's future financial development. It will also be the way the central government steers regional development (say, in defining the pace, scale and scope of the Pan-Pearl River Delta development) that will structure Hong Kong's future development in the areas of logistics, business services and tourism. The point is not that Hong Kong needs to prove to Beijing that it is functional to the national project. For a long time, Hong Kong has demonstrated its value to China. Indeed, its existence as a British colony in 1949–97 largely hinged upon such contributions. However, as China globalizes, there emerges a growing number of rising cities in competition with Hong Kong for its once almost unchallenged position and status. More importantly, it will be the central government that assumes the active and leading role in shaping the future course of national economic development wherein Hong Kong is eager to find its place. Paradoxically, Hong Kong has repositioned itself only to find itself placed in the back seat.

The incorporation of Hong Kong into the plan of national development is double-edged. On the one side, there will be plenty of opportunities. On the other, Hong Kong is becoming a Chinese global city. More precisely, it will become one of several Chinese global cities with Shanghai, Beijing, and perhaps Tianjin, Shenzhen and others. In the past two centuries Hong Kong prospered because of its Chinese connection. As discussed in Chapters 1–3, Hong Kong has been able to grow economically and to climb the hierarchy of global cities because of its connectivity with overseas Chinese business networks, and its unique ability to mediate between China and the world economy. It was, and still is, a very special Chinese city. It strikes a balance between being global and being Chinese by building an institutional structure that would fit in comfortably with the requirements of global business and finance and, at the same time, by working through Chinese networks on the mainland and abroad. Its special blend of Chinese global business and finance is the strength of Hong Kong in maintaining its position and status in the global urban hierarchy. Yet, its eagerness to be incorporated within China's national economic development and the turn towards the mainland for new opportunities may upset the previous balance of being both global and Chinese. In the short term, becoming a Chinese global city would help Hong Kong recover from its economic recession, but the long-term implications of such a strategy are far from clear.

In the last analysis, the very notion of Hong Kong as a global city suggests that it has to maintain its embeddedness in both the regional economy and the global economy. It also implies that it is both a central node of the national governance as well as the global governance system. It has to understand Chinese culture but tap into the pulses of global culture. It has to be both embedded and autonomous at the same time. Losing either one of the two strands of its development would spell trouble for Hong Kong. The challenge to Hong Kong's future as a global city is exactly about how to maintain its global connectivity and outlook and to become a Chinese city (of a very different brand) at the same time. To be Chinese but retain its distinctive character and a measure of autonomy from China is the tightrope that Hong Kong has to walk to secure its economic and political future. We hope this book will contribute to the understanding of Hong Kong's place in China and the world.

Notes

Introduction

1 See Olds and Yeung (2004) on how Singapore's entrepreneurial state takes the lead in going global. The character of the state in Hong Kong is very different. But instead of being irrelevant, the effects of the state in Hong Kong's case manifest themselves in a different form.

2 An industrial colony: Hong Kong manufacturing from boom to bust

1 LCD serves the display function in a wide range of gadgets, from calculators to laptop computers, whereas CRT has so far been the prominent type of colour picture tube for TV and computer monitors.
2 The Census and Statistics Department does not use the same categories as we use in this chapter. To facilitate sector analysis, 'consumer electronics' includes 'electronic toys', 'electronic watches and clocks', 'transistor radios', 'television receivers and communication equipment', 'sound reproducing and recording equipment and apparatus'; 'parts and components' includes 'electronics parts and components'; 'computer products' includes 'computing machinery and equipment'; 'office automation equipment' includes 'office machinery and equipment except computing and accounting machinery'; and 'others' includes those electronics products not specified elsewhere.
3 We are well aware of the limitations of a functionalist explanation of state provisions of public housing in Hong Kong. For a historical analysis emphasizing the broader political context in shaping the colonial government's policy on resettlement and public housing, see Smart (2006).
4 Goodstadt (2005, 2007) sees 'positive non-interventionism' as an ideological weapon of the colonial government that allowed the colonial bureaucrats to resist pressures from the business and professional elites: 'Officials never saw themselves as locked into non-interventionism by colonial tradition. For them, laissez faire was not a matter of principle but motivated by political convenience and economic expediency. The continued governability of Hong Kong was their overwhelming concern' (Goodstadt 2007: 16).
5 The survey on the garment-making and electronics industries was carried out in the period June–September 1992. The sampling frame was provided by the Census and Statistics Department. It consisted of a randomly selected 20 per cent of all establishments of our chosen industries, and gave an updated record of their addresses (as at December 1991). Manufacturing establishments of all sizes were included in this address list. Manufacturing establishments were selected by stratified random sampling according to establishment size. In other words, samples of different size categories were chosen in proportion to the size distribution of manufacturing establishments of the two industries. Altogether, 211 establishments were selected for interview. A letter explaining the background of the survey was sent to the owner or manager of the selected

establishments. This was then followed by a face-to-face interview with the owner or appointed managerial staff for the completion of the questionnaire. The number of successfully completed questionnaires for garment-making and electronics establishments were 69 and 50 respectively. Since quite a number of the sampled establishments had closed their business, relocated or stopped production, the response rate was in the range of 67.6–73.5 per cent. Details of the survey can be found in Chiu, Ho and Lui (1997).

6 Drawing upon bank archival materials, Schenk (2004a) argues that banks in Hong Kong were quite eager to engage in industrial lending. They had made efforts – such as setting up dedicated departments to deal with the manufacturers – to overcome potential obstacles, cultural as well as institutional, to the building of a closer business connection between the manufacturing and the banking sectors. Goodstadt (2007) was more cautious in analysing this question concerning financial support of industrial development. He noted the complaints made by the manufacturers concerning lack of funding and support, and was careful not to jump too quickly to the conclusion that they were more political pressures than genuine voices from the industrial sector. He suggests that banks in Hong Kong were slow in recognizing the significance of industrial lending. Complaints about the neglect of industry could be traced back to the manufacturers' experiences in the initial phase of industrial development. From the 1960s onwards, the banking sector had become quite active in financing industrial projects. The points made by Schenk and Goodstadt are pertinent. Yet, it should be noted that the persistent perception of having difficulties in securing loans from local banks cannot easily be brushed aside as misperception, especially by the small firms. Furthermore, it must be emphasized that the issue of an institutional separation between industry and finance raised in our discussion is less about lending in general but more specifically about the availability of loans for projects of a longer duration and those involving risk and uncertainty (e.g. loans for fixed capital and other investments for upgrading) (see Table 2.5).

7 How Hong Kong can tap in to the growing economic sectors in the PRD and provide producer services to mainland corporations is still an open-ended question. A survey conducted by Yeh (2006: 157) in 2002, on manufacturing firms in Dongguan and Zhongshan, found that only a small fraction of the domestic factories (10.2 per cent) used external producer services.

3 The building of an international financial centre

1 The competence of the colonial administrators in responding to crisis and carrying out prudent supervision and monitoring should not be overstated. See Goodstadt's discussion of the top bureaucrats' mismanagement and their slowness in bringing professionals into the colonial administration's management of financial affairs (2007: Ch. 1).

4 A divided city?

1 This is also reflected in the publication of a research report on income distribution by the Census and Statistics Department (2007a), with detailed analyses of the patterns of income distribution (at both individual and household levels) and the effects of taxation and social benefits on reducing income inequalities.

2 Also see Tai (2006) for a comparative analysis of Asian cities, namely Singapore, Hong Kong and Taipei.

3 Baum's article, however, does not specify whether the analysis was based on income measured in current prices or constant prices.

4 The data file is a full sample of the 'long form' of the census questionnaire, which covers about one-seventh of the total population in Hong Kong at the time of the census.

5 Official publications only report the Gini Coefficients of income inequality at the household level. According to Hong Kong Census and Statistics Department (2002a: 82), the Gini Coefficient rose from 0.476 in 1991 to 0.525 in 2001, or by 10.29 per cent.

6 Although the concept of ethnic minorities is not identical with migrants, the two overlap considerably. A total of 343,950 ethnic minorities was reported in the 2001 Population Census, or 5.1 per cent of the total population (Census and Statistics Department 2002d: 5). Of these, only 13,249, or 3.9 per cent, were of Chinese nationality with place of domicile in Hong Kong (Census and Statistics Department 2002d: 17).

7 This discussion of the importation of foreign workers is based on Chiu and Levin (1993).

8 We are grateful to the Labour Department for pointing out the difference between 'foreign worker' and 'imported' worker as the majority of the workers imported under the various schemes are from the mainland. In this book, we refer to the workers coming from outside Hong Kong (whether from the mainland or elsewhere) as 'imported' or 'guest' workers rather than 'foreign' workers to highlight this fact (private correspondence from Hong Kong Labour Department on 23 January 1998 and also 19 January 2000).

9 An exploratory attempt was carried out by Forrest, La Grange and Yip (2004). They argue that 'multivariate analysis does not generate a statistically significant spatial concentration of multiple deprivation and this suggests that the kinds of urban ghettos found in other major cities do not exist on a large scale' (Forrest, La Grange and Yip 2004: 223). However, it is important to note that their analysis was carried out at the tertiary planning unit level. Such a level of analysis does not allow the authors to look into social inequalities at the neighbourhood level.

5 Decolonization, political restructuring and post-colonial governance crisis

1 See, for instance, the 'Hong Kong Core Values' campaign launched by local professionals in 2004. For details, consult http://www.hkcorevalues.net.

2 Lau is not totally unaware of the issue of diversity of interests. He discusses the impacts of the political transition, particularly the emergence of the China-centred networks, on the fragmentation of elite politics (see Lau 1999: 68). However, his discussion is largely confined to the cleavages created by the decolonization process. Diversity in class interests is basically ignored.

3 Cultural analysis of Hong Kong politics promises to go beyond class analysis of politics, see Ku (2001). Ku (2001: 122) argues that '[in the case of the bird flu crisis in Hong Kong] the challenge was powerfully presented not so much because of capitalist forces or class interests but because *the crisis became a dramatic moment of meaning reconstruction through ironic narration and democratic encoding in the public sphere*' (original emphasis). Despite reference to Gramsci (1971) and his notion of hegemony, nowhere is it clear that the widening of narrative cracks and credibility crisis are grounded upon and made possible by realpolitik and contest of meaning and interests carried by political actors with specific interests in a certain course of development. The civil service has long been bureaucratic and institutionally not accountable to the public. Why and how there was a narrative displacement to facilitate the rise of a hegemonic discourse on the civil servants, and then why and how the same civil service was de-heroized are questions left unanswered. As a result, conjunctural analysis becomes free-floating cultural construction of politics.

4 It would, of course, be overly simplistic to assume that the colonial government had not made changes in its ruling strategy in dealing with social and political changes in Hong Kong. On the move from selecting the old rich in Hong Kong to absorbing the younger and emerging professionals and managers since the late 1960s, see Tang (1973).

5 One crucial difference between our sample and previous ones is that, by the late 1990s, a new type of director was appointed to corporate boards, namely the 'independent non-executive director'. As they are 'outsiders' to the management team, an interlock that involves this kind of director should have a much less significant impact on the networking relationship between two companies. Under the current listing rules of the Hong Kong Exchange, at least three independent non-executive directors must be appointed to

the boards of listed public companies. As the number of this type of director increased quite dramatically between the three time points – from 0 to 503 in 1997 and 855 in 2004 – and they are typically found among those director groups with the largest membership, we have decided to exclude them in our analysis of the 1998 and 2004 panels in order to control for their presence over time. For a definition of independent non-executive directors in the context of banking, please refer to the HKMA website at http://www.info.gov.hk/hkma/gdbook/eng/n/non-exec_directors.htm.

6 Latter (2007b: Ch. 3) offers a sceptic's view of the government's attitude towards interventionism and becoming proactive. In his words, 'During his almost eight years as chief executive, Tung appeared forever anxious to please everyone, and he seemed to feel a need always to be seen to be doing something' (Latter 2007b: 38).

7 See, for example, *South China Morning Post* (1999a, 1999b).

8 The claim came back to the political scene in 2005 prompting the government to release 24 letters between the government and the PCC Group to prove an absence of collusion with the business sector (see *South China Morning Post* 2005).

6 The return of the regional and the national

1 See, for example, Olds and Yeung (2004), who focus on the role of the developmental state in understanding Singapore's global reach. The difference between our discussion and theirs on the role of the state and the national reflects the very different character of the state in Hong Kong and Singapore.

2 A regional headquarters (RHQ) is defined as 'an office that has control over the operation of other offices or branches in the region, and manages the business in the region without frequent referrals to its parent company outside Hong Kong'. A regional office (RO) is 'an office that coordinates offices/operations elsewhere in the region, in addition to the city in which it is located, and manages the business but with frequent referrals to its parent company outside Hong Kong or a regional headquarters' (see Census and Statistics Department 2001a: 5). These definitions have been slightly revised (in fact, simplified) since 2006. There have not been major changes in the meanings of the terms.

3 Thompson's observations are based on his own questionnaire survey of 159 MNCs in Hong Kong. No details are provided in his paper on the timing of data collection or sampling methods.

4 In addition to geographical proximity, the 'soft' side of Hong Kong's connection with China is also very important. On Hong Kong's advantage of being Chinese and at the same time 'not too Chinese', see Crawford (2001). Also see Chan (2002) for the relevance of Hong Kong businessmen's tacit knowledge in doing business and developing personal networks in China to attract Japanese companies to come to Hong Kong and see it as a springboard for moving into China.

7 A Chinese global city?

1 In the survey carried out by the Census and Statistics Department, 'Hong Kong residents working in the Mainland' refers to 'employed persons in the Hong Kong Residential Population who were required to work in the Mainland in their present job, irrespective of the number of times they had traveled to work in the Mainland during the 12-month period and the duration of each stay' (Census and Statistics Department 2006: FB2). Employed persons who were required to travel to the mainland only for inspection and business negotiation, and/or participating in trade fairs and/or exhibitions, meetings and business-related entertainment would not be included in the category of Hong Kong residents working on the mainland. Transport workers and fishermen or seamen who had to work within China's territory would also be excluded. It also does not cover those Hong Kong people who have already settled on the mainland on a permanent basis.

Bibliography

Abrahamson, M. (2004) *Global Cities*. New York: Oxford University Press.

Abu-Lughod, J.L. (1999) *New York, Chicago, Los Angeles: America's Global Cities*. Minneapolis: University of Minnesota Press.

Advisory Committee on Diversification (1979) *Report of the Advisory Committee on Diversification*. Hong Kong: Government Printer.

Amsden, A. (1989) *Asia's Next Giant*, New York: Oxford University Press.

Andersson, A.E. (2000) 'Gateway regions of the world', in A.E. Andersson and D.E. Andersson (eds) *Gateways to the Global Economy*. Cheltenham: Edward Elgar, 3–16.

Bard, S. (1993) *Traders of Hong Kong: Some Foreign Merchant Houses, 1841–1899*. Hong Kong: Urban Council.

Barker, B. and Goto, A. (1998) 'Technological systems, innovation and transfer', in G. Thompson (ed.) *Economic Dynamism in the Asia-Pacific: the Growth of Integration and Competitiveness*. London: Routledge, 250–73.

Baum, S. (1997) 'Sydney, Australia: a global city? Testing the social polarisation thesis', *Urban Studies*, 34(11), 1881–901.

Baum, S. (1999) 'Social transformations in the global city: Singapore', *Urban Studies*, 36(7), 1095–117.

Beaverstock, J.V., Taylor, P.J. and Smith, R.G. (1999) 'A roster of world cities', *Cities*, 16(6), 445–58.

Berger, S. and Lester, R.K. (eds) (1997) *Made by Hong Kong*. Hong Kong: Oxford University Press.

Berger, S. and Lester, R.K. (2005) *Global Taiwan*. Armonk: M.E. Sharpe.

Birnbaum, D. (1993) *Importing Garments Through Hong Kong*. Hong Kong: Third Horizon.

Boston Consulting Group (1995) *Report on Techno-economic and Market Research Study on Hong Kong's Electronics Industry 1993–94 Vol. 2*. Hong Kong: Hong Kong Government, Industry Department.

Breitung, W. and Gunter, M. (2006) 'Local and social change in a globalizing city: the case of Hong Kong', in F. Wu (ed.) *Globalization and the Chinese City*. London: Routledge, 85–107.

Brenner, N. (1998) 'Global cities, global states', *Review of International Political Economy*, 5(1), 1–37.

Brenner, N. and Keil, R. (eds) (2006) *The Global Cities Reader*. London: Routledge.

Bruegel, I. (1996) 'Gendering the polarisation debate: a comment on Hamnett's "social polarisation, economic restructuring and welfare state regimes"', *Urban Studies*, 33(8), 1431–9.

Burgers, J. and Musterd, S. (2002) 'Understanding urban inequality: a model based on existing theories and an empirical illustration', *International Journal of Urban and Regional Research*, 26(2), 403–13.

Business Week (1996) 'Taiwan's high-tech race', 6 May.

Carroll, J.M. (2005) *Edge of Empires: Chinese Elites and British Colonials in Hong Kong*. Cambridge: Harvard University Press.

Castells, M., Goh, L. and Kwok, R.Y.W. (1990) *The Shek Kip Mei Syndrome: Economic Development and Public Housing in Hong Kong and Singapore*. London: Pion Ltd.

Census and Statistics Department, Hong Kong (1982) *Hong Kong 1981 Census Main Report, Volume 1: Analysis*. Hong Kong: Government Printer.

Census and Statistics Department, Hong Kong (1991) *Estimates of Gross Domestic Product: 1966–1990*. Hong Kong: Government Printer.

Census and Statistics Department, Hong Kong (1995) 'Trade involving outward processing in China, 1989–1994', *Hong Kong Monthly Digest of Statistics*, June, F1–F16.

Census and Statistics Department, Hong Kong (1996) 'Trading firms with manufacturing-related activities', *Hong Kong Monthly Digest of Statistics*, August, FA1–FA10.

Census and Statistics Department, Hong Kong (1998) *Estimates of Gross Domestic Product*. Hong Kong: Government Printer.

Census and Statistics Department, Hong Kong (2001a) *Report on 2001 Annual Survey of Regional Offices Representing Overseas Companies in Hong Kong*. Hong Kong: Government Printer.

Census and Statistics Department, Hong Kong (2001b) 'Trading firms with manufacturing-related activities', *Hong Kong Monthly Digest of Statistics*, September, FB1–FB11.

Census and Statistics Department, Hong Kong (2002a) *2001 Population Census: Main Report Volume 1*. Hong Kong: Printing Department.

Census and Statistics Department, Hong Kong (2002b) *2001 Population Census Thematic Report – Persons from the Mainland Having Resided in Hong Kong for Less Than 7 Years*. Hong Kong: Printing Department.

Census and Statistics Department, Hong Kong (2002c) *2001 Population Census Thematic Report – Women and Men*. Hong Kong: Printing Department.

Census and Statistics Department, Hong Kong (2002d) *2001 Population Census Thematic Report – Ethnic Minorities*. Hong Kong: Printing Department.

Census and Statistics Department, Hong Kong (2005a) 'Trading firms with manufacturing-related activities', *Hong Kong Monthly Digest of Statistics*, February, FA1–FA12.

Census and Statistics Department, Hong Kong (2005b) 'Development of trade in services of Hong Kong', *Hong Kong Monthly Digest of Statistics*, October, FB1–FB12.

Census and Statistics Department, Hong Kong (2006) 'Hong Kong residents working in the mainland of China, 1995–2005', *Hong Kong Monthly Digest of Statistics*, January, FB2–FB9.

Census and Statistics Department, Hong Kong (2007a) *Thematic Report: Household Income Distribution in Hong Kong*. Hong Kong: Government Printer.

Census and Statistics Department, Hong Kong (2007b) *Report on 2007 Annual Survey of Companies in Hong Kong Representing Parent Companies Located Outside Hong Kong*. Hong Kong: Government Printer.

Census and Statistics Department, Hong Kong (various years) *Annual Survey of Industrial Production*. Hong Kong: Government Printer.

Census and Statistics Department, Hong Kong (various years) *Annual Survey of Regional Offices representing Overseas Companies in Hong Kong*. Hong Kong: Government Printer.

Census and Statistics Department, Hong Kong (various years) *Hong Kong Annual Digest of Statistics*. Hong Kong: Information Services Department.

Census and Statistics Department, Hong Kong (various years) *Hong Kong Trade Statistics*. Hong Kong: Government Printer.

Census and Statistics Department, Hong Kong (various years) *Quarterly Report on General Household Survey*. Hong Kong: Government Printer.

Census and Statistics Department, Hong Kong (various years) *Statistical Digest of the Services Sector*. Hong Kong: Information Services Department.

Chan, K.S. (2002) 'Japanese small and medium electronics firms in south China'. Unpublished MPhil thesis, University of Hong Kong.

Chan, M.K. and So, A.Y. (eds) (2002) *Crisis and Transformation in China's Hong Kong*. Armonk: M.E. Sharpe.

Chan, W.K. (1991) *The Making of Hong Kong Society*. Oxford: Clarendon Press.

Chen, E.K.Y. (1984) 'The economic setting', in D. Lethbridge (ed.) *The Business Environment in Hong Kong* (2nd edn). Hong Kong: Oxford University Press, 1–51.

Chen, E.K.Y. and Li, K.W. (1988) 'Industry', in H.C.Y. Ho and L.C. Chau (eds) *The Economic System of Hong Kong*. Hong Kong: Asian Research Service, 113–39.

Chen, X.M. (2005) *As Borders Bend: Transnational Spaces on the Pacific Rim*. Lanham: Rowan & Littlefield Publishers.

Cheung, L. and Yeung, V. (2007) 'Hong Kong as an international financial centre: measuring its position and determinants', Working Paper 14/2007, Hong Kong Monetary Authority.

Cheung, M.K.W. (1994) 'The applicability of four theoretical perspectives of economic power to the corporate market in Hong Kong'. Unpublished PhD thesis, Sociology Department, University of California, Los Angeles.

Chiu, S.W.K. (1994) 'The changing world order and the East Asian newly industrialized countries: challenges and responses', in D. Jacobson (ed.) *Old Nations, New World: Conceptions of World Order*. Boulder: Westview Press, 75–114.

Chiu, S.W.K. (1996) 'Unravelling Hong Kong's exceptionalism: the politics of laissez-faire in the industrial takeoff', *Political Power and Social Theory*, 10, 229–56.

Chiu, S.W.K. (2003) 'Recent trends in migration movements and policies in Asia: Hong Kong region report'. Paper presented at Workshop on International Migration and Labour Markets in Asia, Japan Institute of Labour, Tokyo.

Chiu, S.W.K. and Levin, D. (1993) 'Labour under industrial restructuring in Hong Kong: a comparison of textiles and garments'. Occasional Paper no. 21 of Hong Kong Institute of Asia-Pacific Studies, Hong Kong: Hong Kong Institute of Asia-Pacific Studies, The Chinese University of Hong Kong.

Chiu, S.W.K. and Levin, D. (2003) 'HRM in Hong Kong since 1997', *Asia Pacific Business Review*, 9(4), 32–54.

Chiu, SW.K. and Lui, T.L. (1995) 'Hong Kong: unorganized industrialism', in G. Clarke and W.B. Kim (eds) *Asian NIEs and the Global Economy*. Baltimore: Johns Hopkins University Press, 85–112.

Chiu, SW.K. and Lui, T.L. (2004) 'Testing the global city – social polarization thesis: Hong Kong since the 1990s', *Urban Studies*, 41(10), 1863–88.

Chiu, S.W.K. and Wong, K.C. (1998) 'The Hong Kong LCD industry: surviving the global technology race', *Industry and Innovation*, 5(1), 51–71.

Chiu, S.W.K., Ho, K.C. and Lui, T.L. (1997) *City-States in the Global Economy*. Boulder: Westview Press.

Choi, A.H.K. (1997) 'The political economy of Hong Kong's industrial upgrading: a lost opportunity', *China Information*, 12(1/2), 157–88.

Chu, Y.W. (1988) 'Dependent industrialization: the case of Hong Kong garment industry'. Unpublished MPhil thesis, Sociology Department, University of Hong Kong, Hong Kong.

Chu, Y.W. (2008) 'Deconstructing the global city: unraveling the linkages that underlie Hong Kong's world city status', *Urban Studies*, 45(8), 1625–46.

Clifford, M. and Engardio, P. (2000) *Meltdown: Asia's Boom, Bust and Beyond*. Paramus: Prentice Hall.

Crawford, D. (2001) 'Globalization and *guanxi*', *New Political Economy*, 6(1), 45–65.

Crisswell, C.N. (1991) *The Taipans: Hong Kong's Merchant Princes*. Hong Kong: Oxford University Press.

Dataquest Inc. (1991) *Techno-economic and Market Research: Study on Hong Kong's Electronics Industry, 1988–1989*. Hong Kong: Government Printer.

Davies, S.G.N. (1977) 'One brand of politics rekindled', *Hong Kong Law Journal*, 7(1), 44–80.

Davis, D. (2005) 'Urban consumer culture', in M. Hockx and J. Strauss (eds) *Culture in the Contemporary PRC*. Cambridge: Cambridge University Press, 170–87.

Deyo, F. (1987) 'Coalitions, institutions, and linkage sequencing – toward a strategic capacity model of East Asian development', in F. Deyo (ed.) *The Political Economy of the New Asian Industrialism*. Ithaca: Cornell University Press, 227–47.

Dicken, P. (1986) *Global Shift*. London: Harper & Row.

Economist Intelligence Unit (1962) *Industry in Hong Kong*. Hong Kong: South China Morning Post.

Edgington, D.W. and Hayter, R. (2006) 'Hong Kong's changing role as a global city: the perspective of Japanese electronic MNCs', in P.W. Daniels, K.C. Ho and T.A. Hutton (eds) *Service Industries and Asia-Pacific Cities*. London: Routledge, 173–98.

Eitel, E.J. (1983) *Europe in China*. Hong Kong: Oxford University Press.

Endacott, G.B. (1964a) *An Eastern Entrepot: A Collection of Documents Illustrating the History of Hong Kong*. London: Her Majesty's Stationery Office.

Endacott, G.B. (1964b) *Government and People in Hong Kong*. Hong Kong: Hong Kong University Press.

Endacott, G.B. (1973) *A History of Hong Kong* (2nd edn). Hong Kong: Oxford University Press.

Eng, I. (1997) 'Flexible production in late industrialization: the case of Hong Kong', *Economic Geography*, 73(1), 26–43.

England, J. (1989) *Industrial Relations and Law in Hong Kong* (2nd edn). Hong Kong: Oxford University Press.

England, J. and Rear, J. (1981) *Industrial Relations and Law in Hong Kong*. Hong Kong: Oxford University Press.

Enright, M.J., Scott, E.E. and Chang, K.M. (2005) *Regional Powerhouse: The Greater Pearl River Delta and the Rise of China*. Singapore: John Wiley & Sons (Asia) Pte Ltd.

Enright, M.J., Scott, E.E. and Dodwell, D. (1997) *The Hong Kong Advantage*. Hong Kong: Oxford University Press.

Ernst, D. and O'Connor, D. (1992) *Competing in Electronics Industry: The Experience of Newly Industrialising Economies*. Paris: OECD Publications Service.

Esping-Andersen, G. (1990) *The Three Worlds of Welfare Capitalism*. Cambridge: Polity Press.

Esping-Andersen, G. (ed.) (1993) *Changing Classes: Stratification and Mobility in Post-industrial Societies*. London: Sage.

Evans, P.B. (1995) *Embedded Autonomy: States and Industrial Transformation*. Princeton: Princeton University Press.

Fairbank, J.K. (1969) *Trade and Diplomacy on the China Coast*. Stanford: Stanford University Press.

Fan, S.C. (1974) *The Population of Hong Kong*. Hong Kong: Swindon Book Co. Ltd.

Faure, D. and Lee, P.T. (eds) (2004) *Economy: A Documentary History of Hong Kong*. Hong Kong: Hong Kong University Press.

Federation of Hong Kong Industries (1992) *Hong Kong's Industrial Investment in the Pearl River Delta: 1991 Survey Among Members of the Federation of Hong Kong Industries*. Hong Kong: Federation of Hong Kong Industries.

Federation of Hong Kong Industries (1993) *Investment in China*. Hong Kong: Federation of Hong Kong Industries.

Federation of Hong Kong Industries (2003) *Made in PRD: The Changing Face of HK Manufacturers*. Hong Kong: Federation of Hong Kong Industries.

Federation of Hong Kong Industries (2007) *Made in PRD: Challenges and Opportunities for HK Industry*. Hong Kong: Federation of Hong Kong Industries.

Fell, R. (1992) *Crisis and Change: The Maturing of Hong Kong's Financial Markets, 1981–1989*. Hong Kong: Longman.

Fong, A.H.S. (1992) 'Just-in-time inventory system: the case of Hong Kong'. Business Research Centre Working Paper Series, School Of Business, Hong Kong Baptist College.

Forrest, R., La Grange, A. and Yip, N.M. (2004) 'Hong Kong as a global city? Social distance and spatial differentiation', *Urban Studies*, 41(1), 207–27.

Fortune (1995) 'The death of Hong Kong', 26 June.

Fortune (2002) 'Who needs Hong Kong?', 20 May.

Friedman, M. (2006) 'Death of the Hong Kong model', *Wall Street Journal Asia*, 6 October.

Friedman, M. and Friedman, R. (1980) *Free to Choose*. Harmondsworth: Penguin Books.

Friedmann, J. (1986) 'The world city hypothesis', *Development and Change*, 17(1), 69–84.

Friedmann, J. (1995) 'Where we stand: a decade of world city research', in P.L. Knox and P.J. Taylor (eds) *World Cities in a World-System*. Cambridge: Cambridge University Press, 21–47.

Friedmann, J. and Wolff, G. (1982) 'World city formation', *International Journal of Urban and Regional Research*, 6(3), 309–44.

Frobel, F. *et al.* (1980) *The New International Division of Labour*. Cambridge: Cambridge University Press.

Fung, V.K. *et al.* (2008) *Competing in a Flat World*. Upper Saddle River: Wharton School Publishing.

Gereffi, G. (1994) 'The organization of buyer-driven global commodity chains: how US retailers shape overseas production networks', in G. Gereffi and M. Korzeniewicz (eds) *Commodity Chains and Global Capitalism*. Westport: Praeger Publishers, 95–122.

Gereffi, G. and Korzeniewicz, M. (eds) (1994) *Commodity Chains and Global Capitalism*. Westport: Praeger.

Germidis, D. (ed.) (1980) *International Subcontracting*. Paris: OECD.

Gerschenkron, A. (1966) *Economic Backwardness in Historical Perspective*. Cambridge: Cambridge University Press.

Ghose, T.K. (1987) *The Banking System of Hong Kong*. Singapore: Butterworths.

Goodman, D. (ed.) (2008) *The New Rich in China*. London: Routledge.

Goodstadt, L.F. (2005) *Uneasy Partners: The Conflict Between Public Interest and Private Profit in Hong Kong*. Hong Kong: Hong Kong University Press.

Goodstadt, L.F. (2007) *Profits, Politics and Panics*. Hong Kong: Hong Kong University Press.

Gordon, I. and Harloe, M. (1991) 'A dual to New York? London in the 1980s', in J.H. Mollenkopf and M. Castells (eds) *Dual City: Restructuring New York*. New York: Russell Sage Foundation, 377–95.

Gottmann, J. (1989) 'What are cities becoming centres of?', in R.V. Knight and G. Gappert (eds) *Cities in a Global Society*. Newbury Park: Sage, 58–67.

Gramsci, A. (1971) *Selections From the Prison Notebooks*. London: Lawrence & Wishart.

Greenwood, J. (1990) 'Hong Kong: the changing structure and competitiveness of the Hong Kong economy', *Asian Monetary Monitor*, 14(6), 21–31.

Gregory, G. (1985) *Japanese Electronics Technology: Enterprise*. Tokyo: Japan Times.

Guangdongsheng Tongjiju (2006) *Guangdong Tongji Nianjian [Guangdong Statistical Yearbook]*. Beijing: Zhongguo Tongji Chubanshe (in Chinese).

Gugler, J. (2003) 'World cities in poor countries', *International Journal of Urban and Regional Research*, 27(3), 707–12.

Haddon-Cave, P. (1984) 'Introduction', in D. Lethbridge (ed.) *The Business Environment in Hong Kong* (2nd edn). Hong Kong: Oxford University Press, xv–xx.

Hall, P. (1966) *The World Cities*. London: Heinemann.

Hamashita, T. (1997a) *Xianggang Dashiye [Hong Kong in Macro Perspective]*. Hong Kong: Commercial Press (in Chinese).

Hamashita, T. (1997b) 'The intra-regional system in East Asia in modern times', in P.J. Katzenstein and T. Shiraishi (eds) *Network Power: Japan and Asia*. Ithaca: Cornell University Press, 113–35.

Hamashita, T. (2003) 'Tribute and treaties: maritime Asia and treaty port networks in the era of negotiation, 1800–1900', in G. Arrighi, T. Hamashita and M. Selden (eds) *The Resurgence of East Asia: 500, 150 and 50 Year Perspectives*. London: Routledge, 17–50.

Hamilton, G.G. (1999) 'Hong Kong and the rise of capitalism in Asia', in G.G. Hamilton (ed.) *Cosmopolitan Capitalists*. Seattle: University of Washington Press, 14–34.

Hamnett, C. (1994) 'Social polarisation in global cities: theory and evidence', *Urban Studies*, 31(3), 401–24.

Hamnett, C. (1996) 'Social polarisation, economic restructuring and welfare state regimes', *Urban Studies*, 33(8), 1407–30.

Hang Seng Bank (2006) 'Strategies for further enhancing Hong Kong's status as an international financial centre', *Hang Seng Economic Monthly*, October.

Hao, Y.P. (1970) *The Comprador in Nineteenth-century China*. Cambridge: Harvard University Press.

Hao, Y.P. (1986) *The Commercial Revolution in Nineteenth-century China*. Berkeley: University of California Press.

Harding, A. (1995) 'Elite theory and growth machines', in D. Judge *et al.* (eds) *Theories of Urban Politics*. London: Sage Publications, 35–53.

Hayes, J. (1977) *The Hong Kong Region 1850–1911*. Hamden, Connecticut: Archon Books.

Henderson, J. (1989) *The Globalization of High Technology Production*. London: Routledge.

Henderson, J. (1991) 'Urbanization in the Hong Kong–south China region: an introduction to dynamics and dilemmas', *International Journal of Urban and Regional Research*, 15(2), 169–79.

Hill, R. and Kim, J.W. (2000) 'Global cities and developmental states: New York, Tokyo and Seoul', *Urban Studies*, 37(12), 2167–95.

Ho, P.Y. (2004) *Challenges for an Evolving City: 160 Years of Port and Land Development in Hong Kong.* Hong Kong: The Commercial Press.

Ho, R.Y.K. (1991) 'The regulatory framework of the banking sector', in R.Y.K. Ho, R.H. Scott and K.A. Wong (eds) *The Hong Kong Financial System.* Hong Kong: Oxford University Press, 91–118.

Hobday, M. (1995) *Innovation in East Asia: The Challenge to Japan.* Aldershot: Edward Elgar.

Hong, S.G. (1992) 'Path of glory: semiconductor leapfrogging in Taiwan and South Korea', *Pacific Focus*, 7, 59–88.

Hong Kong: Central Policy Unit (2007) *Our Way Forward: Report on Economic Summit on 'China's 11th Five-Year Plan and the Development of Hong Kong', Action Agenda.* Hong Kong: Central Policy Unit, Hong Kong SAR Government.

Hong Kong Core Values (n.d.) Online, available at http://www.hkcorevalues.net (accessed 12 September 2008).

Hong Kong Government Information Services (various years) *Hong Kong Yearbook.* Hong Kong: Government Printer.

Hong Kong Immigration Department (2001) *Annual Department Report 2000–2001.* Hong Kong: Government Printer.

Hong Kong Monetary Authority (1994) *The Practice of Central Banking in Hong Kong.* Hong Kong: Hong Kong Monetary Authority.

Hong Kong Monetary Authority (1995) *Money and Banking in Hong Kong.* Hong Kong: Hong Kong Monetary Authority.

Hong Kong Monetary Authority (1998) *Annual Report 1997.* Online, available at http://www.info.gov.hk/hkma/eng/public/ar97/toc.htm (accessed 2 August 2008).

Hong Kong Monetary Authority (1999) *Annual Report 1998.* Online, available at http://www.info.gov.hk/hkma/eng/public/ar98/toc.htm (accessed 2 August 2008).

Hong Kong Productivity Centre (1983) *Report on the Hong Kong Electronics Industry 1982.* Hong Kong: Industry Development Board.

Hong Kong Productivity Council (1992) *Report on Industrial Automation Study.* Hong Kong: Government Printer.

Hong Kong Special Administrative Region Government (2003) *Report of the Task Force on Population Policy.* Hong Kong: Government Printer.

Hong Kong Special Administrative Region Government (2008) *Hong Kong Yearbook.* Hong Kong: Government Printer.

Hong Kong Special Administrative Region Government (n.d.) 'Policy address'. Online, available at http://www.policyaddress.gov.hk (accessed 12 September 2008).

Hong Kong Special Administrative Region Government (n.d.) 'Quality migrant admission scheme'. Online, available at http://www.immd.gov.hk/ehtml/QMAS.htm (accessed 12 September 2008).

Hong Kong Special Administrative Region Government (n.d.) 'Brand Hong Kong'. Online, available at http://www.brandhk.gov.hk/brandhk/emesstop.htm (accessed 12 September 2008).

Hong Kong Trade Development Council (1984) *Hong Kong Radio and Cassette Recorder Industry and the Canadian Market for Radios and Cassette Recorders.* Hong Kong: Hong Kong Trade Development Council.

Hong Kong Trade Development Council (1988) *Hong Kong's Electronics Industry and Exports.* Hong Kong: Hong Kong Trade Development Council.

Hong Kong Trade Development Council (1990) *Hong Kong's Electronics Industries.* Hong Kong: Hong Kong Trade Development Council.

Hong Kong Trade Development Council (1991) *Survey on Hong Kong Domestic Exports and Re-exports and Triangular Trade*. Hong Kong: Hong Kong Trade Development Council.

Hong Kong Trade Development Council (1997) *Profile of Hong Kong's Major Manufacturing Industries*. Hong Kong: Hong Kong Trade Development Council.

Hong Kong Trade Development Council (2003) *Hong Kong as a Sourcing Centre for China-made Goods: Buyers' View*. Hong Kong: Hong Kong Trade Development Council.

Hong Kong Trade Development Council (2004) *Reaching Out, Not Hollowing Out: Hong Kong Industry and Trade Development Trends Under Globalisation*. Hong Kong: Hong Kong Trade Development Council.

Hsing, Y.T. (1998) *Making Capitalism in China: the Taiwan Connection*. New York: Oxford University Press.

Hsu, B.F.C. (1998) *Laws of Banking and Finance in the Hong Kong SAR*. Hong Kong: Open University of Hong Kong Press and Hong Kong University Press.

Hsu, D.L. (1986) 'Deposit-taking companies and merchant banking', in R.H. Scott, K.A. Wong and Y.K. Ho (eds) *Hong Kong's Financial Institutions and Markets*. Hong Kong: Oxford University Press, 19–34.

Hua, M. and Cao, H.C. (2006) 'Goujian guoji jinrong zhongxin de lujing [Pathways to an international financial centre]'. Occasional paper No. 15, Shanghai-Hong Kong Development Institute, Chinese University of Hong Kong (in Chinese).

Hughes, R. (1976) *Borrowed Place Borrowed Time* (revised edn). London: Andre Deutsch.

Hung, C.L. (1984) 'Foreign investment', in D. Lethbridge (ed.) *The Business Environment of Hong Kong* (2nd edn). Hong Kong: Oxford University Press, 180–209.

Industry Department (1992) *Hong Kong's Manufacturing Industries*. Hong Kong: Government Printer.

Industry Department (various years) *Annual Survey of Regional Representation by Overseas Companies in Hong Kong*. Hong Kong: Government Printer.

Ingham, G.K. (1984) *Capitalism Divided? The City and Industry in British Social Development*. London: Macmillan.

International Herald Tribune (2006) 'Hong Kong passes New York in value of IPOs', 26 December.

Jacobs, J. (1986) *Cities and the Wealth of Nations*. Harmondsworth: Penguin Books.

Jao, Y.C. (1974) *Banking and Currency in Hong Kong: A Study of Postwar Financial Development*. London: Macmillan.

Jao, Y.C. (1979) 'The rise of Hong Kong as a financial center', *Asian Survey*, 19: 674–94.

Jao, Y.C. (1980) 'Hong Kong as a regional financial centre: evolution and prospects', in C.K. Leung, J.W. Cushman and G.W. Wang (eds) *Hong Kong: Dilemmas of Growth*. Canberra: Research School of Pacific Studies, Australian National University and Hong Kong: Centre of Asian Studies, University of Hong Kong, 161–94.

Jao, Y.C. (1988) 'Monetary system and banking structure', in H.C.Y. Ho and L.C. Lau (eds) *The Economic System of Hong Kong*. Hong Kong: Asian Research Service, 43–85.

Jao, Y.C. (1991) 'On central banking in Hong Kong', in Y.C. Jao (ed.) *Monetary Management in Hong Kong: The Changing Role of the Exchange Fund*. Hong Kong: Chartered Institute of Bankers, Hong Kong Centre.

Jao, Y.C. (1993) *Zou Xiang Wei Lai de Xianggang Jin Rong (Hong Kong Finance Moving Towards the Future)*. Hong Kong: Joint Publication.

Jao, Y.C. (1997) *Hong Kong as an International Financial Centre: Evolution, Prospects and Policies*. Hong Kong: City University of Hong Kong Press.

Jao, Y.C. (2001) *The Asian Financial Crisis and the Ordeal of Hong Kong*. Westport: Quorum Books.

Jao, Y.C. (2006) 'Hong Kong as a financial centre of China and the world', in L.S. Ho and R. Ash (eds) *China, Hong Kong and the World Economy*. London: Palgrave, 121–51.

Jarman, R.L. (1996) *Hong Kong Annual Administration Reports 1841–1941 – Volume 1: 1841–1886*. Southampton: Archive Editions.

Johnson, C. (1987) 'Political institutions and economic performance: the government–business relationship in Japan, South Korea, and Taiwan', in F.C. Deyo (ed.) *The Political Economy of the New Asian Industrialization*. Ithaca: Cornell University Press, 136–64.

Joint Associations Working Group (1989) 'Report on Hong Kong's labour shortage'. Mimeo, Chinese General Chamber of Commerce.

Jonas, A.E.G. and Wilson, D. (eds) (1999) *The Urban Growth Machine: Critical Perspectives, Two Decades Later*. Albany: State University of New York Press.

Keating, M. (2001) 'Governing cities and regions: territorial restructuring in a global age', in A.J. Scott (ed.) *Global City-Regions*. Oxford: Oxford University Press, 371–90.

Kim, L. (1997) *Imitation to Innovation: The Dynamics of Korea's Technology Learning*. Boston: Harvard Business School Press.

King, A.D. (1991) *Global Cities*. London: Routledge.

King, F.H.H. (1988) *The Hong Kong Bank in the Period of Imperialism and War, 1895–1918*. Cambridge: Cambridge University Press.

Kose, H. (1994) 'Chinese merchants and Chinese inter-port trade', in A.J.H. Latham and H. Kawakatsu (eds) *Japanese Industrialization and the Asian Economy*. London: Routledge, 129–44.

Ku, A.S. (2001) 'The "public" up against the state: narrative cracks and credibility crisis in postcolonial Hong Kong', *Theory, Culture & Society*, 18(1), 121–44.

Landsberg, M. (1979) 'Export-led industrialization in the third world', *Review of Radical Political Economics*, 11, 50–63.

Latham, A.J.H. (1994) 'The dynamics of intra-Asian trade, 1868–1913: the great entrepots of Singapore and Hong Kong', in A.J.H. Latham and H. Kawakatsu (eds) *Japanese Industrialization and the Asian Economy*. London: Routledge, 145–93.

Latter, T. (2007a) *Hong Kong's Money: The History, Logic and Operation of the Currency Peg*. Hong Kong: Hong Kong University Press.

Latter, T. (2007b) *Hands On or Hands Off? The Nature and Process of Economic Policy in Hong Kong*. Hong Kong: Hong Kong University Press.

Lau, S.K. (1999) 'Political order and democratisation in Hong Kong: the separation of elite and mass politics', in G.W. Wang and S.L. Wong (eds) *Towards a New Millennium: Building on Hong Kong's Strengths*. Hong Kong: Centre of Asian Studies, 62–79.

Lau, S.K. (2000) 'Xingzheng zhudaodi zhengzhi tizhi: xhexiang yu xianshi [An executive-led political system: design and reality]', in S.K. Lau (ed.) *Xianggang 21 Shiji Lantu [The 21st Century Blueprint of Hong Kong]*. Hong Kong: Chinese University Press, 1–36 (in Chinese).

Lau, S.K. (2002) 'Tung Chee-hwa's governing strategy: the shortfall in politics', in S.K. Lau (ed.) *The First Five Years of the Hong Kong Special Administrative Region*. Hong Kong: Chinese University Press, 1–39.

Lauria, M. (ed.) (1997) *Reconstructing Urban Regime Theory*. Thousand Oaks: Sage Publications.

Le Gales, P. (2002) *European Cities*. Oxford: Oxford University Press.

Lee, C.S. and Pecht, M. (1997) *The Taiwan Electronics Industry*. Boca Raton, Florida: CRC Press.

Lee, E.W.Y. (1999) 'Governing post-colonial Hong Kong', *Asian Survey*, 39(6), 940–59.

Lee, M.K. (2001) 'Class, inequality and conflict', in S.K. Lau *et al.* (eds) *Indicators of Social Development: Hong Kong 1999*. Hong Kong: Hong Kong Institute of Asia-Pacific Studies, 115–35.

Leeming, F. (1975) 'The earlier industrialization of Hong Kong', *Modern Asian Studies*, 9(2), 337–42.

Lethbridge, D. and S.H. Ng (1984) 'The business environment and employment', in D. Lethbridge (ed.) *The Business Environment in Hong Kong* 2nd Ed., Hong Kong: Oxford University Press, 52–69.

Leung, A. (2002) Speech at the Hong Kong Business Community Luncheon, 14 March 2002. Online, available at http://www.info.gov.hk/gia/general/200203/14/0314152.htm (accessed 12 September 2008).

Leung, B.K.P. (1990) 'Power and politics: a critical analysis', in B.K.P. Leung (ed.) *Social Issues in Hong Kong*. Hong Kong: Oxford University Press, 13–26.

Leung, C.K. (1993) 'Personal contacts, subcontracting linkages, and development in the Hong Kong-Zhujiang delta region', *Annals of the Association of American Geographers*, 83(2), 272–302.

Leung, F. *et al.* (2008) 'Service exports: the next engine of growth for Hong Kong'. Working paper 04/2008, Hong Kong Monetary Authority.

Li, C.L. (2005) *Duanlie yu Suipian [Cleavage and Fragment: An Empirical Analysis on the Social Stratification of Contemporary China]*. Beijing: Social Sciences Academic Press.

Li, D.K.P. (2004) 'Document VI.8: Hong Kong as a financial centre', in D. Faure and P.T. Lee (eds) *Economy: A Documentary History of Hong Kong*. Hong Kong: Hong Kong University Press, 234–50.

Li, K.W. (2006) *The Hong Kong Economy: Recovery and Restructuring*. Singapore: McGraw-Hill Education (Asia).

Logan, J.R. and Molotch, H.L. (1987) *Urban Fortunes*. Berkeley: University of California Press.

Lui, T.L. (1999) 'Hong Kong society: anxiety in the post-1997 days', *Journal of Contemporary China*, 8(20), 89–101.

Lui, T.L. (2005) 'Under fire: Hong Kong's middle class after 1997', in J.Y.S. Cheng (ed.) *The July 1 Protest Rally: Interpreting a Historic Event*. Hong Kong: City University of Hong Kong Press, 277–301.

Lui, T.L. and Chiu, S.W.K. (1993) 'Industrial restructuring and labour-market adjustment under positive noninterventionism: the case of Hong Kong', *Environment and Planning A*, 25(1), 63–79.

Lui, T.L. and Chiu, S.W.K. (1994) 'A tale of two industries: the restructuring of Hong Kong's garment-making and electronics industries', *Environment and Planning A*, 26(1), 53–70.

Lui, T.L. and Chiu, S.W.K. (1996) 'Merchants, small employers and a non-interventionist state: Hong Kong as a case of unorganized late industrialization', in J. Borrego *et al.* (eds) *Capital, the State and Late Industrialization*. Boulder: Westview Press, 221–46.

Lui, T.L. and Chiu, S.W.K. (2001) 'Flexibility under unorganized industrialism?', in F.C. Deyo, R.F. Doner and E. Hershberg (eds) *Economic Governance and the Challenge of Flexibility in East Asia*. Lanham: Rowman & Littlefield Publishers, 55–77.

Lui, T.L. and Wong, C.T. (2003) *Xianggang Zhongchan Jieji Chujing Guancha [Observations of Hong Kong's Middle Class]*. Hong Kong: Joint Publications (in Chinese).

Ma, N. (2007) *Political Development in Hong Kong*. Hong Kong: Hong Kong University Press.

Mackintosh Consultants Ltd (1982) *Profile of the Worldwide Semiconductor Industry*. Luton: Benn Electronics Publications Ltd.

Marcuse, P. (1989) 'Dual city: a muddy metaphor for a quartered city', *International Journal of Urban and Regional Research*, 13(4), 697–708.

Massey, D. (2007) *World City*. Cambridge: Polity Press.

Matheson Connell, C. (2004) *A Business in Risk*. Westport: CT: Praeger.

Mathews, G., Ma, E. and Lui, T.L. (2008) *Hong Kong, China: Learning to Belong to a Nation*. London: Routledge.

McDermott, M.C. (1992) 'The internationalization of the South Korean and Taiwanese electronics industries: the European dimension', in S. Young and J. Hamill (eds) *Europe and the Multinationals: Issues and Responses for the 1990s*. Aldershot: Edward Elgar, 206–33.

McKenzie, R.D. (1968 [1927]) 'The concept of dominance and world-organization', in A. Hawley (ed.) *On Human Ecology*. Chicago: Chicago University Press, 205–19.

McLaughlin, E. (1993) 'Hong Kong: a residual welfare regime', in A. Cochrane and J. Clarke (eds) *Comparing Welfare States: Britain in International Context*. London: Sage, 105–40.

Meyer, D.R. (2000) *Hong Kong as a Global Metropolis*. Cambridge: Cambridge University Press.

Miners, N. (1996) 'Consultation with business interests: the case of Hong Kong', *Asian Journal of Public Administration* 18(2), 245–56.

Mitchell, M. (2000) 'On to the streets', *Far Eastern Economic Review*, 27 (July).

Mollenkopf, J.H. and Castells, M. (eds) (1991) *Dual City: Restructuring New York*. New York: Russell Sage Foundation.

Molotch, H.L. (1976) 'The city as a growth machine', *American Journal of Sociology*, 82(2), 309–32.

Montes, M.F. (1999) 'Tokyo, Hong Kong and Singapore as competing financial centres', in G. de Brouwer and W. Pupphavesa (eds) *Asia Pacific Financial Deregulation*. London: Routledge, 151–70.

Munn, C. (2001) *Anglo-China: Chinese People and British Rule in Hong Kong, 1841–1880*. Richmond: Curzon Press.

Next Magazine (2002) 'Caituan jiagong chaoren neimu [An insider's report on the business groups' organized attack on the "superman"]', *Next Magazine*, 21 November.

Ng, S.H., Chan, F.T. and Wong, K.K. (1989) *A Report on Labour Supply Studies*. Hong Kong Economic Research Centre.

Ng, S.H., Lui, T.L. and Chan, F.T. (1987) *Report on the Survey on the Conditions of Work for Female Workers in Tsuen Wan*. Hong Kong: Government Printer.

Ngo, T.W. (1999a) 'Colonialism in Hong Kong revisited', in T.W. Ngo (ed.) *Hong Kong's History*. London: Routledge.

Ngo, T.W. (1999b) 'Social values and consensus politics in colonial Hong Kong', in H. Antlov and T.W. Ngo (eds) *The Cultural Construction of Politics in Asia*. New York: St Martin's Press, 131–53.

Ngo, T.W. (2000) 'Changing government-business relations and the governance of Hong Kong', in R. Ash *et al.* (eds) *Hong Kong in Transition: The Handover Years*. London: Macmillan Press, 26–41.

Ngo, T.W. (2002) 'Money, power, and the problem of legitimacy in the Hong Kong Special Administrative Region', in F. Mengin and J. Rocca (eds) *Politics in China: Moving Frontiers*. New York: Palgrave Macmillan, 95–117.

Olds, K. and Yeung, H. (2004) 'Pathways to global city formation: a view from the developmental city-state of Singapore', *Review of International Political Economy*, 11(3), 489–521.

Pearson, M.M. (1997) *China's New Business Elite*. Berkeley: University of California Press.

Peng, J.L. (1981) 'Shijiu shiji xifang qinluezhe dui zhongguo laogong di lulue [Western invaders' seizure of Chinese labour in the nineteenth century]', in Wendi Lu *et al.* (eds) *Huagong Chuguoshi Huibian Disiji [Collection of Historical Materials on Chinese Labourers Working Abroad Vol. 4]*. Beijing: Zhonghua Shuju, 174–229.

Prime Magazine (2005a) 'Fuhao mailuo [Tycoons' networks]', *Prime Magazine*, No. 6, 14–55.

Prime Magazine (2005b) 'Fuhao mailuo [Tycoons' networks] II', *Prime Magazine*, No. 7, 14–45.

Rabushaka, A. (1976) *Value for Money*. Stanford: Hoover Institution Press.

Rating and Valuation Department (1991) *Property Review: 1991*. Hong Kong: Government Printer.

Rear, J. (1971) 'One brand of politics', in K. Hopkins (ed.) *Hong Kong: The Industrial Colony*. Hong Kong: Oxford University Press, 55–139.

Reed, H.C. (1981) *The Preeminence of International Financial Centers*. New York: Praeger.

Reidel, J. (1973) *The Hong Kong Model of Industrialization*. Kiel: Institut fur Weltwirtschaft.

Reif, R. and Sodini, C.G. (1997) 'The Hong Kong electronics industry', in S. Berger and R. Lester (eds) *Made By Hong Kong*. Hong Kong: Oxford University Press, 186–215.

Robinson, J. (2002) 'Global and world cities: a view from off the map', *International Journal of Urban and Regional Research*, 26(3), 531–54.

Sassen, S. (1991) *The Global City*. Princeton: Princeton University Press.

Sassen, S. (1998) *Globalization and its Discontents*. New York: The New Press.

Sassen, S. (1999) 'Global financial centers', *Foreign Affairs*, 78(1), 75–87.

Sassen, S. (2000) *Cities in a World Economy* (2nd edn). Thousand Oaks: Pine Forge Press.

Sassen, S. (2001) *The Global City* (2nd edn). Princeton: Princeton University Press.

Sassen, S. (ed.) (2002) *Global Networks, Linked Cities*. London: Routledge.

Sassen, S. (2006) 'Why Hong Kong is happening', *Newsweek*, 31 July.

Schenk, C.R. (1995) 'The Hong Kong gold market and the Southeast Asian gold trade in the 1950s', *Modern Asian Studies*, 29(2), 387–402.

Schenk, C.R. (2000) 'Another Asian financial crisis: monetary links between Hong Kong and China 1945–50', *Modern Asian Studies*, 34(3), 739–64.

Schenk, C.R. (2001) *Hong Kong as an International Financial Centre: Emergence and Development 1945–65*. London: Routledge.

Schenk, C.R. (2003) 'Banking crises and the evolution of the regulatory framework in Hong Kong 1945–1970', *Australian Economic History Review*, 43(2), 140–54.

Schenk, C.R. (2004a) 'Finance of industry in Hong Kong 1950–70: a case of market failure?', *Business History*, 46(4), 583–608.

Schenk, C.R. (2004b) 'Regulatory reform in an emerging stock market: the case of Hong Kong, 1945–86', *Financial History Review*, 11(2), 139–63.

Schiffer, J. (1991) 'State policy and economic growth: a note on the Hong Kong model', *International Journal of Urban and Regional Research*, 15(2), 180–96.

Scott, A.J. (ed.) (2001) *Global City-Regions*. Oxford: Oxford University Press.

Short, J.R. and Kim, Y.H. (1999) *Globalization and the City*. Harlow: Longman.

Short, J.R. *et al.* (2000) 'From world cities to gateway cities', *City*, 4(3), 317–40.

Sit, V.F.S. (1982) 'Dynamism in small industries – the case of Hong Kong', *Asian Survey*, 22(4), 399–409.

Sit, V.F.S. (1998) 'Hong Kong's 'transferred' industrialization and industrial geography', *Asian Survey*, 28(9), 880–904.

Sit, V.F.S. (2006) 'Dynamic Hong Kong – Pearl River Delta relationship under globalization and one country – two systems', in A.G.O. Yeh *et al.* (eds) *Developing a Competitive Pearl River Delta*. Hong Kong: Hong Kong University Press, 3–26.

Sit, V.F.S. and Wong, S.L. (1989) *Small and Medium Industries in an Export-oriented Economy*. Hong Kong: Centre of Asian Studies, University of Hong Kong.

Sit, V.F.S. and Yang, C. (1997) 'Foreign-investment-induced exo-urbanization in the Pearl River Delta, China', *Urban Studies*, 34(4), 647–78.

Sit, V.F.S., Wong, S.L. and Kiang, T.S. (1979) *Small Scale Industry in a Laissez-faire Economy*. Hong Kong: Centre of Asian Studies, University of Hong Kong.

Skeldon, R. (1986) 'Hong Kong and its hinterland: a case of international rural-to-urban migration?', *Asian Geographer*, 5(1), 1–24.

Smart, A. (2006) *The Shek Kip Mei Myth: Squatters, Fires and Colonial Rule in Hong Kong, 1950–1963*. Hong Kong: Hong Kong University Press.

Smith, M.P. (2001) *Transnational Urbanism: Locating Globalization*. Oxford: Blackwell Publishers.

So, A. (1986) 'The economic success of Hong Kong: insights from a world-system perspective', *Sociological Perspective*, 29(2), 241–58.

So, A. (1999) 'Hong Kong's pathway to a global city: a regional analysis', in J. Gulger (ed.) *World Cities Beyond the West*. Cambridge: Cambridge University Press, 212–39.

Stoker, G. (1995) 'Regime theory and urban politics', in D. Judge *et al.* (eds) *Theories of Urban Politics*. London: Sage Publications, 54–71.

Stoler, A.L. and Cooper, F. (1997) 'Between metropole and colony', in F. Cooper and A.L. Stoler (eds) *Tensions of Empire*. Berkeley: University of California Press, 1–56.

Soulard, F. (1997) *The Restructuring of Hong Kong Industries and the Urbanization of Zhujiang Delta, 1979–1989*. Hong Kong: The Chinese University Press.

South China Morning Post (1999a) 'Tycoons urge Cyberport tender', 19 March.

South China Morning Post (1999b) 'Pressure to block Cyberport funding', 12 May.

South China Morning Post (2002a) 'Red chips set for cash flood from mainland', 17 March.

South China Morning Post (2002b) 'Developers step up campaign over electricity charges', 12 November.

South China Morning Post (2005) 'Tung faces Cyberport pressure', 3 February.

South China Morning Post (2006a) 'HK's got it all, says China-wide survey of competitiveness', 21 March.

South China Morning Post (2006b) 'Mainland cities won't usurp HK: NPC chief', 21 March.

South China Morning Post (2006c) 'State fund becomes market player', 21 March.

South China Morning Post (2007) 'As HIS door swings open, the risks widen', 4 March.

Sudjic, D. (1992) *The 100 Mile City*. San Diego: Harcourt Brace & Co.

Sung, Y.W. (2006) 'The evolving role of Hong Kong as China's middleman', in L.S. Ho and R. Ash (eds) *China, Hong Kong and the World Economy*. Basingstoke: Palgrave Macmillan, 152–69.

Susser, I. (1991) 'The separation of mothers and children', in J.H. Mollenkopf and M. Castells (eds) *Dual City: Restructuring New York*. New York: Russell Sage Foundation, 207–24.

SynergyNet (2007) 'Implications of cross-boundary economic integration for Hong Kong's managerial and professional workers'. Research Paper, SynergyNet.

Tai, L.S.T. (1986) 'Commercial banking', in R.H. Scott, K.A. Wong and Y.K. Ho (eds) *Hong Kong's Financial Institutions and Markets*. Hong Kong: Oxford University Press, 1–18.

Tai, P.F. (2006) 'Social polarisation: comparing Singapore, Hong Kong and Taipei', *Urban Studies*, 43(10), 1737–56.

Tang, L.W.S. (1973) 'The power structure in a colonial society – a sociological study of the unofficial members of the Legislative Council in Hong Kong (1948–1971)'. Unpublished senior thesis, Department of Sociology, Chinese University of Hong Kong.

Tao, Z. and Wong, Y.C.R. (2002) 'Hong Kong: from an industrialised city to a centre of manufacturing-related services', *Urban Studies* 39(12), 2345–58.

Taylor, P.J. (2004) *World City Network: A Global Urban Analysis*. London: Routledge.

Taylor, P.J. (2006) 'Shanghai, Hong Kong, Taipei and Beijing within the world city network: positions, trends and prospects'. Online, available at http://www.lboro.ac.uk/gawc/rb/rb204.html (accessed 18 August 2008).

Thompson, E.R. (2000) 'Hong Kong as a regional strategic hub for manufacturing multinationals', in A.E. Andersson and D.E. Andersson (eds) *Gateways to the Global Economy*. Cheltenham: Edward Elgar, 169–89.

Time (2007) 'Hong Kong, China', *Time*, 18 June.

Time (2008) 'Ny-lon-kong', *Time*, 28 January.

Trade and Industry Department (2001) *Techno-economic and Market Research Study on Hong Kong's Textiles, Clothing and Footwear Industries, 2000 Vol. II*. Hong Kong: Government Printer.

Tsai, J.F. (1993) *Hong Kong in Chinese History*. New York: Columbia University Press.

Tsang, D. (2006) 'Big market, small government'. Online, available at www.ceo.gov.hk/eng/press/oped.htm (accessed 27 August 2008).

Tsang, S. (2004) *A Modern History of Hong Kong*. Hong Kong: Hong Kong University Press.

Tse, Y.K. and Yip, P.S.L. (2003) 'The impacts of Hong Kong's currency board reforms on the interbank market', *Journal of Banking and Finance*, 27, 2273–96.

Tung, C.W. (2003) *The Chief Executive's Policy Address*. Online, available at http://www.policyaddress.gov.hk/pa03/eng/policy.htm.

Vogel, S.K. (1996) *Freer Markets, More Rules: Regulatory Reform in Advanced Industrial Countries*. Ithaca: Cornell University Press.

Wade, R. (1990) *Governing the Market*. Princeton: Princeton University Press.

Wan, S.P.S and Wong, T.K.Y. (2005) 'Social conflicts in Hong Kong: 1996–2002'. Occasional paper No. 156. Hong Kong: Hong Kong Institute of Asia-Pacific Studies, Chinese University of Hong Kong.

Wang, J.H. (2004) 'World city formation, geopolitics and local political process: Taipei's ambiguous development', *International Journal of Urban and Regional Research*, 28(2), 384–400.

Ward, P.M. (1995) 'The successful management and administration of world cities: mission impossible?', in P.L. Knox and P.J. Taylor (eds) *World Cities in a World-system*. Cambridge: Cambridge University Press, 298–314.

Weiss, L. (1998) *The Myth of the Powerless State*. Cambridge: Polity Press.

Weiss, L. and Hobson, J. (1995) *States and Economic Development: A Comparative Historical Analysis*. Cambridge: Polity Press.

Welsh, F. (1997) *A History of Hong Kong* (revised edn). London: Harper Collins Publishers.

Wessel, T. (2000) 'Social polarisation and socioeconomic segregation in a welfare state: the case of Oslo', *Urban Studies*, 37(11), 1947–67.

Wong, G. (1996) 'Business groups in a dynamic environment: Hong Kong 1976–1986', in G. Hamilton (ed.) *Asian Business Networks*. Berlin: Walter de Gruyter, 87–113.

Wong, H. (2000) 'Globalisation and marginalisation of labour: the case of Hong Kong'. Paper presented at the 12th Annual Meeting of the Society for the Advancement of Socio-Economics, London.

Wong, H. (2007) 'Misled intervention by a misplaced diagnosis: the Hong Kong SAR government's policies for alleviating poverty and social exclusion', *The China Review*, 7(2), 123–47.

Wong, K.A. (1986) 'The Hong Kong stock-market: its development and control', in R.H. Scott, K.A. Wong and Y.K. Ho (eds) *Hong Kong's Financial Institutions and Markets*. Hong Kong: Oxford University Press, 57–78.

Wong, K.A. (1991) 'The Hong Kong stock-market', in R.Y.K. Ho, R.H. Scott and K.A. Wong (eds) *The Hong Kong Financial System*. Hong Kong: Oxford University Press, 215–34.

Wong, P.K. (2001) 'Flexible production, high-tech commodities, and public policies: the hard disk drive industry in Singapore', in F.C. Deyo, R.F. Doner and E. Hershberg (eds) *Economic Governance and the Challenge of Flexibility in East Asia*. Lanham: Rowan & Littlefield Publishers.

Wong, S.L. (1986) 'Modernization and Chinese culture in Hong Kong', *The China Quarterly*, 106, 306–25.

Wong, S.L. (1988) *Emigrant Entrepreneur*. Hong Kong: Oxford University Press.

Wong, T.Y.C. (1991) 'A comparative study of the industrial policy of Hong Kong and Singapore in the 1980s', in E.K.Y. Chen, M.K. Nyaw and R.Y.C. Wong (eds) *Industrial and Trade Development in Hong Kong*. Hong Kong: Centre of Asian Studies, 256–96.

World Federation of Exchanges (various years) 'Statistics: annual: equity markets'. Online, available at http://www.world-exchanges.org/statistics/annual (accessed 2 September 2008).

Wu, J. (1988) 'Entrepreneurship', in H.C.Y. Ho and L.C. Chau (eds) *The Economic System of Hong Kong*. Hong Kong: Asian Research Service, 155–68.

Yang, C. (2006) 'Cross-boundary integration of the Pearl River Delta and Hong Kong: an emerging global city-region in China', in F.L. Wu (ed.) *Globalization and the Chinese City*. London: Routledge, 125–46.

Yeh, A.G.O. (2006) 'Producer services and industrial linkages in the Hong Kong-Pearl River Delta region', in P.W. Daniels, K.C. Ho and T.A. Hutton (eds) *Service Industries and Asia-Pacific Cities*. London: Routledge, 150–72.

Yeh, A.G.O. and Xu, J. (2006) 'Turning of the dragon head: changing role of Hong Kong in the regional development of the Pearl River Delta', in A.G.O. Yeh *et al.* (eds) *Developing a Competitive Pearl River Delta in South China Under One Country-Two Systems*. Hong Kong: Hong Kong University Press, 63–95.

Youngson, A.J. (1982) *Hong Kong: Economic Growth and Policy*. Hong Kong: Oxford University Press.

Yu, T.F.L. (1997) *Entrepreneurship and Economic Development in Hong Kong*. London: Routledge.

Yusuf, S. and Nabeshima, K. (2006) *Postindustrial East Asian Cities*. Palo Alto: Stanford University Press and the World Bank.

Yusuf, S. and Wu, W. (2002) 'Pathways to a world city: Shanghai rising in an era of globalisation', *Urban Studies*, 39(7), 1213–40.

Zhang, X.H. (2001) *Xianggang jindai jingjishi [Economic History of Modern Hong Kong (1840–1949)]*. Guangzhou: Guangdong renmin chubanshe (in Chinese).

Zheng, D. (1987) *Xiandai Xiang Gang Jingji [Modern Hong Kong Economy]*. Beijing: China's Financial, Political and Economic Publisher (in Chinese).

Index